The Economic Growth Debate

An Assessment

E. J. MISHAN

The London School of Economics and Political Science
and *The University of Maryland*

London
GEORGE ALLEN & UNWIN LTD
Ruskin House Museum Street

First published in 1977

ISBN 0 04 330280 7 hardback
0 04 330281 5 paperback

Printed in Great Britain by
Biddles Ltd, Guildford, Surrey

Preface

This book is not intended to be a new version of my earlier book, *The Costs of Economic Growth* (1967), although some of the arguments which first appeared in that essay cannot be left out of the present volume without leaving gaps in the development of its thesis. It goes without saying, however, that the present work, like the first, departs from the economist's conventional treatment of social welfare which tends to the conclusion that economic growth would indeed raise social welfare in the absence of those effects which are classified in the literature as 'external diseconomies'.

These effects have been treated extensively in the journals with the object, mainly, of discovering fiscal devices and institutional alterations that might promote a more efficient allocation of resources. Through this concept of external diseconomies, the economist is coming close to making useful contributions to environmental improvements, though drawing on the results of biologists, ecologists, toxicologists and others.

On the other hand, the more intimate human consequences of economic expansion are far less extensively treated by economists. Such research is more congenial to other disciplines: history, sociology, psychology, philosophy, biology and medicine. Nevertheless, in an informal way a number of economists have shown awareness of the problem, to the extent at least of refusing to be bound by the traditional assumption that a net increase in goods entails a net increase in welfare, either at the individual or at the social level. This liberty I have taken in discussing the human consequences of economic growth both in my earlier and in my present work.

However, the approach adopted here differs from that in my earlier work in two respects. First, the space devoted to economics is much smaller. Indeed, after a short opening section (Part I) critical of economic methods for calculating real income and for treating pollution and allied problems, economic criteria play a decidedly inferior role. Second, this volume is divided into two Books. For those who have not followed the economic growth debate over the last few years, and for those who are predisposed to favour continued economic growth, Book 1 is essential reading. Whether or not reflection on the arguments in this Book will cause them to revise their opinions, they should be better able to defend them after their attention is drawn to the range of issues involved. There are others, however, who have followed this debate and have not been impressed by the pro-growth brief. For such people it is more profitable to begin with Book 2 in which the central thesis is unfolded. There, beginning with some ideas of the basic material and psychological needs of ordinary men, and of their aspirations towards the good life, I look at the main economic and social developments over the last few decades in the endeavour to determine whether, on balance, these basic needs and aspirations are in fact being realised or not.

Many of the ideas and some of the passages are taken from recent articles, some of which have appeared in the columns of *Encounter*. Others are the outcome of animated discussions at conferences. Yet others have arisen from reading the articles and books of writers in a number of disciplines. My intellectual debts are many, and I acknowledge them wherever I can trace them.

Finally, I owe a debt of gratitude to Mrs Diane Giles for transforming my scrawled-over first draft into a faultlessly typed manuscript, in the course of which she discreetly called my attention to a number of expositional malapropisms. I am indebted also to Mrs Scheila Collins who cheerfully assisted her in checking the manuscript, and to Mrs Betty McCormack, the copy-editor, for correcting a large number of grammatical errors and ambiguities.

Foreword

More than ten years have passed since I finished writing *Costs of Economic Growth*. That book was an attempt, among other things, to draw the reader's attention to a real issue that was being frequently misrepresented by the 'Establishment'. This real issue is not, as it was then misrepresented (and often still is), whether poor people, or ordinary people, want or need more of 'the good things of life'. All of us, from the poorest to the richest, from the meanest to the noblest, would probably be glad to have some extra income or wealth. Neither is the real issue that of the moral worth or justification of amassing material goods in comparison with less worldly pursuits, nor that of the distribution of the world's annual product among its population. Certainly it is not a class issue or an ideological issue.

To place the issue in perspective, it is a distinct advantage to imagine that some ideal distribution of income already exists, at least within each of the affluent countries of the world. We do not, however, have to suppose that the prevalence of these ideal distributions of income has any perceptible effect in abating people's material appetites. We may, indeed, continue to suppose that in this new dispensation each one of us would like to have more worldly goods and as soon as possible. The real issue – or, to be more precise, the issue that I regard as dominant today – is whether we are ready seriously to recognise that the collective pursuit of economic growth, which depends, in the main, on scientific advance and technological progress, has begun to have complex and far-reaching consequences both on the biosphere and on the 'sociosphere', consequences that are by no means entirely benign. They demand the most searching study and surmise. For it is now reasonable to believe that, despite the abundance of man-made goods produced by continued economic growth, its net effect on human health and happiness could be adverse and possibly disastrous.

Indeed, the broad conclusion of my polemic essay referred to above was that a continuation of economic growth, as conventionally understood, and assuming it to be possible, could not be counted upon to improve social wellbeing. If wellbeing is society's objective, we should do better to think more directly and carefully about the ways in which this might be improved rather than to allow ourselves to be guided by orthodox doctrine and put our trust in economic growth.

To my genuine surprise, this essay of mine was well received by the public, even by economists. But today nothing dates so quickly as success, unless it be a modest success. Observations that looked novel enough at the time now seem jaded, and much of what passed for ingenuity then has come to appear increasingly obvious. For all that, the essay helped to start a debate that had been too long deferred and the interest in which has grown and spread rapidly.

Participation in this debate for over a decade has not altered my views. Indeed, events have confirmed them. Some of the tendencies that could be described in the 1950s and early 1960s, when I began tentatively to write on the subject in several of the journals, look today to be almost irreversible trends. The uglification of once-handsome cities the world over continues unabated. Noise levels and gas levels are still rising and, despite the erection of concrete freeways over city centres, unending processions of motorised traffic lurch through its main thoroughfares. Areas of outstanding natural beauty are still being sacrificed to the tourist trade, and traditional communities to the exigencies of 'development'. Pollution of air, soil and ocean spreads over the globe. The Mediterranean now serves as a sewer for over 400 million people, and also for innumerable oil-powered craft, as a result of which the beaches of nearly every once-beautiful coastal resort are sifted with pellets of tar. The upward movement in the indicators of social disintegration – divorce, suicide, delinquency, petty theft, drug taking, sexual deviance, crime and violence – has never faltered over the last two decades. And the unchecked erosion of standards of taste and propriety is reflected in the resigned acceptance by the quality press of obscene language and allusion, and in the diffusion of porno-erotic literature, display and entertainment.

These and other unhappy developments of the postwar period were then identified as being among the bitter fruits of our much vaunted prosperity. And it is no less ironic now than it was then that the official exhortations to faster economic growth are so often rationalised by reference to immense resources needed to deal with the mounting social and environmental problems that are themselves the chief legacy of rapid economic growth.

As a number of writers have observed, the original Puritan ethic which suffused nineteenth-century capitalism has spent its force. It could hardly be otherwise. For the justification of hard work and accumulation in terms of a need, or an historic task, to lift the masses out of poverty and provide them with the material conditions and the leisure necessary for their enlightenment and moral improvement, has become wholly implausible in the West in the latter part of the twentieth century. If capitalism, true to its nature, continues the search for profits and expansion in already-wealthy societies and in conditions of near-surfeit, anything will be produced that may add, temporarily, an iota of gratification to an increasingly indiscriminate consumer market – a fact which would be more cheering if the system could boast any great success over the past decade or so in making life more enjoyable rather than more exhausting. Nonetheless, the imperative towards greater efficiency, expansion and innovation has become so much a part of our commercial conscience, so deeply embedded in our commercial institutions, that the habits of hard work, self-discipline, and worldly ambition and enterprise are still lauded as prime social virtues.

Though aware of these developments, I have forborne from casting my thesis in terms of such categories as capitalism, socialism and the like, simply because I want to shift current preoccupation away from politics and ideologies towards the role of technology in shaping our civilisation. The problems noted by writers such as Walter Weisskopf (1971) or Daniel Bell (1975), in connection with the rise of the so-called consumer society, result principally from the impulse of modern technology in conditions of material plenty and irrespective of the political complexions of the countries in question.

I have, then, sought not to elaborate any existing doctrine of economic and social development, nor to create a new system of ideas designed to integrate such developments over the centuries – which is just as well, since I am not likely to succeed. My method has been quite different. It is to assess each and every consideration by reference to its contribution to the broad theme of my inquiry: whether continued economic growth can be expected to enhance social wellbeing.

Although my basic misgivings about the growth process have not altered, as indicated earlier, my views broadened in response to new facts and their interpretation, and to pondering on the arguments and counterarguments of professionals in a number of disciplines. As a result I became aware of the need for a more systematic treatment of the subject that would enable the layman to place in orderly perspective the multitude of factors pertinent to the economic growth debate.

Three years ago, prompted by Dr Chester Cooper of the Smithsonian Institution in Washington DC, I surrendered to the ambition to devise a framework about which all the critical issues in the debate might be arranged. But since I had no wish to encumber the public by editing yet another volume of unevenly written papers by a group of diverse specialists, which seldom produces effects on the ordinary reader other than inarticulate dismay and exasperation, I decided bravely to write it all myself, though easing my task by dividing it over time. My plan was first to write a volume on the question of the social desirability of continued economic growth, to be followed later by at least one more volume on the physical limitations to further economic growth.

This order was dictated by necessity. The literature bearing on the physical limitations to continued economic growth encompasses a wide range of disciplines within the physical sciences. At one end of the spectrum are the articles and monographs written about world models, of which the best known today are those of Forrester (1971) and of Dennis and Donella Meadows (1972). At the other end of the spectrum are the volumes of collected papers and highly specialised treatises on ecological mechanisms and toxic technologies. Starting from a very imperfect knowledge of any aspect of this vast subject, it would take me some time before I began to feel comfortable with this literature – comfortable enough, at least, to be able to distil from it the nature of the chief factors and to arrange them in a form designed to foster a common perspective. In contrast, a treatment of the social consequences of economic growth, the literature with which I was already fairly familiar, would require less time and less specialised knowledge, though possibly more imagination and judgment.

The choice of this subject matter, incidentally, explains why I have so little to say in this volume about the global contribution to ecological imbalance of the population boom of the twentieth century, itself a product of scientific and technological advances especially in the fields of medicine and agronomy. Although I am persistently and painfully aware of the mounting distress and poverty being suffered today by millions of families in the subcontinents of Asia, and in South America and Africa, arising in the main from the relentless pressure of swelling human populations on limited natural resources and the limited absorptive powers of the ecosphere, I shall have to leave the systematic treatment of such problems to a forthcoming volume.

The business of war, it is said, is too serious to be left to the generals. And the study of economic growth is too serious to be left to the economists. Speaking from inside the profession, I am sensible of the drastically simplified assumptions, and the abstractions from reality, on which the policy prescriptions of the economist have to rest. Indeed, my Part I is a brief attempt to convey to the non-economist some idea of the limitations of the economist's approach to the growth question.

However, if the study of economics alone does not fit a man to pronounce with confidence on the chief consequences of economic growth, neither does the study of any of the physical sciences. True, subjects such as anthropology, sociology, psychology, politics, philosophy and history can all be expected to throw some light on at least some aspects of economic growth. But the light thrown by any one subject has too narrow a focus to reveal the full extent of any relationship between economic growth and welfare.

Thus, although there is call enough for more comprehensive approaches to social problems, no less a figure than Arthur Koestler has dwelt on the follies committed by specialists who stop specialising and start generalising. The reader is being given fair warning, though he will, I hope, perceive the dilemma. Until such time as the universities discover the secret of producing enlightened generalisers, a commitment to the highest standards of scholarship must severely restrict social relevance. On the other hand, a primary commitment to social relevance imposes limits to fastidious scholarship. If the option of being meticulous but irrelevant is rejected, we have to accept the risk of being relevant but wrong.

A word now about the text and the themes that emerge from it. The assortment of environmental and social problems, which is the daily bread of our preoccupation, would not have taken us unawares had we not already been gulled by the growing hubris of the last two centuries into the belief that man's increasing powers of control over nature could be made to serve his ambition to engineer his future.

Such a belief is in stark contrast to the conservative wisdom generally associated with Edmund Burke, a wisdom expressed in the presumption in favour of the existing institutions of a stable society, institutions that have come into being by the slow process of social selection and have endured the passage of time. Contrary, then, to our current prejudice in favour of 'change', the conservative doctrine bids us in effect to resist proposals that entail significant changes in the existing social order unless the alleged benefits are believed substantial and the belief is backed by powerful arguments or overwhelming evidence.

Bearing in mind that the accumulation of technological innovations produces both environmental and institutional changes that cannot but influence the style of life and the character of men, and therefore necessarily influences for better or worse their capacity for enjoyment, the pertinence at least of the conservative doctrine is beyond question. For, carefully interpreted, its import is to inhibit social change, though not necessarily to prevent it.

By the lights of this doctrine, however, we have thrown caution to the winds. We have chosen to act with increasing boldness on the basis of new scientific and technical knowledge. And everywhere about us now are the visible consequences, sorry testimony to the power of modern expertise. The point can be illustrated by noting the words of a distinguished American civil servant, Harland Cleveland, quoted by Warner Wick (1976): 'There isn't anything we don't know about the modern city – its demography, its water table, its engineering design, its art, its slums, its economics, its politics. We just don't seem to know how to make it beautiful, accessible, safe, and clean.' And Wick adds: 'He could say similar things about almost any topic of general concern: inflation, pollution, unemployment, energy and food supplies, and so on.' In this 'and so on' I should include our social arrangements, our beliefs, our aims and our whole way of life, all of them the unwilled and unforeseen consequences of two centuries of increasingly rapid technological innovation and economic expansion.

Inevitably so, for the knowledge we are amassing and on which, commercially and politically, we do not hesitate to act, is scientific and technical only. As such it addresses itself to specific and immediate ends: namely, those it aims to control. What such knowledge cannot control, indeed, what it cannot foretell, are the manifold and complex consequences that come to affect both the smaller and larger ends of society. In particular, when such knowledge advances rapidly, and is no less rapidly harnessed to the task of changing the world, it is not possible for society as a whole to perceive the growing range of social repercussions, much less to appraise and debate them. It follows that society has no control over the larger destiny to which it is impelled by the forces of science and technology.

Nevertheless, we might want to press the question: are there any grounds, additional to the considerations adduced above, for believing that this destiny must necessarily be an ignoble one?

Of course, generations of economists, taking their inspiration from Adam Smith, have repeatedly and blithely affirmed that the collective economic outcome that results from a vast diversity of individual enterprise is also no part of any man's intention, nor indeed within any man's control. In this, they are subscribing to Smith's celebrated doctrine of 'the invisible hand' whereby the efforts of each man who seeks only his own commercial interest, channelled through a system of competitive markets, produces an outcome that is beneficial to society. The analysis, however, is invariably conducted within an economic context in which technology plays no part other than, perhaps, lowering production costs or improving the quality of the consumer goods.

Once we move into a world in which the vast and innovative powers of technology have become the primary force, the resulting impact in changing society – which again is not willed or foreseen by anyone – can no longer draw on the elements of Smith's analysis to create for us a comforting conclusion. There is already, as indicated, ample evidence to suggest that the effects on society are far from being uniformly benevolent. And there can be no longer a presumption either that they are *on balance* favourable.

With these observations in mind, the tasks I attempt in this volume include the following: to make clear to the reader why economic analysis is of little use in this context; to understand more intimately the nature of the social consequences of technological and economic growth; to assess them in the light of some acceptable norm; and, finally, to establish a presumption that continued technological and economic growth will act to worsen the human condition.

The writing of this first volume would have been far less enjoyable if I had insisted at all times on maintaining a tone of judicious detachment in presenting the arguments. For a determination to conceal my alarm about some development, or my disdain of some argument, behind an imperturbable facade would have sorely taxed my patience and ingenuity. It would have made the task both of writing and of reading this first volume more tiresome. The important thing, after all, is not to contrive to persuade the reader of an impartiality I do not feel, or to make the arguments always look evenly balanced when they seem to me to be quite otherwise. The important thing is to raise all the main issues, to eschew superficiality, to assess the importance of the issues, and to arrange them in some schematic way. This much can be accomplished irrespective of the particular views of the writer.

If on putting the book down the reader is better able to sort out the agenda of the economic growth debate from the non-agenda, if he is able to rank on the scale of significance the many elements comprising the agenda, and if he is able to think more clearly about any of these elements, the book will have achieved its main purpose. The reader cannot reasonably be expected to reach conclusions similar to mine in all details. Nor is he expected to afflict himself with the same degree of impatience and pessimism at the current turn of events – although, of course, I would be gratified if he should do so.

E.J.M.
May 1976

Contents

BOOK 1

Agenda and Non-Agenda in the Economic Growth Debate

Part I

Why a Strictly Economic Approach Will not Serve

Chapter 1

The Thraldom of Economic Growth

'Does money buy happiness?' is the title of a recent article by Professor Richard Easterlin (1973). Drawing its inspiration from the data of public opinion surveys, it concluded, tentatively, that in cross-country comparisons there was no clear relationship between average per capita income and degree of happiness. Within countries over time, however, there was evidence of a relationship. Americans, on balance, believed themselves to be less happy in 1970 than they were in 1957.

Such evidence, based as it has to be on 'self-anchoring' scales, is not entirely convincing. The data are certainly open to interpretation. Yet the figures for America between 1957 and 1970 are significant if only because, until comparatively recently, no people were more prone to regard themselves as the most fortunate of mortals than the Americans. More seriously, their significance lies in their contribution to the doubts being expressed about the social benefits of further economic growth.

The transition, in the West, from the Middle Ages to the Rennaisance was marked by a shift of the focus of concern from man's wellbeing in the hereafter to man's wellbeing here on earth. From the Enlightenment of the eighteenth century sprang the idea of the perfectibility of man, the product not of any divine intervention but of a deliberate social process. The Future – the secular Future – began to be seen as a promised land towards which, despite possible setbacks, mankind would unerringly be drawn. And, notwithstanding the traumatic experience of the 'Industrial Revolution' in Britain, the notion of progress as a continuing process, the product of man's ingenuity and purpose, took root in society well before the middle of the nineteenth century.

As the nineteenth century wore on, and society at large became increasingly aware of the contributions of science and technology to material improvements, which were diffused among the populace through the accumulation of capital and the spread of industry, there were few, very few – the eccentric genius of Ruskin or of Carlyle comes to mind – who did not seriously believe that economic progress was a wholly beneficent phenomenon. There were, of course, any number of movements organised to remedy social deficiences, to eliminate particular abuses, and to promote political and economic reform. In the first half of the nineteenth century in particular, militant revolts and Luddite incidents were far from rare. On more than one occasion, Britain seemed to be dangerously close to revolution. But none of these things succeeded in shaking the growing belief that economic progress, taken as a whole, was socially beneficial. Indeed, until the 1960s, the belief in economic progress had so pervaded our thinking as to become, in effect, a tacit presupposition about the working of Providence. Even those profoundly discontented with the existing distribution of wealth, with the class structure, or with any other feature of the economic or social system, never doubted its dynamic wealth-producing potential which, they believed, could be harnessed for the good of all. Political utopias, whether of Right or Left, were, and still are, predicated on the notion of releasing the potential of science, and directing its force to serve 'the needs of the people'. In short, whatever the shape of the future envisaged, it was to be realised through continued economic growth.

Since World War II, the more specific economic concept of growth has become not merely one of the economic goals of social policy. Like Aaron's rod, when transformed into a serpent, it was seen to swallow all its rivals – or almost all. For governments did, in fact, continue to concern themselves with the level of employment, with the balance of payments, with the distribution of national income and, more recently, with the pace of inflation. Nevertheless, in considering alternative remedies for any problems they posed, governments were always mindful of their implications for the pace of economic growth, regarded as a paramount long-term objective for society.

The economic growth rate is the one indicator of progress to which politicians of every party pay homage. As a criterion by which the nation's overall performance is judged, and by which the current worths of nations are compared, the index of economic growth has achieved international recognition as the common standard of virtue. Over the last fifteen years, for instance, fashionable newspaper articles on Britain's 'Failure in the modern world',

Britain's 'Plight', Britain's 'Decline', etc. have had practically nothing to say on any aspect of British life save the economic. And that itself focused on economic *growth* or, rather, on the British growth performance in comparison with the performances of other countries, chiefly those of Western Europe. For a decade and a half, then, the British people were to be represented by successive governments, by industrialists, by journalists and by technocrats – in fact, by all who fondly piqued themselves on being in the vanguard of progress and in amiable alliance with the Future – as the incorrigible laggards of the New Europe. Radio commentary, lectures, orations, sermons, all waxed eloquent at some point on the 'English disease' and, when not facetious, spoke darkly either of our impending eclipse by other more 'thrustful' nations or of our being bypassed by the twentieth century. And such is the power of reiteration that by the early 1970s, with all the modern paraphernalia of prosperity blatantly in evidence, cluttering up our homes and cluttering up our streets, more than half the housewives of Britain, even those who couldn't tell a growth index from a cigarette coupon, had begun to worry about 'Britain's economic survival'.

By then, of course, every facet of our national life, other than the economic, had faded from the horizon. The British contribution to science and literature, to drama and ballet; Britain's unparalleled institutions, her broadcasting services, her police, her law courts, her university system; the political genius of the British people, the humaneness of their society, the prevailing climate of moderation and good sense – inestimable assets, all the products of a complex historical process, were just not agenda for this new economic assessment of the worth of a nation. Indeed, so thoroughly demoralised had the nation become that, when stripped by government fiat (and in the name of economic efficiency, of course) of the emblems of her identity – of her pounds and shillings, her pints and yards, her acres and fathoms – measures that are part of her Anglo-Saxon heritage, words that are resonant with her history and form an essential part of her language, her culture, her literature – nothing could be heard but the muted sounds of baffled antagonism.

However, to return to the broader theme, it is no uncommon occurence in history for a dominant ideology to find itself being undermined at the time of its widest diffusion throughout society. Certainly, the variety of protest movements that have come, over the last ten years, to challenge the policy of continued economic growth have never been more articulate. Doubts expressed today about the ultimate beneficence of economic growth, indeed, of progress in general, are no longer regarded by the intellectual public as an eccentric indulgence. Quite the contrary, scepticism about progress threatens to become one of the fashionable heresies of the day, especially among the 'socially concerned'. And yet, as much from fear as from faith, the world manages to skirt the more pessimistic implications, helped along by growthmen who have a fondness for spinning ingenuous phrases about using further economic growth in order to undo the harmful effects of past and present economic growth, or in order to improve the quality of life, or in order to increase leisure, culture and learning, and, unsurprisingly, in order to reduce poverty. These and other impressive rationalisations for further economic growth (which are examined in Part III) are comprehended by the judicious maxim which today finds a place in the peroration of every pro-growth statesman: economic growth must not be abandoned; it must be given 'a new direction'.

Yet, as doubts have spread and taken root throughout the West, the pro-growth Establishment can be expected for some time to go on making boisterous sounds, to shove on gamely, to go over to the counterattack and to reaffirm its faith in economic growth – such reactions being, also, a part of the good fight against what threatens to be an engulfing sense of purposelessness. For it must be allowed that a reluctance, officially, to face the realities of continuing economic growth is not wholly irrational. Bearing in mind that the trauma of passing from a predominantly religious society to a predominantly secular one over the last three centuries was mitigated by a growing belief that material progress and the advance of learning would bring about universal peace and plenty, it is not going to be easy to abandon that faith today. For we cannot return to an earlier state and believe again what we believed once; lost innocence cannot be retrieved. What is more, there is today no alternative universal ideal to inspire us. Therefore, if we observe that, despite decades of material improvement, all social statistics indicate a growing sense of malaise and unfulfilment, there is a temptation to believe, or at least to hope, that some further growth, plus, perhaps, some special research programme or carefully 'structured' plan, will yet enable us to 'stop the rot'.

This belief or hope is nourished by a popular awareness of the growth and fastidiousness of modern scholarship in the social sciences. In economics, in particular, a good proportion of the professional literature is devoted to the measurement of economic progress and to sophisticated analysis designed to reveal the conditions necessary for improving 'economic welfare'. The first thing to be done, therefore, is to make clear to the general reader just how limited are the conventional economic premises and concepts as they are used in the measurement and the analysis of changes in 'real' income or welfare. Chapters 2 and 3 have been written for this purpose.

Chapter 2

Limitations of the Conventional Economic Premises and Concepts

In the traditional credenda of the economist, more is better. Indeed, the textbook description of economic growth as a process that effectively 'widens the area of choice' would seem to sanction a presumption in favour of an economic system that, over time, produces – among other things – a per capita increase in man-made goods and services.

But even if it could be said of economic growth that it expands unambiguously the options open to the consumer, it would not follow that men should be regarded as being better off. For one thing, these options refer only to the amounts and varieties of goods available to the average person in his capacity of consumer. In his other roles, as worker, citizen, member of the family or part of the larger community, the individual may not be faced with more options as a result of continuing economic growth. If there are new opportunities in some respects, in other respects there can be a withdrawal of opportunities. In general, economic growth has many effects on a man's life, besides expanding the choice of market goods. What is more, even if all the other opportunities available to him do remain unchanged over time as economic growth continues, it is plausible to believe that a stage will be reached beyond which greater levels of output will add virtually nothing to his wellbeing. This is so not only because a point of satiation exists even for the most acquisitive animal, but also because, in high income societies, an individual's satisfaction comes to depend less on his absolute income and more on his income relative to the incomes of others, a topic we shall touch on later.

Notwithstanding these considerations, the traditional approach in economic theory is one which assumes, explicitly, that more is better. It is so convenient an assumption for the economist that unless there is strong evidence to the contrary it is unlikely to be relinquished. However, for the economist, as indeed for the scientist generally, evidence has to be of the measurable sort – able, that is, to withstand statistical scrutiny. Since quantitative relationships tending either to confirm or to deny this convenient premise are hard to come by, we are left with a methodological bias in favour of economic growth, one that can be detected even in statements that appear reasonable and just. For instance, according to Professor Richard Zeckhauser (1973), '*If we could demonstrate* an adverse causal relationship between economic growth and these (welfare) variables, we might wish to slow growth despite the economic consequences' (my italics). As Zeckhauser sees it, then, the burden of proof is to be on those who are sceptical of the benefits of economic growth. In effect, then, ignorance or uncertainty is to be translated into a mandate to continue along the growth path.

In the more orthodox economic inquiry, moreover, it is as well to be aware also of a strong presumption in favour of a number of particular trends that economic growth seems to promote. They include increased mobility, both social and geographical, increased information, increased education, increased medical facilities, increased welfare expenditures, and increased travel and recreation. In more detail, they include increased book sales, increased home ownership and increased sales of refrigerators, washing machines, television sets and other hardware. Greater economic equality is also included among the broader social goods, although its association with modern economic growth is historical rather than causal – a result, primarily, of the political expression in Western democracies of the rise in egalitarian sentiment.

It is certainly convenient for social scientists to agree on such measurable indices of social welfare. It enables them to offer more specific advice to governments, and so enhances their status as social scientists. They can devise strategies for accelerating this or that agreeable trend. And if the phenomena they agree on as indicators of social welfare happen also to be those which are, in fact, facilitated or promoted by economic growth, there is the additional satisfaction of seeing their aspirations realised and their recommendations taking effect over time. In consequence, they will be regarded by the Establishment as being among the more diligent and dependable 'forward-lookers'.

But the choice of the above trends as indicators of social welfare has not been closely argued in the standard economic literature on the subject.[1] In effect they are, as stated, no more than presumptions and, as such, have been strongly influenced by the spirit of economic growth and the prevailing democratic sentiment. Such presumptions are inadmissible in a study that seeks to raise more searching questions about the effects of economic growth in general, and of these trends in particular, on people's experience of wellbeing.

SOURCES OF COMPLACENCY

In response to the growing concern at the rate of depletion of non-renewable resources, the economist has recourse to three arguments. (a) First, he informs the supposedly simple-minded ecologist that, although many currently used resources will indeed eventually come to an end, they will not do so abruptly. In the absence of technical improvements or new discoveries of reserves, the price of scarce materials will rise over time, a movement that causes producers and consumers to economise increasingly on its use and that provides industry with the incentive necessary to discover or invent substitute materials. (b) Secondly, and as an extension of the first argument, it is pointed out that there is an 'optimal time path' for the price and output of each non-renewable resource, whether fossil fuel or mineral, and also that a well-functioning market (by which is usually meant a highly competitive market) tends to bring such optimal paths into existence. (c) Thirdly, the economist shares a fondness with the technocrat for producing instances of unwarranted alarms, in the past, about the running-out of this or that resource, and seeks to clinch his arguments by producing evidence of some decline in the relative prices of important raw materials over time.[2]

Now these arguments are not very reassuring. First, the fact that, in the absence of technical innovation, the increasing scarcity of a material is accompanied by a rising price (leading to the forms of adaptation mentioned) does not solve the problem of scarcity. The rising price is no more than the simple economic mechanism which translates scarcity into an increase in the cost of living.

As for this much-vaunted concept of the optimal time path, along which the rate of price rise of the depleting resource is directly related to the expected yield on current investment,[3] its correct determination over the immediate future, and over the lifetime of the scarce material in question, depends upon present knowledge of all future demand and supply schedules (including those of sources yet to be discovered) as well as of future yields on investment. Such a time profile is not actually known, and the mere fact that the price of the material happens to be rising over the present period cannot be taken as evidence that we are exploiting it at the socially correct rate.

What is more, the most perfectly competitive market for the

depleting material cannot ensure that the price path follows the optimal. Only perfect foreknowledge of demand and supply conditions, and of investment yields, either by the competing firms or else by competing speculators operating a futures' market, could do that – which amounts to saying that the competitive economy cannot realise the optimal time path.

Finally, in the same connection, even if, by some miracle, this optimal time path could be followed, the problem of depletion would not be resolved. It would be resolved only if the current generation were the only generation, for it is optimal only in virtue of its generating the maximum present value of expected net social benefits over the future. But since this maximum present value is obtained by *discounting* (at a rate equal to the investment yield) the future net benefits, it is a maximum only for persons living today – not for persons yet to be born. Thus, conditions of expected demand and supply of the depletable material might be such that, on this calculation of optimality, the whole of the world's existing stocks should be used up within, say, twenty or thirty years. And there is nothing in the calculations to prevent the lot from being consumed within that period, leaving nothing at all for future generations.

Turning, thirdly, to the somewhat dated evidence of a relative decline of important raw materials over time, it is hard to believe that the apparent success story of the last 200 years can be repeated, when the scale of depletion today is incomparably greater than what it was 200 or even 100 or 50 years ago. We have had no previous experience of running out of a large number of currently important materials on a world scale. And it is entirely possible that technology will not, after all, succeed in producing adequate substitutes, and, certainly, not without increasing the ecological risks which are associated with the production and consumption of synthetic substances.[4]

Complacency can also be found in the response of some economists to the topical concern with pollution.[5] The phenomenon is subsumed under the more comprehensive concept of 'external diseconomies', 'spillover effects' or 'spillovers'. These can be described briefly as the direct,[6] though incidental, consequences on other people's welfare of the legitimate activities of some persons, firms or industries.

So rapidly has our awareness of pollutants grown since 1960 that a new process having no discernible spillovers is apt to be regarded today as the exception to the rule: ' 'Tis a good wind that blows no one any harm.' At all events, even the most conservative economist now agrees that changes in GNP are no longer acceptable as an index of changes in social welfare or in social product – at least not without there first being made a number of corrections, chief among which is the subtraction from GNP of some estimate of the damage sustained by the proliferation of adverse spillovers.

There are, not surprisingly, formidable problems to be faced in attempts to estimate the social costs of adverse spillovers.[7] But recognition of them cannot lead to the conclusion supposed by some economists[8] that, unless it can be shown that the value of spillover damage exceeds the value of the additional product, the nation must on balance have improved its welfare. As indicated earlier, such statements pluck an affirmative from ignorance by arbitrary imposition of the burden of proof.

But economists have other ways of sheltering themselves from the winds of public passion. Many feel satisfied after acknowledging the incidence of current spillovers, after classifying them, after tracing their origin to institutional inadequacies, or after making the standard (often impractical) proposals for their correction. Seldom do they miss an opportunity to explain patiently to the innocent layman that zero pollution would be an absurd target to aim for – since the social benefits of incurring some pollution will exceed the social cost of the damage. And this observation often tempts them onwards to describe the attractive characteristics of the 'optimal' or 'just right' amount of pollution – which, in practice, would be of great value if only people today had the information necessary to estimate the extent of the damage, or of the risk of damage, falling on themselves and their descendants, of any of these pollutants taken singly or in combination. Nonetheless, the pro-growth economist continues to descant on the problem and, for good measure, will offer a few instances – which is not too tiresome since, in fact, there are only a few – of recent cleaning-up operations, in order to convey the impression that the Establishment has such matters well under control.[9]

SPILLOVERS ARE NOT THE ONLY PROBLEM

There is today a growing number of economists who are deeply troubled by the environmental problems that arise from the application of sophisticated technologies. Compared with the situation in the profession ten years ago, this is a remarkable improvement. Nevertheless, the number of economists who are professionally concerned with the *social* consequences of technological progress, or, more generally, of economic growth, is less impressive. It is safe to say, then, that, of those economists working on problems of the impact of technology or economic growth on the quality of life, by far the greater proportion regard the concept of 'external diseconomies' (or adverse spillovers), and their incidence in the economy, as central to the question of social welfare.

Now I should be the first to admit that the continuing economic analysis and debate about these spillovers, about their institutional genesis, about the group conflicts they engender, and about the alternative methods open to society for dealing with such problems, are highly informative and sophisticated.[10] Yet the impression they convey is generally the same: that if, somehow, all adverse spillover effects could properly be corrected, any residual economic growth could not but produce an improvement of social welfare. This view is wholly misleading. However important these spillover problems are, their successful resolution would, if possible, contribute to making life more enjoyable only in limited respects. The really significant issues may have more to do with the array of social consequences that stem from the nature of the innovations produced by economic growth – including, of course, the consequences on the attitudes, values and institutions of society.

If we grant that, for the same 'real' productive power per capita, life can be either rich and wholesome or sick and threadbare, then clearly there are dimensions to welfare other than the freedom to choose – at prices equal to social marginal costs – among a variety of man-made goods. Thus we might imagine two communities, A and B, both having the same size and composition of population, and both inhabiting much the same kind of geographical area. In so far as private competitive enterprise or economic efficiency is the criterion, or output per capita is the criterion, we may assume that there is nothing to choose between them. But there can be other acceptable criteria.

Society A, let us suppose, has much beautiful architecture, broad tree-lined boulevards and spacious parks. It has quiet, frequent and efficient public transport services within and between towns and cities, none of which, however, exceed half a million in population. People dress well, but not ostentatiously. Society A is regulated by a strong code of ethics and strong sense of propriety, which attributes appear to be entirely compatible with cheerfulness and good fellowship. There is no commercial advertising, and no television. But there is an abundance of good music and good theatre. Apart from sports and outdoor recreation, citizens of country A entertain themselves through a variety of different social clubs and by extending their hospitality to family and friends. Travel is limited, and so life is leisurely and the environment unspoilt. The people on the whole are contented and, in the main, seek civic distinction rather than personal aggrandisement. Not surprisingly, there is little crime and drug taking.

Citizens of country B, on the other hand, spend much of their time gazing listlessly at their television screens, or motoring vast distances in congested traffic in attempts to escape the desolation of the vast urban wastelands, placarded with commercial posters, strewn with litter, clamorous with noise, rent by traffic and steeped in dust and gas fumes. The citizens think of themselves as 'dynamic' and 'highly motivated', which is to say that they have become restive and desperate to advance their material status. Moral checks are weak; almost 'anything goes' with respect to dress and behaviour. Pornographic theatre and pornographic literature are expanding industries. There is much drug taking, alcoholism, gun toting and street violence; in consequence, there is little trust between neighbours and suspicion between strangers.

Society A is a mythical one. Technically, it is wholly feasible, though it must seem implausible to those nurtured in a commercial economy whose continued expansion demands a continuous whetting of consumers' appetites to the margin of insatiability. Society B, on the other hand, is all too plausible. However, their respective plausibility does not matter in this context. They could be regarded as hypothetical societies, both having, as indicated, free competitive markets for all goods in the private sector, while goods in the public sector are determined by voting mechanisms based on universal suffrage. We can further suppose that the familiar range of environmental spillovers in B – urban pollution, traffic congestion, etc. – is held in check by a system of 'optimal taxes', notwithstanding which there remains a depressing amount of pollution and traffic congestion.

Are we now to follow the conventional self-denying ordinances of the professional economist and forbear from ranking societies A and B on the scale of better or worse? Are we, in other words, to assert that any statement that A is the better society must be regarded as an unwarranted imposition of one's personal values? If we elect to do so, the debate on the welfare implications of economic growth would have to end here. We should then be conceding that the only valid criteria in judging the welfare of alternative societies are conventional economic criteria – the competitiveness of markets for goods and 'bads' (adverse spillovers),[11] ideal taxes, the volume of goods produced and possibly, also, their distribution among society's members.

But if we are genuinely interested in the welfare, and the character, of society, we should be unwilling to reconcile ourselves to this restriction on our judgment – to accept that the smooth operation of competitive markets, and the level and distribution of outputs, are the only criteria to be respected.

It does not matter, in this connection, whether the profession itself has resolved to exclude any other criteria in comparing alternative situations from the scope of economics. For, at this juncture, I am writing to doff my professional cap and to speak without the authority of economic analysis – to appeal to imagination, reason and good sense, only. Nor does it matter that other criteria may be difficult to agree upon, or that their adoption raises problems. Such difficulties and problems have to be faced simply because the conventional economic criteria are patently inadequate; for example, acceptance of them would mean that we should be indifferent in any choice between societies A and B. Worse, such conventional economic criteria can be wholly misleading. For who doubts that the wealthier and economically more efficient society can also be the less healthy, the less honest, the less secure and the less contented?

Thus, under conditions familiar to economists, the market may be a perfect instrument of rational choice. Yet at the same time it can be morally blind. Both Nazism and Quakerism, both a society of free men and a slave society, are compatible with perfectly functioning markets and high productivity.[12] Certainly, increasing wealth and competitive markets – also an economy in which there were no effective labour unions and a minimum of government intervention in industry – existed side by side with the fourteen-hour workday, with soul-destroying occupations for men and women and with the heartless exploitation of child labour, in the England of the first half of the nineteenth century. Confining oneself to the conventional economic criteria, no criticism of the epoch is possible – save, possibly, that the distribution of income was less egalitarian than it is now. By the light of these conventional economic criteria we should not discover that, for the mass of the working class families, life was ugly, cruel and often degrading.

To be brief, then, the market will indeed serve to express and facilitate the aesthetic propensities of an aesthetic society, and it will serve also to express and facilitate the good propensities of a good society. But the market will also express and facilitate the sadistic propensities of a sadistic society, and, for that matter, the licentious and vicious propensities of a society that is itself becoming licentious and vicious. And, in all these cases, the market serves the character and purposes of society as efficiently, irrespective of the level of wealth and its distribution.

Thus, the studies for which economists are, by conventional training, most fitted, and in the pursuit of which they can bring to bear their theory and refined statistical techniques – namely, the measurement of changes in the levels of production, in distribution and in the incidence of spillover effects – though undeniably useful, may be of small consequence. For improvements in any of these respects contribute only in limited ways to social welfare. They are overshadowed, in affluent countries at least, by social tendencies, arising from the economic growth process itself, that have far-reaching influences on welfare. This being the case, we should not regard an inverse relation between wealth and welfare, in some social contexts, as being in any way paradoxical. Economic growth is neither necessary nor sufficient for the growth of social welfare; indeed, we must be prepared to discover that further pursuit of economic growth is inimical to the good life we aspire to.

Chapter 3

How Real Income and its Growth Are Over-stated

In Chapter 2, I have suggested that any presumption of a connection between economic growth and social welfare should be treated with scepticism. This scepticism can be reinforced by some brief consideration of the ways in which current estimates of 'real'[13] income, viewed (as they almost invariably are) as indicators of national well-being, if not of national virtue, tend to overstate the magnitude of the net achievement and, also, to exaggerate the improvement over time – even when we abstract entirely from considerations that enter into the quality of life.

The tenor of my observations is not unfamiliar to economists, many of whom make ingenious suggestions and calculations from time to time in the attempt to correct for sources of bias in national income comparisons. Since the purpose is only to impress on the general reader the restricted and sometimes misleading nature of national income comparisons over time, I shall not go beyond discussion of a number of examples that reveal the nature and extent of the problem.

The problem in question is this. A large proportion of the goods that enter into estimates of national income,[14] or a nation's per capita income, are not, in fact, finished goods, or goods 'wanted for their own sake', as they ought to be. Rather they are *intermediate* goods, or goods that are only instrumental in the production of finished goods and also, therefore, by extension, instrumental in the reduction of the incidental damages caused in the production or use of the finished goods. There is, as always in such cases, some uncertainty about where the line should be drawn, and discussions about particular cases could take us far afield. But, to repeat, we are not interested here in exploring the problem in general. I shall therefore illustrate relevant aspects of the problem with instances on which there is widespread agreement, plus a few also which may be thought controversial.

INTERNAL AND EXTERNAL DEFENCE

It is generally agreed that additional expenditures on internal and/or external defence do not betoken any increase in social welfare – at least, not when the comparison is made with some preceding period in which the need for these additional expenditures was not felt. If, for example, in response to an increased threat of crime, an existing expenditure of $20 billion on the police has to be raised to $30 billion in order to afford the community the same sense of security, the additional $10 billion spent on the police adds nothing to social welfare. In the circumstances, the additional resources may be regarded as an increase simply in costs of providing the same amount of the finished good, security. Like remarks apply to any increase in expenditures on external defence.

To avoid misunderstanding, however, I ought to add that it does not follow that such additional expenditures are *wasted* in the economic sense of the word. Aware of the increased dangers to itself, the community may collectively agree that the additional resources used in its defence could not, in fact, be put to any better use; better to incur these additional expenses, it is believed, than to submit to the increased dangers. But this quite rational choice is entirely consistent with the conclusion that social welfare itself has not increased as compared with the original (less dangerous) situation, in spite of this additional expenditure of $10 billion.

It follows that if US citizens today feel no more secure from internal or external threat than they did, say, fifty years ago, even though they are spending $100 billion more (at 1975 prices), then in any comparison of net national incomes (regarded as indices of net wellbeing) of the two years a subtraction of at least $100 billion has to be made in today's net national income.

TRAVEL

Unless all the time spent travelling is enjoyed for its own sake, the increase in hours travelled, or the increase in travel expenditures, ought not to be counted as an increase in the amounts of finished goods. That part of travel time, or that part of the travel expenditure, that is needed simply as a means of reaching a destination should properly be regarded as an intermediate good. Expenditure on this latter kind of travel is not then a part of real net national income. Since it does in fact enter as such, it ought then to be subtracted from net national income.

What is the proportion of such intermediate travel to total travel? Some guesses have put it at more than 50 per cent, which figure, I am inclined to think, is on the low side. For such intermediate travel includes not only journeys to work, and business travel, but some portion also of travel in pursuit of recreational activities. Unless one is constantly deriving pleasure from the motion of the vehicle, from the view, or from the steering in traffic, the time and expenditure on travel towards some non-business destination cannot be treated as though it were a desirable good in itself.

In a pre-industrial economy, in contrast, one lived close to one's work. A few minutes' walk from one's home town or village, and one was in broad country. The amount of cross-country movement and foreign travel was incomparably smaller than it is today. In response to the coming of the motor car, we have built urban areas of such extent that very few today are able to walk to work. In many conurbations of America, it has become highly inconvenient, if not impossible, to travel any way other than by private automobile.

The relevant question is whether the proportion of travel time and expenditure that is properly an intermediate good has been growing over the last few decades. And the answer is clearly yes for all Western countries. It is not enough, however, to subtract the value of this intermediate good from its inclusion in the value of finished goods. Some further subtraction should be effected for the actual inconvenience suffered in having to undertake such journeys.

What has been said of ground travel extends also to air travel, much of which again is an intermediate good only and, indeed, a good which is for the most part suffered rather than enjoyed.

EDUCATION

A very large part of modern education, both of child and adult, is a form of current expenditure necessary to replenish the stock of skilled human capital, without which the running of a highly industrialised economy would be impossible. The fruit of these expenditures, along with the expenditures on capital equipment, is the high standard of living the citizens of such an economy are deemed to enjoy.

Again, we have to make the usual distinction between new capital (or net additions to the stock of existing capital) and replacement capital. By far the greater portion of annual investment in plant and industrial equipment is excluded from net national income, for the simple reason that it serves only to replace capital that is used up in the current production of goods. Such replacement investment is, then, really no more than a part of the cost of maintaining the industrial machine that produces current output (though its quality, or efficiency, does indeed increase over time).

Another part of this annual cost of maintaining the industrial machine, however, is the bulk of annual education expenditure. Assuming all educational expenditure to be vocational in nature, in the sense of training children and adults to take their place in industry, all of it would be maintenance costs or replacement investment (in human skills) – at least in a stationary economy operating at a high level of productivity. For, in such an economy, the stock both of physical capital and of human capital would remain constant over time.

However, the assumption that all educational expenditure is vocational in the above sense is too severe; some part is indeed valued in its own right, even where it has no market value. We should not, therefore, be justified in subtracting from net national income the whole of educational expenditure, only a part – though the larger part in a modern economy. Again, in a growing economy, the stock of skilled human capital may increase during the year just as the stock of physical capital may. Any such net addition to current capital, physical or human, will, by definition, be a part of net national product.

MEDIA INFORMATION

What is said of education can be said, also, of books, newspapers and a lot of television and radio broadcasting. Information of what is happening within the country and abroad, a part of which is necessary to the economic and political operation of modern society, partakes of the nature of an intermediate good. A lot of such information, that is, can be regarded as indispensable for social reasons. A person who is not *au courant* with the news will feel himself to be at a disadvantage in company. And if, over time, there is more news to be absorbed, he will try to absorb it if for no other reason.

Thus such information can increase over time without anyone's feeling the better for it and, indeed, with many people's feeling the worse for it. For the additional time, effort and expenditures incurred in trying to keep up with the growing spate of information can be regarded as unavoidable efforts and defensive expenditures. In as much as the expenditures, at least, on books, newspapers and media enter the net national income as finished goods, a substantial proportion of them can be subtracted. More yet should be subtracted when account is taken of the time, effort and anxiety involved in this process of keeping up.

MEDICINE

If it could be assumed that medical services continued over time to maintain the population in the same state of health, then there would be a case for deducting all expenditure on health and medicine from net national product – regarding it, that is, as an intermediate expense necessary to keep the industrial machine going. If this correction were not made, an increase, say, of $30 billion this year, compared with last year, on medical expenditure would have then to be subtracted from this year's net national income before a fair comparison could be made. The case would be analogous to a rise by $30 billion in the cost of producing exactly the same assortment of manufactured goods. If this were the only change to have taken place this year as compared with last year, the economy would be $30 billion worse off as a result of this extra cost.

However, there have been two forces at work over the last two centuries. On the one hand, medical knowledge has been advancing and, by itself, would have tended to produce a higher standard of health in the community. On the other hand, the economic growth process has been associated with a number of factors bearing on health, some beneficial, others deleterious. Among the latter factors, industrialisation, urbanisation, more noise and pollution, more specialisation and study, and an increase in the pace and competitiveness of life all are generally held to have adverse effects on health, and to be partly responsible for an increase in the incidence of coronary, carcinogous, bronchial and nervous diseases. Moreover, in trying to cope with the stress of urban living, a proportion of the adult population is becoming increasingly dependent upon a wide variety of drugs, from alcohol and tobacco to tranquillisers and narcotics (additional expenditures on which would not then signify a commensurate increase in real income).

Striking a balance is a very impressionistic business. Even if we had precise figures on every malady over the years, and an agreed system of weights, we should hardly be able to say with conviction that the population today is healthier than it was, say, before World War II, or indeed, than it was in some pre-industrial age when continual physical exercise, fresh air, a fairly quiet and unhurried existence, an undisturbed routine, and an absence of 'motivation and anxiety all contributed to health of ordinary people.

We conclude that there is a case for subtracting from net nationa income all medical and health expenditure over the period in question, save to the extent that there has been some distinc improvement in health. This improvement in health is not, however, to be measured in terms of longevity alone. Survival up to age 70 as a result of new medical techniques that enable a man to overcome a succession of maladies is not the same thing as the enjoyment of good health up to that age.

It should be borne in mind, incidentally, that the figures given for longevity tend to mislead. True, infantile mortality has declined over the last hundred years, and it is certainly lower today than it was in pre-industrial times. To that extent the overall expectation of life has increased. But if we exclude infant mortality and, instead, compare the expected longevity of those surviving their fifth or tenth year, this marked superiority of modern times disappears.

VACATIONS

In a civilisation where stress diseases are commonplace, vacations may also be thought of as fitting into the category of medical expenditures. They may also be enjoyable in themselves, but they are necessary for the maintenance of physical and mental health. Without them, people could not long continue to function efficiently, and the industrial economy would break down. So regarded, they are, in part, intermediate goods – part of the costs of running the industrial machine.

In particular, it should be noted that the growth of these expenditures does not necessarily imply a growth in the enjoyment of vacations. As the strains become greater, longer and perhaps more frequent, recuperation periods are necessary, and the costs too become higher. With the rapid spread of urban and suburban development, and the growth in the popularity of mass travel, it becomes more costly to travel farther afield in the attempt to 'get away from it all'.

CLOTHING

Expenditure on clothing poses similar problems. The matter is least controversial wherever the job carries with it an obligation to wear particular clothing either for protection, for identification or for conformity. Outside such categories there is a lot of latitude in allocating how much of a person's clothing expenditure should be classified either as finished goods expenditure or as expenditure on intermediate goods.

Neither are fashion goods to be thought of as entirely finished goods. There can be a strong element of social or vocational compulsion about their choice. A person may, of course, ignore fashion on some occasions. But he can only go so far without suffering discomfort, and without risk to his occupational or other pecuniary prospects.

One might go on to argue that food expenditures in the richer countries, being in excess of what is required for an adequate and varied diet, are also partly intermediate expenditures. Some of it is certainly business-dictated and fashion-dictated. The same can be said of expenditures in recreation over time in response to rising levels of productivity. Recreation assumes more expensive forms, though not necessarily more enjoyable ones. It is not plausible to believe that the yeomen of fourteenth-century England enjoyed their longbow archery tournaments any less than today's executives enjoy their boating or golfing. But pursuit of this line of thought raises philosophical questions about the relation between goods and satisfaction, that we defer to later.

INSTITUTIONAL LUBRICANTS

This is a category that is large and indeterminate. As the economy becomes more complex, new institutions and services come into being that were unnecessary in a simpler economy. The values of these new services appear as finished goods in the national accounts and are added to the net product. Yet they are used, not for the direct enjoyment they offer to customers, but simply because – in the more complex society associated with higher living standards – they serve, like the postal and telephone services, to facilitate the business of living, and to reduce the sources of friction and frustration arising therefrom.

Many of the services provided by banks, labour unions, employment agencies, stockbrokers, travel agents, marriage agencies, and such like are those which were just not needed in a traditional society. Indeed, many of the legislative, administrative and judicial functions that abound in a modern economy are the result of its size, complexity and communications system. In a country the size of the United States, the cost of such services would be of the order of several score billion dollars. Over time, therefore, a proportion of the apparent increase in net national product will be from this category of services.

A controversial, but an increasingly important, amendment to the conventional calculation of net national income might also be touched upon in passing. In so far as the definition of income is the increase in the value of the product above all the expenditure necessary to maintain capital intact, there will have to be further deductions from net national income if – as can reasonably be claimed – the earth's finite resources are regarded as part of the stock of our capital wealth. Thus, from the annual income derived, say, from mining, which is made up of rents (or profits) and wages and salaries paid out in the process of using up the minerals, we must, on this logic, subtract the net value of the minerals that are consumed.

In addition to these sources of bias, there has been over the last century a number of services, hitherto unpriced, that are increasingly entered into the national product. The most common textbook example is housewives' domestic work, which includes cooking, washing, house cleaning, laundering, dressmaking and looking after the children. Much of this once-unpriced traditional housework is now divided into new services industries: laundries, dry-cleaners and precooked and processed foodstuffs. In as much as the housewife today uses modern gadgets – dishwashers, clothes washers, vacuum cleaners, electric mixers and other implements – a substantial part of the services she used to provide in the home is now provided (more efficiently) by specialised capital and labour. But the services the housewife provides in the home were never priced, and did not therefore enter the national product, whereas those who today provide – via gadgets or directly – a large part of these services earn incomes that do enter the value of the national product. To that extent, again, historical comparisons tend to overstate the improvement.

Similarly, in days gone by, the work done by a man in his garden, or the wood he chopped for fuel, did not enter the national accounts. In contrast, when some part of this work is done today by modern garden implements, or when his home is heated by coal or oil, all the income of those who provide him with these services does indeed enter the national income. Yet a bit more of the apparent growth of national income over time is illusory.

Again, although costly domestic sanitary arrangements, and the disposal of rubbish and sewage, are essential to public health in densely populated areas, such expenditures were not necessary in small rural communities.

The rapid growth in population mobility has led inevitably to a collapse of the social life of town and village, the primary condition for which is a settled population. The consequent search for new forms of solace and entertainment led to the music halls, carnivals and brass bands of the latter part of the nineteenth century, to the cinema and radio of the twentieth century and, since World War II, to television and stereophonics supplemented by an indigestible diet of 'human interest' items and fantasy sex in our newspapers and magazines.

Indeed, it is difficult to call a halt to the train of examples of those innovations that, looking at first blush like contributions to a higher standard of living, appear on further surmise to be more like contributions to a higher cost of living. So much of the nation's effort and ingenuity is spent in producing sophisticated products and specialised services that cater to basic biological and psychic needs which were more easily, and often more fully, met in pre-industrial societies.[15]

Finally, some part of both public and private expenditure is today allocated to the goal of restoring once-free amenities that have become damaged in the process of economic growth. Under such 'regrettable' expenditures are those used for reducing toxicity of air and water; for reducing noise levels, fire hazards and motor accidents; for removing mountains of slag or metal tailings; for filling in pits; for cleaning coastlines, lakes and rivers – in effect, for trying to restore the natural assets man has been destroying for decades. From one year to the next, such expenditure on restoring the environment is indeed a good, and represents an improvement. But in comparison with an earlier age, one having an undamaged environment, such expenditures have to be regarded as intermediate goods; that is, as a part of the costs of production that have to be incurred in the endeavour to maintain intact the natural (environmental) capital of the country. Including such restorative expenditures as part of the national income therefore also overstates real income today as compared with the real income of an earlier age.

It is important to emphasise this last amendment, since some economists have misperceived the implications of this process of restoration. For instance, Edwin Mills (1975) alleges that there is an antigrowth bias in the environmental literature arising from a failure to realise that, with continued growth, resources can be directed to environmental protection as well as to the production of manufactures. The statement evokes a picture of the economy sunk under an accumulation of pollutants waiting patiently for economic growth to provide the resources necessary to remove them. That we have sadly damaged our global environment (as a consequence of economic growth) is alas true, and that resources can always be devoted to making some improvement is also true. What is *not* true, however, is that environmental restoration or desirable improvements have to wait upon further economic growth.

In fact, the economic analysis pertinent to pollutants, or 'spillovers' (as the economist loosely calls them), is wholly independent of economic growth. This is true whether the analysis addresses itself to the determination of 'optimal' pollution levels or to the cost-benefit calculations of installing antipollutant equipment. The fact that economic growth is or is not occurring alters neither the analysis nor the economically 'ideal' solution at any moment of time. What is more, any effect that economic growth may have on real incomes does not necessarily produce 'ideal' or optimal solutions having less residual pollution.

It may be true that higher incomes from economic growth result in the placing of a higher value on the damage suffered from pollution. But economic growth itself introduces new, often more insidious, spillovers and, to boot, new consumer and producer interests to prevent corrective legislation from being effective (see Chapter 11).

NOTES FOR PART 1

Chapter 2

1 A recent, and welcome, swerve from adherence to the standard economic indicators of welfare mentioned above is to be found in the US document *Toward a Social Report,* published by the US Department of Health, Education and Welfare under the direction of Professor Mancur Olson (1969). In addition to the old favourites – income distribution, health, social mobility and education – there were chapters on indicators of environmental damage, crime and alienation.

2 More often than not, the figures are those given by Harold Barnett and Charles Morse (1963). However, many of the figures there have since been revised, both to take account of later years and to include elements of social (environmental) costs. A more scholarly treatment of depleting resources is given by Talbot Page (1976).

3 For unless the price is expected to be sufficiently higher at some future date than it is today, it would be more profitable to mine the material today, and to invest the proceeds in industry at current yields.

Thinking along such lines, it transpires that the mine owner is indifferent between mining this year and mining next year when the annual rate of price rise is that for which the annual increase in royalty or net price (that is, price *less* marginal cost) is just equal to the expected yield on current investment. This equilibrium price rise is also equal to the optimal rate of price rise, at least under simplifying conditions.

However, even if the actual rate of price rise happens to be equal to the optimal rate, the path being followed may be above, or below, the optimal path.

4 The ecological consequences of the production and uses of many modern synthetics are described in Barry Commoner's popular book, *The Closing Circle* (1971).

5 Problems of depletion and pollution are closely related. The depletion of clean water or clean air can arise from its pollution.

6 The word 'direct' is used in the particular economic sense to imply that such effects are not conveyed through prices. In fact, the problems arise just because such effects escape the price mechanism, even though they have an impact on outputs or welfare generally.

7 Among some recent attempts to correct the measure of national product for environmental spillovers, perhaps the best known is that by W. Nordhaus and J. Tobin, *Is Economic Growth Obsolete?* (1972), in which technical finesse makes no amends for some sweeping and wholly unacceptable assumptions.

8 For instance, by Wilfred Beckerman (1971).

9 This pattern of argument was well represented by Wilfred Beckerman in 1973.

10 The non-economist should be able to form a good idea of the quality of this sort of literature by perusing the contributions of the economists in *The Corporate Society*, edited by Robin Marris (1974). (The economists represented there, other than myself, are Kenneth Arrow, Robin Marris, Richard Musgrave, Mancur Olson and Thomas Schelling.)

11 By definition, the economist's spillover effect is an *unpriced* effect on society's welfare. It therefore escapes the market or pricing system. Ideally, the economist would like to 'internalise' these spillover effects into the economic system by setting up markets in them. If this could be done for all of them (without incurring costs that would exceed the benefits from this method of 'internalisation'), competitive markets in all goods and 'bads' would produce the economist's ideal allocation of resources.

Since, in fact, this solution is unfeasible for most spillover effects, other institutions must be established which impute to them a social value or cost. In some instances, a system of excise taxes (or subsidies) will serve.

12 Any reader who doubts that efficient methods of production can prevail in a slave society should consult R. W. Fogel and S. L. Engerman's stimulating work, *Time on the Cross* (1974).

Chapter 3

13 In the economist's parlance, 'real' income is distinguished from money income, in its being corrected for changes in the level of prices. So corrected, it is regarded as a measure of actual output.

14 Gross National Product (GNP) overstates Net National Income (NNI) or Net National Output (NNO), roughly by the value of capital amortisation over the period, usually a year. Thus, in order to move from GNP to NNI, we subtract from the gross investment during the year that part of it that is deemed to 'replace' capital equipment that is used up during the year. Put otherwise, GNP is the sum of expenditure on finished consumer goods during the year. In contrast, NNI is the sum of expenditures on finished consumer goods and on net additions only to the stock of capital goods. However, proportional changes in GNP are taken to be a good index of proportional changes of NNI.

15 This view that 'economic progress over the last two centuries has succeeded only in making life increasingly complex, frantic and wearing' has been elaborated in my book, *The Costs of Economic Growth* (1967) (see especially my digression to Part 3), and more recently in Richard Wilkinson's *Poverty and Progress* (1971) (see especially Chapter 9).

Part II

An Alternative Approach to the Debate

Chapter 4

The Expanding Horizon of Hazard

Broadly speaking, we are concerned in this volume with the question of the desirability of further economic growth in already prosperous countries. But desirable by what lights? It is possible to assert that the growth of knowledge itself, or the power it bestows on man, is the sole end of human activity. If this were conceded, the debate about the desirability of economic growth could end here. For not only is the growth of knowledge a precondition of continuing economic growth, economic growth itself is all but a precondition of the former. Certainly, economic growth promotes the advance of the applied sciences.

However, the assertion will not be conceded. If knowledge and power were recognised as the chief ends of human endeavour, no exception could be taken to adapting men to scientific and technological developments that were believed to serve those ends. There could then be no valid objections to the use of genetical engineering, or brain-activating chemicals, or psycho-surgery, for the express purpose of reducing emotional 'interference' so as to enable the human brain vastly to increase its thinking power and capacity.

Alternatively, it may be contended that the growth of knowledge should be regarded as the chief goal of human activity, in the belief that it exerts a humanising influence on mankind. This is a disputable proposition at any time, and particularly so where the kind of knowledge that is growing is, by and large, highly specialised scientific and technical knowledge. Nevertheless, the contention itself does have the merit of presupposing a more acceptable end of human activity: 'humanisation', by which the growth of knowledge, or other developments for that matter, are to be judged. This ungainly word, 'humanisation', is in some respects more appropriate as a criterion of desirability than the word 'happiness' – bearing in mind the old tag: 'Better Socrates unhappy, than a pig happy.' And certainly examples from history and literature come to mind of societies of beings that were only vestigially human. Indeed, in these scientific days, no stretch of imagination is needed to visualise a society in which the mass of people live in a permanent condition of drug-induced euphoria. Such a state – the culmination, perhaps, of continued medical advance in drugs innovation – is not the good society we are to envisage.

At some fundamental level of experience, there may be no contradiction between the state of wellbeing and integrity of character; it may be that human fulfilment is incompatible with the cultivation of base pursuits, and that, as Aldous Huxley observes in his *Point Counterpoint*, true happiness is simply a byproduct of right living. Yet since there is a clear distinction between happiness and integrity, even though they are thought to be inseparable in fact, it is as well to be explicit about our concern here with both of them. If, therefore, for brevity's sake, we talk of society's welfare, well-being, contentment, happiness or some other synonym (the advisability of making a distinction between them being considered in Chapter 7), we do so without ever losing sight of the moral values of society's character and institutions.

The related and, perhaps, logically prior question, whether in fact continued economic growth is physically possible – or, more generally, what alternative growth paths can be sustained, for what periods of time for particular areas of the world, or for the world as a whole – is one I do not raise in this volume. Not only is it beyond my present competence; but also I am already conscious of straining the bounds of ambition by attempting to erect some framework about which to organise reflection and investigation on so controversial a topic as the desirability of continued economic growth, on the explicit assumption that it is physically possible.

Nonetheless, there are two considerations which are so closely linked with both aspects of the growth debate – the physical possibility and the social desirability – that brief mention of them is necessary before defining more carefully the terms of our inquiry.

THE EFFECTS OF COMPOUNDING INCOME

A proper respect for the awesome multiplicative power of compound interest should act to jar anyone's optimism about the prospect of perpetual economic growth. For example, a per capita rate of economic growth for the next 500 years in the United States that averages 3 per cent a year – not high, judged by postwar economic performance in the West – implies a per capita income there that will be in excess of 1 *million* times as high as it is today. Even if world population could, by some miracle, be stabilised at about ten billion souls, the amounts of energy and materials that would be required to maintain such fantastic standards even in only a part of the world, or even in the United States alone, are of an order of magnitude far, far beyond our historical experience. How each person will manage to 'live it up' so as to dispose of such amounts of energy and materials entailed by so fantastic a statistic is a problem which, if contemplated for long, is likely to unhinge the imagination. Anyone having the slightest familiarity with the physics of heat, energy and matter will realise that, in terms of historical time, the end of economic growth, as we currently experience it, cannot be that far off.

SOURCES OF DANGER TO CIVILISATION

There are many emerging sources of physical danger and social instability, the direct consequences of scientific advance and technological innovation, that appear increasingly to threaten the survival of modern civilisations, if not also of the human species itself. The more familiar of them can be grouped into four broad categories.

A. Transport and Communications

The postwar expansion in world transport and communications has given rise to four sources of danger.

(1) The threat of civil disturbances and internecine warfare, especially within the *poorer* countries, arising from the continued frustration of material expectations that are aggravated by the growth in tourism, and by mass media. This growth-generated dissatisfaction, which is easily transformed into disaffection and turbulence or channelled into ideological extremism, is one of the reasons why liberal democratic institutions are not likely to flourish in poor countries.

(2) The conflicts and resentments between countries, and within the host countries, that will grow along with the scale of illegal immigration from the poorer countries in Africa, Asia and South America, to the richer countries of the West.

(3) The danger of political antagonism and confrontation between blocs of nations, arising directly from a growing awareness among the less developed countries of the extent to which the affluent West has come to depend upon their production and reserves of a limited number of scarce resources – aluminium, copper, tin, tungsten, mercury and, of course, oil. The

temptation of each of a group of the poorer countries, which between them provide the bulk of the world's requirements of a particular mineral, collectively to arrange to exploit their monopoly position, is not likely to be resisted once it becomes technically feasible to exploit it. Unless the West is able soon to discover low cost substitutes or synthetics for such essential resources, serious international friction is almost sure to arise between, on the one hand, the primary producers anxious to squeeze the utmost from their current economic advantages, and, on the other, the highly industrialised nations which perceive a growing threat to their living standards and to their economic expansion.

(4) The spread of disease through rapid travel. In earlier times, when a journey from the West to some tropical or Mediterranean country took weeks, the traveller intended to sojourn there for months, if not years. If he survived some tropical disease, he was unlikely to be unaware of it on his return home. The increasing risks of epidemics, or 'pandemics' today, arise from the simple fact that each year tens of millions of people are transported by air within a few short hours from one area of the world to another. Without being aware of it, many become the carriers of infection from one country to another.

B. Rapid Innovation

Some examples of dangers arising from rapid innovation follow.

(1) The risk of ecological disruption resulting from large scale intervention in the biosphere. The ultimate effects of DDT and other pesticides on animal and human life are as yet unknown. Again, the deliberate and incidental destruction by man of any number of species, from the blue whale to other large mammals, from birds and butterflies to plant varieties, is indeed a cause for lament. But their full ecological effects, which may take years to work out, may give the human race far greater cause to lament. As for the ecological havoc wrought by the construction of mighty dams, by vast irrigation projects, and by the levelling of forests, they have already exacted a heavy price in Africa and Asia, in terms of lives through flood, drought and disease.

(2) The more insidious threat to human health and survival from the evolution of more resistant pests and microbes in response to widespread use of more powerful drugs. Through the mechanism of natural selection, that is, nature replies to man's 'miracle drugs' by the production of 'miracle microbes' – and, for that matter, increasingly pest-resistant insects, and swifter

and hardier rodents. Perhaps one reason why these threats to human health and survival are taken less seriously than they ought to be is the greater likelihood of their full effect falling on future generations – which, we fondly hope, will be better equipped to deal with an increasing range of dangerous problems that they will inherit from us.

(3) The risk of genetic calamity arising from increased radiation and from thousands of new chemicals coming on to the market each year about whose long run effects, singly or in combination, we know practically nothing. We were lucky in discovering the mutative effects of Thalidomide in time. We may not be so lucky next time, if only because the genetic effects of some of the new drugs will take longer before their effects are understood – by which time, of course, the damage may be irreversible.

Indeed, according to a recent leaflet put out by the US National Foundation, *March of Dimes*, 'Seemingly harmless drugs like aspirin, "diet pills", tranquillizers, "cold pills", nose drops, and vitamins, are under scrutiny as possible causes of birth defects. . . . The number of new drugs on the market is increasing at an enormous rate. No one knows just what these can do to an unborn baby.'

C. *Weapons Technology*

There is also the more obvious threat to our survival arising from the continuing advances being made in weapons technology.

(1) Though we are reluctant to dwell upon the fact, there is today a clear and present danger of a nuclear catastrophe, or of the annihilation of a critical portion of the world's population by more horrible means, as a larger number of smaller countries come to acquire the secrets of thermonuclear destruction and biochemical warfare. And it is not only the increase in the number of nuclear-capable countries that is taking us closer to the brink, but also the advances being made by the world powers. According to a report in *The Times* of London (17 January 1974), innovations in nuclear technology have so increased the accuracy and power of nuclear missiles as to make a first strike a highly effective and possibly decisive strategem. At the time of writing, the concept of 'the balance of terror' is far from reassuring.

Moreover, accidents cannot be ruled out. Human error has always been a factor and now there is also the risk of computer error. In January 1974, a computer expert spoke on the BBC of the 'glitch' – a term used when a perfectly good computer apparently goes wild. Nobody knows when this will happen or how to prevent it. It has nothing to do with the human element or with any fault in the construction of these incredibly complex machines. According to the expert's estimate, about half of the number of existing computers have a 'glitch' some time or other. Since the atomic missiles of the great powers are, in fact, computer-controlled, it is not altogether impossible, the expert concluded, that a 'glitch' could start a third world war.

(2) In addition to advances being made in nuclear and biochemical warfare, there have been many gruesome developments in small weapons technology: miniature explosives, blinding-flash devices, laser beams, deafening detonations, and other devices that poison or cripple from a distance. All, incidentally, are apt to accelerate the postwar trend towards increasing violence, crime and sabotage.

D. Urban Size and Concentration

Finally, there are the dangers arising from the growth in urban size and concentration. A prescription for ecological stability is the fostering of variety. It ought also to be a principle for economic stability. But developments have been otherwise as the following instances show.

(1) As a result of habitual endeavours to exploit the economies of large scale operation, either of electricity generation through giant stations and link-up systems, or of other public utilities, such as gas production, sewage disposal, and water purification and distribution, large urban areas have become vulnerable to widespread disorganisation following any breakdown of such systems. In 1965, there was an electricity failure in the city of New York which lasted but a few hours. Yet its impact was devastating. Had it lasted a week, the city would have been paralysed, with its food deliveries and traffic brought to a standstill (since trucks and cars could not be fuelled if the electric-powered petrol pumps were rendered useless), and its police force immobilised.

(2) In the case of other public utilities, air transport, mail delivery, telephones and communications, there is no choice about size; it must follow the growth of population, in size and wealth, within the urban area in question. After the system in question has reached a certain size, significant diseconomies of scale are unavoidable. A telephone system connecting 100 million subscribers is more than twice as complex, and, therefore, more than twice as expensive to operate at the same level of efficiency, as a system serving 50 million subscribers. In the event, however, the larger system tends to be less efficient, and

to be more prone to overloading and breakdown. And just because larger numbers are involved, the occasional breakdown causes greater social disarray. Indeed, as Roberto Vacca (1972) points out, a breakdown in one system, say transport, leads to breakdowns in related systems, say the telephone system and the post office, since the extra load becomes shifted from one system to another.

(3) What is at least as serious a hazard is the recognition of this urban vulnerability by criminals, hooligans and fanatics. Successful sabotage, even the threat of sabotage, could create havoc in areas containing millions and tens of millions of people.

With sadness, one must record the fact that this growing vulnerability of our highly urbanised civilisation has not been lost on organised labour either. In their tactical struggles for higher pay or for maintaining what they believe to be their rightful place in the structure of wages, workers in key areas or occupations are not above threats to hold the country to ransom. Through obstinacy or miscalculation they may succeed in bringing the life of the city, or the country, to a standstill, and causing a collapse of the civil authority.

After mentioning these emerging sources of danger to our civilisation, the question is whether we should abstract from them in appraising the prospects for continued economic growth. Each specific threat has arisen from the process of economic growth, and, it is not unlikely that each will be aggravated by further economic growth. And if we tend to harp on these unseemlier aspects of economic progress, it is not for lack of spirit or magnanimity. We just cannot afford to let bygones be bygones at this stage in our history. 'The past is prologue.' In order to answer the question whether in fact economic growth can continue unchecked into the near or far future, we cannot reasonably exclude from our calculations the risks of events which, should they occur, would cripple our form of society or blot it out completely.

Awareness of these risks is spreading. Reluctantly, the public is beginning to realise that economic growth produces not only the 'widening of the area of choice', beloved of economic textbooks, but also a widening of the area of hazards. The unrepentant growthman is, of course, also aware of these new risks, though he is usually more acutely aware of the dangers to his position of the growing recognition of such risks. His immediate reaction to allegations of new risks can take either or both of two forms. The first reaction is ostentatiously to acknowledge them while affirming his faith in the ability of science ultimately to overcome all those problems that have been created by the applications of science. This position is boldly exemplified by a passage from Sir Peter Medawar's address quoted in Chapter 51. Since much of this volume is given to illustrating the many unsuspected consequences on our lives of scientific and technological progress, no further comment is needed here.

The growthman's second reaction is to adduce examples of gloomy prophecies made in the past in the hope of allaying public anxiety and confounding the opposition. Yet taunts of 'doomsdayism' are not enough to carry the day on this level of debate. For if it is true that history is littered with false prophecies, it is also true that they were not all pessimistic ones. 'Prosperity' Robinson, the British Chancellor of the Exchequer who, in the spring of 1825, assured his countrymen that they were about to enter an era of unprecedented prosperity, had to wait only to the autumn of that year to witness the beginning of what turned out to be one of the biggest economic crises of the nineteenth century, one that was not to lift until 1830. And while American politicians have learned caution from recalling President Hoover's repeated assurances of imminent prosperity following the Wall Street crash of 1929, neither are economists likely to forget some of the more sanguine forecasts made at about the same time by the more eminent members of the fraternity. No less a figure than Irving Fisher, then doyen of American economists, announced that 'stock market prices have reached what looks like a permanently high plateau'. This was just prior to the stock market collapse in the autumn of 1929. And in June 1930, the Harvard Economic Society went on record as saying that 'irregular and conflicting movements of business should soon give way to sustained recovery'. It is just possible that the optimistic prophecies of growthmen and technocrats will fare no better than those of economists in the past, whether optimistic or pessimistic.

On a more philosophical level, however, from the mere fact that there have been millennial prophecies at different times in the past, nothing at all can be inferred about the future. Calling 'Wolf' frequently and mistakenly, does not mean that wolves do not exist. The new dangers that beset our civilisation, some of which were mentioned earlier, are not imaginary. Scientists and scholars today may hold different opinions about the extent of particular risks or about the likelihood of specific occurences. But there is general agreement among them that nothing comparable to such dangers existed, say, at the beginning of the century. And, so far as I know, none has argued that the dangers are receding.

These remarks on growthmen's reactions to the alleged dangers of technological progress will suffice in the present context. More detailed consideration to the issues they raise is given in Chapter 8 on the 'Doomsday syndrome'. However, having taken due note of the real and growing dangers associated with the advance of science and technology, we shall, for argument's sake, refrain from further mention of them – at least in connection with the physical possibility of continued economic growth. They will be considered again only in connection with the quality of life. For, as will be argued in Part VI, awareness of the more dangerous world we are entering has an obvious influence on society's wellbeing, through its effect on the level of anxiety and on the curtailment of personal liberty.

Chapter 5

The Focus of our Inquiry

If we take social welfare, or some other synonymous concept as the touchstone of our inquiry, the inquiry itself may take a number of different directions.

First we might seek an answer to the question: are we getting our money's worth of satisfaction from the postwar affluence? If this is the question, the answer is surely no. Even the most conservative economist will agree that a little collective wisdom, could it be translated into political initiative, would rid us of a lot of economically unwarranted overspill.

Eighteenth-century believers in progress, could they witness our civilisation today, would be astounded at our technological capability. And they would be dismayed at what we have done with it. On what arguments could we justify to them the sheer ugliness and sprawling abandon of our urban areas; the endless clamour, the litter, stench, and tawdiness; the acres of seamless desolation! Let us concede, without further intermission, that we could have used our resources and technical expertise to create a saner physical environment and to encourage more sensible ways of living, before turning to other directions of inquiry.

Secondly, we might want to compare the quality or wholesomness of life today with that of bygone ages. And, to tell the truth, growthmen are ever quick for such comparisons. But the comparisons they make are invariably unfair. They use what smattering of history they have to select the bleaker aspects of particular periods in the past – 'the dark satanic mills' and other grim features of the earlier part of the 'Industrial Revolution' being favourite points of reference (conveniently overlooking the fact that these were the bitter fruits of Britain's initiation into the era of sustained economic growth). Other favourite instances are the ancient slave economies of the East, the coarse and ignorant peasantry of medieval Europe, the savagery and superstition of primitive tribes, or the imagined lives of prehistoric cavemen, 'nasty, brutish and short'.

But although such allusions make effective rhetoric, their relevance is doubtful. It is a commonplace that people alive at any time will want to go on living, less because they love life than because they fear death. The matter stands in much the same countenance in any hypothetical choice between living in the present and living in an earlier age. The present is chosen not so much from joy of the present as from revulsion at the thought of physical discomforts, which we tend to associate with life in the last. The thought of a world without anaesthetics, or painless dentistry or deodorants, is consideration enough for the unheroic denizen of our modern subtopia; he would not be wooed into the past for any sum or any privilege.

It is, then, an obvious tactic for growthmen to accent all those aspects of modern life which, as a result of rising affluence and indiscriminate consumerism, have come to assume a disproportionate influence in our scale of values: hygiene, youthfulness, mobility, instant entertainment, physical comfort and effort avoidance. By implication, growthmen also fail to stress the distinguishing features common to pre-industrial civilisations that lie beyond the experience and, all too often, beyond the imagination and sympathy of post-industrial man: for example, the (by our standards) inordinate number of holy days and holidays, the vaster sense of time and space (owing to slow travel and few timepieces), an unhurried complaisancy in the rhythm of nature, greater communal intimacy and a pervasive sense of hierarchy and belonging, itself the product of an elaborate network of rights and customs, privileges and obligations. To this more settled way of life another feature should be added: easy access to the countryside, to clean air, to lakes, rivers, quiet fields and woodlands. Above all, there was a merciful Deity to turn to, and a faith that gave hope beyond the grave.[1]

Again, in connection with this second approach, we sometimes meet with the assertion, common among 'progressive' thinkers, that the rational spirit informing modern capitalism and its material achievements were both indispensable factors in the creation of the 'open society', as described and defended by Karl Popper (1945), and associated with the expression and toleration of a wide variety of political, religious and social doctrines. In contrast to this 'open' or 'pluralistic' society, pre-industrial societies could be regarded as 'closed' in as much as deviations from prevailing doctrine were apt to be treated as heresies.

Should the reader ever attempt the task of assessing the impact on the experience of liberty and the wellbeing of ordinary people of modern and premodern institutions, he should beware of the ambiguities of language and concept that lend themselves to facile generalisation and, worse perhaps, facile impartiality. It does not do, for instance, merely to conclude that within pre-industrial and post-industrial societies there are both pluralistic and centralistic tendencies. From the simple fact that the kinds of pluralistic and centralistic tendencies were different for the different periods, one may not infer that, with respect to amenity, to wellbeing and to cohesiveness, a ranking of the two periods is impossible.

The pluralism of modern societies takes two forms. First there is the perpetual competition as between various economic groups not merely for material betterment but also for a larger share of 'the national pie'. This continuing struggle takes place directly, either in the form of pressure (or threats) by organised groups on the rest of society, or in the form of interunion rivalry, and less directly through the political process. And it should be noticed, in passing, that faster economic growth cannot of itself alleviate the struggle, since the prize for each group consists of a greater share of the pie and a greater share of power. Indeed, the struggle is sure to become sharper as advances in computation techniques provide power seekers with more frequent and more invidious statistics. This form of pluralist activity, waged by constitutional and extra-constitutional means, is therefore a force disruptive of social harmony.

The other form this pluralism assumes is that of a continuing controversy about the ends of society, and about ethics, propriety and conventions. Such controversy, however, is less the result of a resurgence of new ideas than the product of a collapse of traditional morality. Above all, it is not a pluralism that describes a world of different societies, each society having it own religion and ethics (though these are not basically dissimilar to those of most other societies), and its own customs and conventions in dress, food, art and entertainment. Rather it is a pluralism *within* each of our modern societies, one indicative less of increasing tolerance than of increasing conflict in consequence of the breakdown of those common values, beliefs and customs that produce mutual understanding and social cohesion. Thus the modern state today finds itself in the unhappy position of legislating, or of refusing to legislate, on questions of morality and decency, in the vain endeavour to move with the times and to offend a minimum number of citizens.

These forms of pluralism then reflect currently irreconcilable conflicts of interests and beliefs in modern Western democracies and are, for the most part, productive of social unrest and instability.

The uniformities that are typical of post-industrial societies are no less threatening. The vulnerability of systems of monoculture in agriculture needs no comment, though the vulnerability of 'economic monoculture', especially of our growing dependence on a few large scale plants for a number of necessaries, can bear more emphasis. What is more, the sheer tedium of an admass civilisation, the sheer frustration of effortless availability, can tempt the young and spirited into illegal and dangerous escapades.

In contrast, the sort of pluralism associated with pre-industrial societies acted to stabilise the social structure. Central governments were relatively weak. Political and economic powers were shared locally between overlapping groups: in pre-industrial Britain, for instance, between the Church, the gilds, the landed gentry, the officials of the parish and the municipality, and the merchant companies, each institution having privileges and responsibilities. In the later Middle Ages, pluralism resided also in the hierarchy of society, each person having a role and place within it. And there was a pluralism in the sense of geographic diversity; one did not have to travel far to become aware of the rich local variety in accent, dress, food and customs.

The uniformities of a pre-industrial era contributed to the social stability since they were of an ecumenical character – that is, had a common code of morality based on one or other of the great religions. In some countries, of which England was one, a sense of national pride, harking back to the fourteenth century and earlier, also acted to weld together the different interests and orders of society.

In sum then, closer consideration of both the pluralistic and centralistic tendencies in question suggests that, whereas the tendencies at work in pre-industrial societies acted on balance to stabilise the societies, those found in the post-industrial era act to destabilise them.

A final point, in comparing the quality of life at different periods of history, the concept of some average sort of life does not serve. In all ages, including our own, there are rich and poor, fortunate and unfortunate – though their proportion within a designated community will vary from place to place and from one age to another. A thoughtful historian should be able to pick out certain periods over, say, the last 5,000 years where, for favoured groups in a particular society in some part of the world, life seemed to be good and wholesome while, for a fair proportion of the remainder, it was not burdensome.[2]

Such comparisons are clearly subjective, though there may be more agreement among historians about some civilisations than about others. It is doubtful, however, whether historians would agree to the use of GNP, or any other economic index, as an historical yardstick of wellbeing so as to conclude that life today is transparently better than ever before.

As a third alternative, our inquiry might seek answers to the question whether life is currently becoming more enjoyable; that is, whether we are becoming more contented or better people, in consequence of continuing economic growth. Thus, bearing in mind some facts about human nature (discussed in Chapter 6), we might ask whether contemporary economic developments tend to give rise to modes of living that accord more, or conflict more, with men's biological and psychic needs.

This looks to me the more promising line of inquiry and the one, therefore, I suggest we adopt.

Now, in contemplating the course of social welfare over the foreseeable future, familiarity with the details of scientific phenomena and technological developments is of limited value. In the main, subjective judgements are the vehicles of the debate – judgments of fact, and possibly also, judgments of value.

I say 'possibly also judgments of value' since, in the main, they can be avoided. To illustrate with an extreme example, I might assert that murder is wrong, which is clearly a value judgment. If you agreed with me at once, then we share a common value, and no more need be said. If, however, you did not wholly agree with me, I might try to persuade you. I could quote the golden rule. I could describe the apprehension of honest folk if murderers went unpunished. I could talk of the pity of extinguishing the life of an innocent man, and depict the grief of his family or the loss suffered by the rest of the community. And so, by an appeal to your imagination, to your feelings and to your conscience, I might finally elicit your assent to the value proposition that it is wrong to murder.

But if all I wished for was your co-operation in framing just laws, I could try another tack. Rather than try to persuade you that murder is morally wrong, I could advance the opinion that the consequences that must flow from allowing known murderers to go unpunished are not compatible with the good life, at least not a contented and secure life. If my efforts to convince you that a murder-permissive society is likely to produce a decline in happiness were successful, you would concur with my judgment about the facts.

In view of the above illustration, it is unnecessary to observe that there can be close connections between judgments of values and judgments of facts. But in the current debate on economic growth and the quality of life there are advantages in emphasising the distinction. At all events, the kinds of judgment that are to feature in our inquiry are chiefly, perhaps wholly, judgments of facts. Such judgments will be invoked in detecting the consequences of current and future technological innovations, in gauging the likelihood of their occurrence, and in appraising their impact on people's well-being and character. They include, also, factual judgments about the nature of people's value judgments.

A *caveat* must be entered at this point. We must not unthinkingly attribute all social developments to economic and technological growth. Some significant events, good or bad, may have very tenuous links with such growth, though they may indeed be mitigated or aggravated by it. But, while exercising scruples in this regard, we must not go so far as to omit factors that could be decisive for our conclusions simply because a relationship has not yet been satisfactorily established or is unlikely to be so established.

For example, do we really need exhaustive psychological tests (some of which are described in a recent American symposium, *Where Do You Draw the Line?* (see Victor Cline, 1974)), in order to determine whether the manifest increase in violence and sadistic cruelty depicted in the mass media, especially on television and cinema screens, over the last two decades is likely or not to exercise a bad influence on people's character? Is it not a reflection of the obsession with measurement, which typifies the technological society, that intelligent people today feel impelled to undertake prolonged experimentation, and to employ all the impressive paraphernalia of modern statistics, in order to reach a conclusion, or to confirm a fact of life, that has been part of the common stock of human experience since the dawn of civilisation?

The temptation to retreat into methodological nihilism – to talk and to act on the assumption that there is nothing at all to be learned from history or from human instinct and experience – is well-nigh irresistable to the mediocre academic mind. Such a posture not only is suggestive of an Olympian detachment from the common opinions of mankind, but also helps to create a conviction among the gullible public that there exists a fearful vacuum in our understanding of human nature. Needless to remark, these appointed vacuums have the incidental, but valuable, property of sucking in research funds to finance elaborate facilities which provide occupations for otherwise unemployable graduates.

Indeed, current nihilism goes farther than that. It is seriously contended by some modern writers that prolonged absorption in scenes of crime, violence and carnality has a cleansing effect on the psyche (see, for example, some of the 'evidence' offered in the Arts Council of Great Britain's report on *The Obscenity Laws*, 1969). From this carthartic hypothesis', we should be able to infer that a drunk and obscene father is to be regarded as a distinct advantage in the home, or that a brutalised prison atmosphere offers the best prospects for the rehabilitation of the prisoners. No one really believes this, of course. Yet, in the interests of research and researchers, we are required to suspend the judgment of our senses, of our instincts and of our experience, and to entertain seriously the possibility that scenes of repeated cruelty, calculated violence and sadistic titillation, witnessed day after day by the young and impressionable, will have no influence, other than perhaps a benign one, on their character and behaviour, and on their ideas of what is normal and acceptable.

In a word then, and concerning the causal relations between economic growth and particular social effects, we must append to our first *caveat*, against inadvertently assuming a relationship which is tenuous or non-existent, another *caveat* against disregarding the possibility of a plausible relationship simply because it has not been 'scientifically' established.

Chapter 6

Some Assumptions of Fact

Although other factual judgments will be invoked from time to time in the remainder of this essay, it is as well, at the start, to make explicit a few that are indicative of the author's attitude. They are not critically essential to the inquiry, which is, in the main, exploratory. Yet the general tone of my reactions to many of the issues raised in this volume are influenced by them.

(1) Although it is politically expedient to give equal weight to the different tastes, and equal attention to the different views, of the various members of a community, only a person whose judgment has been perverted by an excess of democratic sentiment can really believe that they are all worthy of equal respect.

For example, a belief that the music of The Beatles will outlast that of Beethoven is not, I submit, an intelligent belief, and I would not waste time affecting to debate it. Nor is the view that the adventures of Superman provides us with as much authentic human insight as Tolstoy's *War and Peace* a view that is worth considering. If society ever abandons itself to such indiscriminate tolerance, literature and art will have no secure place in the curricula of our schools and universities.

In questions of artistic achievement, it is never 'just a matter of taste'. However much opinions vary between specialists, however much fashions vary over time, there is so much art and literature that is undeniably great or beautiful, and so very much more that is irredeemably trivial or hideous, that it is virtually impossible for a civilised society to renounce judgment in these respects.

(2) I believe that the basic nature of man has remained unchanged

for tens of thousands of years. Genetically he is the same animal that huddled close to others for warmth and comfort, and the same animal that hunted in groups in primeval forests. And, what is more, he will continue to be that same animal until science is able, and society is willing, to control mutations in man – or else, through chemical, electric or other means, to produce significant changes in his genetic composition.

Survival mechanisms have produced what we might call his Manichean character. His ruthless and aggressive propensities are an inseparable part of his make-up, as indeed they are of other mammals. Such propensities, however, respond only to specific stimuli. In civilisations, where men are exposed to a wide variety of signals and stimuli, such propensities are overtly controlled by taboos and also by the internal mechanisms of individual repression that they foster.

On the positive side, our basic human feelings have not changed over the millenia of recorded history. Despite profound changes in material standards, in technology, and in culture and fashion, the myths and legends of the past, with their testimony to the strength of human endurance, devotion, heroism and compassion, move and inspire us today as they moved and inspired our ancestors hundreds and thousands of years ago. Thus, while it is true that the absence of historical data makes detailed comparisons of different civilisations difficult, it is conceivable and meaningful to compare the quality of life of different peoples and different classes over the centuries.

(3) An acknowledgment of the natural pleasures of man is a particular instance of the preceding proposition. As distinct from a succession of novelties or fashion goods which offer satisfactions that are alloyed, uncertain and ephemeral – satisfactions that sometimes pall and often (like tobacco or alcoholic beverages, automobiles or household gadgetry) become necessary or addictive – there are always those more basic and perennial forms of enjoyment open to ordinary human beings in all ages and in every sphere of life. These arise from the operation of biological mechanisms that signal the growth of some physical need, whether for food, sleep, sex or warmth. There is joy in anticipating its fulfilment; joy in preparing to satisfy it; and, of course, the joy of the actual gratification itself, and the sense of wellbeing which follows from restoring the biological equilibrium.

With the exception of sexual activity, the opportunity for these basic enjoyments is available to a person in good health to the last days of his life. In recognition of the power of the bodily appetites, in particular for sex and food, there has been a long history of social arrangements of varying degrees of elaboration designed to regulate their expression, some of them sanctioned by religious and secular ceremonies or embodied in feasts and carnivals.

It is hardly necessary to add that not all forms of civilisation serve equally well in providing for these ordinary joys of life. While in some areas of the world food may be too scarce or lacking in variety, in others it may be so abundant and so frequently engorged that appetite has no time to grow. While in some periods and places labour may be exhausting and sleep inadequate, in others natural sleep is difficult from the lack of physical exertion. Again, while discomfort is associated with too little clothing or shelter, the continuous absence of any discomfort from living, say, in a perfectly air-conditioned habitation entails a deprivation of enjoyment; in hot weather, there can be no anticipating the cool of the evening, no slaking one's thirst with a cold drink or immersing oneself in a stream; in cold weather, there can be no foretasting the joy of gathering around the blazing fire. Thus material abundance, plus the priority given to physical comfort, may act to reduce the experience of pleasure.[3]

(4) I shall accept as a fact of life that, notwithstanding the bright visions of eighteenth-century reformers, and their faith in the perfectibility of man, the amount of *haute couture* that can be ingested by the ordinary mortal is strictly limited. It would therefore be rash to assume that much of the increase in the amount of leisure anticipated over the future will be taken up by the mass of people for the pursuit of serious cultural activities.

Taking these ideas to their limit, I assume that the ordinary man cannot retain his self-respect if he comes to feel that he has no productive part to play in society – more particularly, if he feels that his work does not count, or is of no consequence to society. One cannot, therefore, look forwards without apprehension to the culmination of endeavours to 'free man forever from drudgery' that would, in effect, remove from his life the spur of economic necessity.

(5) It should be obvious that I cannot accept the belief that each man knows his own interest best, a view I shall elaborate on in Chapter 19. Indeed, if we conceded the argument that, acting through their economic and political institutions, men were able in fact to promote their own interests best, this inquiry would be superfluous. Of course, it is politically prudent not to dispute such democratic myths in public assembly – more prudent yet, to pay tribute every so often to the fund of common sense and

'grass roots wisdom' to be found in the ordinary people. Nevertheless, I will join my voice to that of the typical Western liberal who is not altogether cynical of democracy, and is ready to affirm that perhaps the least intolerable form of society is that which continues to let men choose freely (in some sense) and, later, freely regret the choices they made. For all that, no one can hope to be a reformer, or to make a contribution to society's wellbeing, if he is so respectful of the judgment of his fellows that he cannot bring himself to announce that, in some respects, attention to his particular opinion may better their lot.

(6) Finally, I reject the view that, in as much as men's tastes and values necessarily differ, consensus on the constituents of the good life is not to be hoped for. Indeed, in the belief that no such consensus can reasonably be expected, growthmen offer us, instead, the vision of increasing opportunities for self-fulfilment within a 'pluralistic society': each person regarded as a consuming unit, a mobile atom, choosing his own lifestyle guided only by his own ideas of the good life.

This is too facile a solution to social problems. Not only is a man's choice of a way of life subject to the laws, institutions, beliefs, customs, and fashions that regulate his intercourse with other members of society – a fact which itself raises questions about the nature of good political constitutions, good laws, good institutions, and good customs and fashions – but also in consequence of rapid and momentous technological change, the society he lives in is increasingly being borne along by powerful currents that cannot be presumed, on balance, to favour his welfare, whether he chooses to act within them or to oppose them.

Indeed, the contrary presumption is the more reasonable one: that the modern citizen has precious little choice about his lifestyle. A society that has reconciled itself to a state of perpetual change comes to adopt a methodology that favours change; it tends unwittingly to place the burden of proof on those who would oppose or delay the change in question. In other words, the traditional conservative doctrine associated with Edmund Burke, – that no alteration in those arrangements of society that have stood the test of time and experience be introduced save, perhaps, in dire emergencies, or else when backed by powerful argument and irresistible evidence – is one that has *de facto* been rejected by today's affluent consumer society. Having cultivated an insatiable appetite for goods and economic opportunities, a prerequisite of sustained economic growth, the consumer society has perforce to accommodate itself also to continuing changes in its institutions, its outlook and its mode of living – these being the byproducts of continuing technical change – irrespective of their intrinsic merit.

This consideration might still seem to leave open the question of the intrinsic merit of the resultant social changes, but for one compelling factor. In consequence of the sheer pace of technological innovation, there is an increasing likelihood that evidence about the range of physical side effects of any one or several innovations will come to light too late to avert misfortune and possible disaster, as argued in Chapter 4. For instance, there has been a growing public concern, especially in the United States, with the effects of supersonic flights, nuclear detonations and aerosols on the earth's protective ozone mantle. The controversy still rages. In the meantime, it is 'business as usual' until evidence of significant ozone dissipation is established beyond reasonable doubt – by which time it is just possible that it will be too late.

Nor is there any immediate and, possibly, no ultimate prospect of establishing conclusive evidence about the intangible but powerful consequences on the cohesion and felicity of society that flow from the range of novel processes and products of a modern growth economy. Yet even if I am only partly right in my general conjecture in this volume about their untoward nature, it is still a matter for grave concern.

I do not doubt that there is, in official circles, the strongest temptation today to uphold a tacit convention that would ignore serious consideration of the range of consequences flowing from continued technological change, in the wilful belief that, on balance, it will, or can be made to, exercise a benign influence on our civilisation. The purpose of this volume, in contrast, is to articulate the dangers of accepting such a convention, and to do so in the endeavour to encourage more searching and systematic thought, particularly into the human and social consequences of the official attempt to maintain the momentum of economic growth. Unless we are prepared to enter full-heartedly into this investigation and debate, we must forgo the option of exercising choice in the vital task of shaping the future; we must resign ourselves, as we do at present, to whatever the future might bring.

Should we ever come to want to control our destiny, however, the exercise of choice that is entailed cannot be individual. It has to be collective. Thus it cannot be effectively exercised without broad agreement on the constituents of the good life, an agreement that arises, ultimately, from our deeper perception of reality, from the experience of history and from prolonged deliberation and debate.

My one article of faith is this: that, given the will, such a consensus can indeed be found. Indeed, Parts V and VI are written on the assumption that the broad essentials of the good life, at least, are discernible and would already command a consensus. If I am wrong about this, then the outlook is indeed a bleak one. Divided among ourselves, we shall have no choice but to drift along, as at present, hoping for the best but fearing the worst.

Chapter 7

Semantic Issues

Once we have decided to ask the question whether life is becoming better or more enjoyable or more worthwhile, the fastidious reader might easily become the victim of philosophical disputes turning on terminological and conceptual niceties. To wit, is happiness reality or illusion? To what extent does it reside in the anticipation of events – in hopes rather than in fulfilment? Does the awareness itself of new possibilities for enjoyment add to a person's satisfaction, even if he never actually experiences them? And are there not pertinent distinctions to be made also between enjoyment and satisfaction, between satisfaction and welfare, between welfare and happiness, between happiness and fulfilment, and so on?

The fact that such semantic issues are frequently deployed by the defenders of current orthodoxies in the attempt to prevent the drawing of unorthodox conclusions, does not mean that they are not worth thinking about. But the attention devoted to them may be limited by clear recognition of the nature of our inquiry, as described in Chapter 5. Thus, in regard to the first set of questions turning on differences between hopes, awareness and fulfilment, we can be brief. Answers to them are clearly judgments of fact, and they will vary with the particular experiences and events that are being debated. As occasion arises, questions such as these will be discussed later in some specific context.

As for the second set of questions, there are indeed difficulties in appointing any one of these terms – enjoyment, satisfaction, welfare, happiness, fulfilment, etc. – to do duty for the others and, more generally, to evoke that condition of society we are to conceive as desirable. All of them suggest desirable states of being, but each has its own connotations. 'Satisfaction', or 'contentment', is admittedly a useful word, but too placid for inspiring an ideal. Animals can achieve contentment if there is enough food about and space to roam without hindrance. One has misgivings about the use of the word 'contentment' to depict the dimensions of life towards which humans aspire.

The terms 'social welfare' and 'social wellbeing' are suggestive while, at the same time, being sufficiently neutral to make them favourites with the social sciences. Economists have no reservations about using the word 'welfare', and go so far, sometimes, as to prefix it with the word *'economic'* – by which they mean, or should mean, the contribution economic arrangements can make to social welfare. But as indicated, 'welfare' is a rather colourless term, and even a depressing one in so far as it has associations with the activities of government welfare agencies.

The word 'happiness' is more specifically human, but it is a state that is difficult to sustain. No man can reasonably expect to remain in a state of happiness for the greater part of his life on earth, though it is not unreasonable for a man to be contented most of the time. Since the state of happiness is generally understood to entail elevation to a more intense level of emotional experience, it is plausible to believe that a man's life may, on balance, be a better life even if, under some new dispensation, it should contain less happiness.

The term 'enrichment of life' might, at first, appear broad enough to secure general agreement. Yet it also tends to suggest the idea of augmenting our daily lives with an abundance of good things, rather like stuffing additional currants into a pudding. Its indiscriminate use in the debate might unwittingly predispose us to favour economic growth.

'Fulfilment' is a more embracing term, though it can presuppose norms or goals which themselves should be the subjects of more searching judgment. For example, since frustration is an antonym of fulfilment, the latter, when regarded as a social goal, may suggest the idea that public policy should be directed, in the main, towards the removal of all sources of existing frustration. Yet it is a commonplace that, without experiencing frustrations and learning to cope with them at some time in his life, a person will be unable to develop emotionally.

'Gratification' covers the spiritual, the aesthetic, the intellectual, the emotional and the carnal. Although, by definition, it is a desirable sensation, in some of its manifestations, it can also come into conflict with any reasonable vision of the good life.

After appraising terms in this way for a time, it may occur to us to try, instead, to touch on the things that ought rather to be avoided. We should not, for example, approve of lives that are aimless, petty, shapeless and dull. We should not approve of a society inhabited by people who are dominated by envy and greed, or by fear and despair.

We should repudiate the idea of a man as a being driven by a single passion, a prisoner of his obsessions, at least as much as we should repudiate that of a man as a being steeped in apathy, without appetite or desire. But, again, it will not take us long to realise that, had we a mind to do so, we could easily stir up a hornet's nest of semantic and philosophic problems.

The main reason why no single term will suffice in this inquiry is that the good life we aspire to cannot be described by a single attribute. Indeed, some transparently undesirable experiences play a necessary role in the good life, by imparting contrast and relief, and by their influence on a man's character. Without learning patience in frustration, fortitude in hardship, resignation in suffering, the soul of man does not grow – or, if the reader prefers it, his psyche does not mature. And the richness and complexity of those emotions that are peculiarly human remain beyond his experience.

From such considerations springs the recognition that, just as a variety of orchestral instruments are needed to produce harmonious sounds, so also is a number of diverse experiences required to produce a harmonious life. The concept of balance or proportion is central to musical harmony. If some instruments are missing, or if some play too loudly, the resulting sound can be harsh and discordant. The analogy with modern living is obvious, in as much as examples of disproportion and imbalance abound in today's civilisation. To press the analogy further, just as the orchestral quality of sound depends not only on a variety of instruments but also on the peculiar sound of each, so that quality of life depends not only on a variety of experiences but also on the particular source and nature of the pleasures and the pains produced in us.

It is one thing if society is so ordered that its pleasures spring, in the main, from a spirit of contentment and acceptance; from friendship and kinship; from the sense of home and family; from surrender and worship; from sacrifice, passion and creation; and from a closeness to nature's breath and pulse. It is quite another if men's primary sources of pleasure are found in self-seeking, in self-display, in vindictive triumphs, in creature comforts and in restless titillation.

So also with 'the slings and arrows of outrageous fortune'. It matters crucially whether the pains that we suffer are physical or spiritual, and whether they are sorrowful and perceptive or else petty and plaintive. Our sufferings, that is, can be dignified and ennobling, or they can be coarse and degrading.

Looking ahead, then, should we not wonder whether the pleasures of living will become more intimate, keen and resonant, or whether, instead, they will become more passive, oafish and dull? It is not a matter of indifference if, in the future we are moving into, the kinds of pleasures we shall come to seek, and the kinds of pains we shall come to endure, act on balance to humanise our lives or else act on balance to dehumanise them.

What emerges from such reflections?

Clearly, that any single attribute alone cannot serve as the touchstone of our inquiry. We may, however, agree provisionally that some vision of what we conveniently refer to as the good life is evoked by such adjectives as 'wholesome', 'complete' or 'rounded', and that such a life is to be thought of as creating a pervasive sense of wellbeing so that, whatever his station, a man will feel that life is abundantly worthwhile not only at times of gladness but also amid inevitable suffering and sorrow.

And there we might leave the matter, save for a proviso necessary to avoid misunderstanding. The import of the preceding paragraph, or earlier passages, is not intended to convey the impression that an ideal life is one that tends so to fortify a man that, irrespective of the extent of adversities endured, he will come through them bravely. Though it is, of course, to his credit if he does so, the degree of moral calibre that is promoted by society is not to be held as the decisive issue. Life on earth will not be so good if it is regarded either as a trial for some future existence or as a crucible of character formation. It must be enjoyable and worthwhile in its own right. Nonetheless, as indicated, without some forms of hardship and frustration, the individual cannot comprehend the pathos and the intimate texture of life. They have, then, an essential part to play in forming that maturity of character and philosophy without which life cannot be fully enjoyed.

These glimpses of aspiration are reflected in each of the various terms by which we shall invoke the concept of the good life or, to be more fastidious, *a* good life. For in order to avoid tedium of expression I propose to choose freely among the terms already mooted – namely, 'welfare', 'wellbeing', 'contentment', 'satisfaction', 'fulfilment', 'gratification', 'happiness' – and also to choose others, wherever the context will suffice to constrain the meaning.

Clearly, there can be a range of alternative civilisations, all of which are compatible with the good life, and also an indefinite number of civilisations, or stages in civilisations, that are incompatible with it. We might well wonder if we are now entering a phase of our civilisation that is becoming increasingly incompatible with the good life. Indeed, our curiosity need not stop there. We might wonder also whether there is not a strong presumption that continuing economic growth in the prosperous countries of the world is moving their people ever farther from even the possibility of achieving any kind of good life.

NOTES FOR PART II

Chapter 5

1 According to Jacques Ellul (1965), the time given in pre-industrial civilisations to the use of techniques was short compared with the leisure devoted to sleep, to conversation, to games and to meditation. For primitive man and for historical man, work, as such, was not a virtue; it was better not to consume than to work hard. Indeed, man worked as little as possible, and was content with a limited amount of consumption goods. Today, comfort means easy chairs, foam rubber mattresses, elegant bathrooms, air conditioning, washing machines, etc. The over-riding objective of the modern consumer is to avoid physical effort, and so he has to become more dependent upon the machine.

In the middle ages, comfort did not mean softness, ease and effort avoidance. Comfort was associated with a moral and aesthetic order. Space was the primary element, according to Giedion (quoted by Ellul). Men sought open spaces and large rooms. They did not care much if the chairs were hard or the rooms poorly heated (by our standards). What mattered to them was proportion and the right use of materials.

2 The reader whose judgment is not petrified by statistics bearing on poverty, inequality or infant mortality rates might agree with me that, for the more recent history of England, the periods that might qualify on this criterion are the time of Chaucer, the Elizabethan age, the mid-eighteenth century and possibly the Edwardian age.

Chapter 6

3 This comfort-versus-pleasure thesis is developed in Tibor Scitovsky's book, *The Joyless Economy* (1976). Though informative and entertaining, the book fails to make the important point that although America, like other Western societies, is 'sexually permissive', it has not been able to evolve satisfactory outlets. For large numbers of people in the West today, the opportunities for enjoyable sexual activity are erratic, fortuitous and limited. A high technology civilisation apparently finds it much easier to offer its citizens salacious entertainment than to provide them with acceptable institutions for extending the area of sexual opportunity.

Part III

The Non-agenda of the Economic Growth Debate

Chapter 8

The 'Doomsday Syndrome'

In the wide-ranging debate about economic growth, a number of assertions and arguments are advanced in favour of economic growth which, although they may be valid in some degree and in some contexts, are not strictly pertinent to the issue as we have conceived it: namely, whether a continuation of the sort of economic growth experienced in the already highly industrialised countries is socially desirable. A person wishing to participate in this debate can save much time and heat by learning to recognise the lineaments of some of the more popular non-starters which are listed and discussed below, beginning, in this chapter, with the 'Doomsday syndrome' (this phrase being the title of a book by John Maddox, 1972).

An effective form of rhetoric for dismissing the more alarming forecasts being made today is to remind the public of earlier warnings or prophecies of impending disaster. We mentioned earlier the fond frequency of reference to Malthus on the population question and to Jevons on the coal question – although, rather than dismiss them as false prophets, it would be more prudent to conclude that, in making insufficient allowance for technical progress, they were premature rather than wholly wrong. Indeed, with respect to population, such prudence concedes too much to growthmen; the Malthusian ghost has been seen stalking through many areas in the so-called Third World, and it will be something of a miracle if widespread famine can be avoided in the new few years in the continent of India, and in parts of North Africa and South America.

Another favourite among this repertory of unconsummated disasters is the alarm that was voiced by New Yorkers less than a century ago, to the effect that, if the traffic in the city continued to grow at the existing rate, it would not be long before the streets of the city would be buried beneath six feet of horse manure. Presumably we are to infer that this indeed would have been the fate of the metropolis had it not been for the providential invention of the automobile. Perhaps we are to suppose that those who today decry the mounting automobile traffic would not have raised their voices against the disruption, stench, clamour and congestion of horse-drawn traffic in large cities. On the other hand, we may be supposed to derive some measure of consolation from the fact that 'alarmists' did raise their voices, and from the belief that they can always be counted on to raise them in time. If the latter, there can be no objection to letting the growth sceptics have their say.

Prophecies of calamity, when expressed in terms of consequences contingent upon the unabated continuation of certain trends, are a form of poetic licence. For society as a whole will respond in a variety of ways as the consequences become increasingly uncomfortable; in the last resort, people will migrate or perish. Regarded in this light, Jevons's prophecy was wrong, simply because his estimates of coal reserves were way out, to say nothing of his assumptions about technological progress. The horse manure alarmists, on the other hand, were right. Certainly something would have been done about the horse-drawn traffic in New York even if the motor car had not come along – later to create its own and more intractable problems. Thus the question of whether society does or does not adapt, in a broad sense, to some untoward trend is not in issue. If the trend continues, society cannot avoid a response, whether controlled, uncontrolled or mixed. The only question, which is the essential question, is the *timeliness* and *appropriateness* of the response.

Thus the *déjà vu* attitude of pro-growthmen to the expressed alarm of modern thinkers is, by itself, not enough. As a general strategem it is also acceptable for a number of fairly obvious reasons.

(1) All sweeping forebodings of mankind's doom made in the past were clearly fallacious. But from the mere fact that humanity has survived to the present, no hope for the future can be salvaged. The human race can perish only once. And if growthmen can spin telling analogies, so can the growth sceptics. A man who falls from a hundred-storey building will survive the first ninety-nine storeys unscathed. Were he as sanguine as some of our technocrats, his confidence would grow with the number of storeys he passed on his downward flight, and would be at its maximum just before his free fall was abruptly halted.

(2) Again, from the fact that at different periods of history the

same sorts of protest were being made as are being made today, no comfort is to be gleaned either. The historian may observe, for instance, that for at least four centuries men have looked back wistfully to an earlier age, and deplored the manifestations of materialism and irreligion, the unnecessary bustle and the vanishing of the old familiar landmarks. From such lamentations, a number of interesting things may be deduced – but *not* that the present age is therefore no more materialistic, no more irreligious or no more rapidly changing than any other in history.

Thus, from the age of Chaucer, British historians have discovered in poems, essays, diaries, sermons, reports and novels a recurring nostalgia for the times when nature was more abundant, when times were more settled, when communities were more intimate and when life was more wholesome and honest. In particular, there is a recurring sadness and dismay at the disappearance of the green forests of England, and at the destruction of the peace and beauty of the English countryside. And if, today, conservationists are heir to this continuing mood of concern, and raise their voices to deplore the unprecedented erosion since World War II of England's coastline, woodland and other scenic heritage, one may legitimately infer that the concern of people at the destruction of the rare, the historic and the beautiful is an abiding characteristic of humanity. What one may *not* infer, however, is that in all these respects things have not changed, and changed for the worse. One cannot deny, that is, that the remaining fraction of accessible natural beauty in Britain is but a tiny fraction of what it was, say, in the eighteenth century; and this at a time when the population today is several times as large as it was then, and its mobility – and therefore its power for further destruction of the natural environment – immeasurably greater.

(3) The many instances of calamities which occurred in the 'bad old days' are not to be entered, either, on the credit side of the growthman's ledger. Plagues, such as the Black Death, which swept through Europe in the fourteenth, fifteenth or seventeenth centuries; the transformation of the once-fertile area of Mesopotamia into the Sahara-type desert of today; or, within a far shorter span of time, the 'mining' of the soil in mid-West areas of the United States which produced the so-called 'Dust Bowl' of the 1930s – these may, all of them, be regarded also as resulting from the short-sightedness of earlier growthmen and expansionists, from their inability to foresee the longer term consequences of their material activities on the urban or natural environment.

The difference between such 'bad old days' and today is that man's global impact today is on a vastly greater scale and in a vastly greater number of ways. We cannot much longer, therefore, continue to despoil the local environment and move into new areas. The world is becoming increasingly packed with human beings, all of them moving about a great deal more than they used to. Should calamity strike, it is more likely than not to encompass the whole world. True, our knowledge is much greater than it was in the past. But in relation to the scale and range of our intervention, it is much smaller. For the full range of ecological and genetic consequences of our current intervention in the biosphere cannot, as indicated, be known for decades, and they could turn out to be disastrous and irrevocable. The very least that should be concluded, then, is that the alleged dangers arising from technological advance should not be dismissed with complacency by adducing instances of premature alarm.[1]

(4) This conclusion applies with special force to the struthious optimism of growthmen in their interpretations of the growing incidence of crime and terror in our towns and cities. Deriving solace from the grimier side of social history, they tend to expostulate as follows: 'What, were there no thugs or marauders in the old days! Was there no pillage, rapine, or terror in the past! Were there no pirates or highwaymen prior to the nineteenth century! ' – and much more tending to the same rhetorical import.

Although this facile rhetoric is, of itself, not very persuasive, let us avail ourselves of its popularity to set down some of the more obvious differences between crime today and crime in the past in order to maintain perspective when assessing current dangers.

First, our knowledge of crime prior to the nineteenth century is hazy and impressionistic. It is also likely to be exaggerated for a number of reasons. In thinking about crime in the past – or, for that matter, invasions, plagues, civil wars or witch hunts – a selection of events and incidents which have occurred over many centuries tend to cluster in the mind, so concentrating the sense of horror. One might reasonably wonder at the terror and incredulity of some eighteenth-century savant were he enabled to read some of the Sunday newspapers which have appeared over the last five years, or to read a potted history of the world's barbarities and follies since the turn of the century, notwithstanding which most families in the West, in fact, have led a tolerable and comfortable life. We should then remind ourselves that the bulk of ordinary people in the 'bad old days' were unaffected by, and indeed often wholly ignorant of, that which appear to us to be the more frightening events of their time. For one thing, populations were much smaller than those today and, by and large, relatively immobile. Whatever the danger that lurked along the main travel routes, or on the high seas or in the larger cities, it did not loom large on the horizon of ordinary people. Until the middle of the nineteenth century, indeed, the bulk of the population, the world over, lived in the comparative safety of the countryside or in small towns or villages; in effect, in small independent communities, within which each family was, for the most part, intimately acquainted with the goings on of the other families. For the working population, the craftsmen and the farmers, travel was for the most part limited to the occasional visit to a local fair, or to a neighbouring town or village.

For another, the technology of crime and terror was primitive compared with that of today. With a spear, an axe, a cross-bow, even a pistol, a man could not kill at one time more than one or two persons, and the amount of damage to property he could do was limited. The machine gun, the bomb, the fast get-away automobile, the airliner, radio communication and other modern contrivances have vastly increased the power of today's criminal, at the same time as the concentration of production in giant plants and the advent of large scale public utilities have increased the vulnerability of populations, especially in metropolitan areas. Two or three determined terrorists, today, can create chaos in a city simply by threatening to poison its water supply or to cut its electricity supply. They can hijack a plane and kidnap scores of people. True, the police also avail themselves of the fruits of technology, and postwar trends show expenditures on internal defence as a rising proportion of GNP. However, the phenomenon of rising crime met by rising police activity does not leave the public feeling equally secure. The expansion of police powers is itself a threat to personal freedom, a subject we treat at length in Chapter 46.

Finally, there is another consideration that ought deeply to disturb the good liberal reformer. Much of the petty crime and the brutal crime before the twentieth century could plausibly be attributed to poverty and to ignorance. Such explanations no longer suffice. In the West today, desperate destitution no longer exists. Since World War II, the welfare state has expanded in all industrial countries. There have, moreover, been a marked improvement in living standards (measured by conventional indices), relatively high levels of employment and, above all, an unprecedented expansion of higher education. And yet, within this same period, there has been an appalling rise in every kind of crime, from shoplifting and hooliganism to arson and bombing, from classroom violence and vandalism to rape and mugging. As we shall have occasion to remark later (see Chapters 36 and 37), one of the more portentous consequences of the spread of science and the spirit of inquiry is that the boundary between good and evil is becoming increasingly fluid and people's sense of right and wrong increasingly blurred. There are today quite a number of so-called philosophical works and popular newspapers that seek to justify, indeed to glorify, violence, terror and anarchy.

More economic growth is hardly the answer to such developments. Indeed, as I shall suggest later, there is every reason to believe that continuing economic growth in the richer countries is actually one of the chief causes of rising crime, perhaps an inevitable cause.

Chapter 9

The Manifest Desire for More Economic Growth

Under this heading I place some of the more common objections to the propriety of challenging the wisdom of policies designed to promote economic growth 'in the face of the clear eagerness of the vast majority of the people . . . everywhere . . . to acquire or to hold on to the benefits of life in an advanced industrial society'.[2]

The phrasing of such a passage acts to confuse the question of rights with the question of facts.

What right, the growthman may ask, have I, Mishan, or has anyone for that matter, to tell others what they should want! (for the growthman likes nothing better than to be heard championing the sacred right of the ordinary man to spend his money just as he pleases). But then, I go along with him. I concede the common man's right to sleep each night on a mattress stuffed with breakfast cereal if he chooses. The growth-sceptic does not, in fact, question people's rights to spend as they please or, for that matter, to vote as they please. What is at issue in the debate are *not* the rights of the consumer or the citizen. What is at issue are the facts or, rather, a judgment of the facts. For the question we seek to answer is simply this: will continuing economic growth in the already affluent society augment, or reduce, social welfare? And whatever my opinion happens to be on this question, I am hardly seeking to *dictate* to others what they should do. I am seeking only to *persuade* them of my own opinion. If my view happens to be a minority view, that is incidental. A minority view may be suspect in a conformist or totalitarian society. But it is yet an impertinence in a liberal democratic society.

Of course, the growthman may still wish to assert that Mishan, or any one else, is presumptuous to think that he *knows* better than others what they really want. The common man, he assures us, knows his own interest best – which dictum, harking back to Adam Smith, he shares with the modern liberal economist. However, it is interesting to note that the confidence reposed by the liberal economist in the judgment of the ordinary man does not extend beyond the ordinary man's choice of market goods. On economic issues that are decided, ultimately, through the polls, liberal economists tend to believe that they, the economists, know what the public really wants better than it does itself. They persist in arguing against this or that welfare programme, this or that tariff or tax, this or that public enterprise or regulatory legislation, despite clear evidence of widespread approval for such measures.

Apparently, the common man is thought to know just what he wants from the assortment of goods offered to him by the market – or, perhaps, it is expedient to suppose that he does so – but he is also thought to be somewhat obtuse when it comes to making a choice of goods offered through the political process. This belief might be questioned, but there is much to be said for it. Every would-be reformer since Socrates must believe that he is in broad sympathy with the ultimate ends sought by the society in which he lives, but also that, by dint of greater imagination or of more systematic thought on specific public issues, he is better able than others to foresee the range of consequences resulting from alternative policies. Thus, the economist may justify his right to challenge the public's political judgment on economic issues, on the grounds that his training and expertise enable him to perceive certain implications that are only imperfectly understood by non-specialists.

It is on just such grounds that economists, including, of course, antigrowth economists, may reasonably challenge political decisions that favour economic growth. For if it is supposed that the ordinary public does not easily discern the chief social implications of enacting specific and relatively simple political measures, it is far less likely that this same public will be aware of the range of consequences, tangible and intangible, short term and long, that bear on society's wellbeing from the persisting pursuit of economic growth. Indeed, if the question, whether further economic growth would improve social welfare, could properly be settled simply by asking people, nobody would be inclined to argue the case either way. His time would better be employed in conducting public opinion polls. Such sample surveys of public opinion would, however, throw light only on people's wants or beliefs with respect to economic growth; not on the question of whether *in fact* further economic growth would make them happier.

Turning to the lesser question of the evidence for the 'clear eagerness of the vast majority of the people' to favour continued economic growth, it is itself far from conclusive. From the observation that today (or during any other period of history) people tend to use up all their income – that is, they do not burn or otherwise destroy their money – and that they all wish they had more of it to spend, one cannot legitimately infer that they all believe further economic growth to be a good thing. I assure my readers that I do not intend ever to throw away any of my money, and that, indeed, I should be glad to receive donations from them at any time. Nevertheless, I believe I am being quite consistent in asserting by belief that further economic growth in the West is unlikely to advance social welfare.

As for the behaviour of the citizen in electing governments evidently committed to economic growth, we must acknowledge that the choice offered to him at any moment of time is restricted, particularly in a two-party system. In modern democracies, political parties are wholly absorbed with ways and means of retaining office or of being returned to office. Of necessity they are conservative, and tend to direct their appeal chiefly to safe bread-and-butter issues – to employment, prices, foreign trade and industrial issues, and to overall growth performance. Perforce, they think largely in terms of the electoral effect of their actions over the next two or three years only, during which period their own assessment of the existing prejudices of their supporters, and of the public at large, figures as part of the unalterable data.

Moreover, where both parties adopt the same policy on critical issues – say, both are habitually wedded to economic growth and to economic efficiency narrowly conceived – the electorate has virtually no choice. Even though a majority of the populace has begun to entertain misgivings about the conventional economic growth wisdom, the launching of a third political party is a Herculean task, requiring time, patience, sacrifices and exorbitant financial and political resources. Even to alter the attitudes and convictions of existing party stalwarts on fundamental issues is a thankless and exhausting task. These observations are relevant to the somewhat Panglossian view put forward by Edward Banfield in *The Unheavenly City* (1968) to the effect that existing social problems cannot, in fact, be severe, for if they were people would surely go to the trouble of solving them. Those problems which continue, therefore, do so simply because the cost of remedy exceeds the expected benefits.

This comfortable view of life was doubtless held to be true by some people during the great depression of the 1930s. But although it is scarcely more than a tautology, this notion of the cost of solving a social problem is worth a moment of our time.

True, any alternative organisation open to society that is manifestly superior to the existing one would be adopted without delay if it were clearly perceived, and if the transition were costless and painless. But a feasible design for specific improvements may not, in fact, occur to anyone for a long time and, when it does so, much effort and expenditure may be necessary to persuade others of its desirability. What is more, great effort and expenditure may be necessary also to overcome the opposition of highly organised commercial interests, or other special groups which, even though they detect long run advantages to society from the adoption of the policy in question, are more alert to their own immediate losses.

It follows that even if eminently attractive proposals are put forward they can founder for lack of funds and sustained endeavours. The welfare of society, we may safely conclude, can be far below the maximum level that is technically attainable.

Chapter 10

No Alternative to Economic Growth

The belief that economic growth may not properly be condemned unless feasible alternatives are presented cannot be justified. A distinction has to be made between a proposal to abandon an existing practice or policy and a proposal to criticise an existing practice or policy.

Thus, if the touchstone of our inquiry is the wellbeing of ordinary mortals, and if by reference to it we are able to undermine the traditional presumption in favour of economic growth, this immanent criticism is not weakened simply because we do not, in addition, suggest positive proposals for an alternative dispensation. Those who, notwithstanding, would continue to support economic growth have the choice either of attacking our criticisms or else of accepting them and, therefore, acceding to the *status quo* only for such time as is necessary to design some feasible alternative. What growthmen cannot reasonably maintain is that any criticism of economic growth is invalid just because there appear to be no feasible alternatives.

One can say more. Not only is such criticism legitimate and of interest to society irrespective of its catalytic potential; but it is also valuable and pertinent in as much as alternative policies will begin to evolve only after people have been undeceived enough to start thinking in all earnestness about swerving away from the growth orbit, and about coming to terms with the reality of a steady state economy.

If, in the end, it transpires that alternatives to continued economic growth are not politically feasible, and that therefore it has to be endured, we are not completely helpless. We can be more philosophical about it. We can do what little we can to discourage it instead of, as at present, striving to accelerate it.

Chapter 11

Economic Growth as the Wellhead of Good

A pro-growth economist began his public address with the observation that, although economic growth could be bad in some circumstances, it could be good in others and, although it might sometimes be too fast, it might also be too slow. Inevitably, he concluded that what was needed was the 'optimal' or just-right rate of economic growth. This is about as vacuous as the all-too-frequent remark that 'economic growth may be bad for you but good for me' or, more generally, bad for some people but good for others. However, the latter is misleading as well as vacuous since the term 'economic growth', which is a social process, is there used to mean individual wealth or welfare with all its invidious associations.

In much the same spirit, however, some economists acknowledge the many disamenities accompanying economic growth but give their unqualified support to 'real' economic growth – much in the same way that ardent socialists abjure the features of self-declared socialist regimes but maintain an unwavering allegiance to 'real' socialism.

Thus, the mere fact that the existing socialist economies have not been remarkably superior (and in some respects have been decidedly inferior) to some of the 'capitalist' economies, or the fact that socialist governments have been dull, repressive and occasionally barbarous, does nothing to damp the fervour of the faithful socialist. In any debate on the subject, he will, unwittingly perhaps, place himself in a position of unfair advantage – there to compare the actual and existing 'capitalist' system (with all its imperfections blown out of proportion by a free press that competes in sensationalism) with an as-yet non-existent and wholly-ideal socialist system.[3]

This forensic tactic seems to have been adopted, possibly inadvertently, by a number of pro-growth economists in as much as they compare any alternative no-growth economy with an idealised growth economy: one that is purified by ideal institutional mechanisms of all harmful spillover effects, these effects being so broadly defined as to ensure net social benefits from the process. Indeed, it is from these traditional aspirations towards the perfectibility of society that the resolution not to jettison economic growth but, instead, to reform it (or to give it 'a new direction') gathers its impetus.

Such inspiration, however, offers no plausible picture of the near future as it has begun to emerge. Economists all know that a narrow range of environmental spillovers might beneficially be reduced, given some political initiative and expenditures. They include air and water pollution, congestion, noise and tourist blight. Yet the mere conceptual possibility of social control is, of itself, nothing to the purpose. In judging the changing quality of life over the past three decades we cannot reasonably ignore the fact that many forms of pollution have already spread over the globe. So also, in foretelling the quality of life over the next three decades, it is not the ideal which economists are able to imagine, and which might spring from some perfect distribution of property rights, that is pertinent. What is pertinent in this debate is *the political likelihood within a growth-bound economy* that significant reductions will actually be made in each of the chief forms of pollution.[4]

The reader must bear in mind that, in the nature of things, by the time a nuisance has come to be recognised as such by the public, organised interests arising out of the new process or activity will have become powerful enough to resist any proposed legislation designed to correct the situation.[5] The winter silence and grandeur of mountain areas were shattered with the advent of the snowmobile, which also produced a train of social and ecological consequences too tedious to narrate here. By the time a protest movement had begun to crystallise, a snowmobile lobby had been formed as determined and resourceful as the Rifle Association of America. The recent popularity of the skimobile, an easier and less expensive sport than waterskiing, has already led to the formation of a lobby in order to combat the more diffused interests of the larger community.

Chapter 12

Economic Growth as the Fount of Cultural Refinement

Animals are simple creatures and have simple needs. In contrast, men are complex creatures and their needs are correspondingly complex. In order to contrive an argument in favour of economic growth from this obvious fact, it is necessary to believe one of two things. (1) That, until economic growth has continued for a longer time, man's complex nature will not be fully satisfied. To some extent, therefore, he still suffers constraints on his powers of enjoyment which only further economic growth can remove. (2) That although, in any period of history, man may think he has enough, and does not seek more complex means of satisfaction, the process of economic growth continues to offer him unforseen opportunities for new experiences which enable his complex nature to attain ever-higher levels of satisfaction. Although no historical evidence can be adduced in favour of such beliefs, they have, in the abstract, a spurious plausibility.

Nevertheless, proposition (1) does not stand up well to a little probing. It can hardly be thought that life was insufficiently complex for the satisfaction of ordinary mortals of an age if for the extraordinary mortals of that age it was apparently complex enough. There is nothing in the works of Aristotle, to choose but one outstanding figure from Antiquity, to suggest that he languished from lack of occupation. Reflecting on the lives of men of genius since the Renaissance – say, Michelangelo, Shakespeare, Rembrandt, Newton, Wren, Beethoven – we may ask if there are any incidents in their lives to suggest that their extraordinary talents were frustrated simply because contemporary life lacked the necessary degree of complexity. Do we imagine that, were they resurrected today, Shakespeare would write more beautiful poetry, or Beethoven compose more beautiful symphonies?

As for proposition (2), while no one denies that man has a complex and subtle psychology, even a casual reading of Greek plays suggests that it was no less complex and subtle then than it is today. That it could conceivably grow yet more complex and subtle can, of course, be argued, though we need not think about it here. For the relevant question is whether the actual goods, and the actual processes and institutions, produced by economic growth act continuously to refine man's sensibilities and so to convolute his psychology as to open him to intenser experiences and enjoyment. Since there is ample illustration in the chapters that follow of the sorts of goods and gadgetry produced by modern economic growth, and of their dubious effects on people's character and welfare, further reading should persuade us that, if anything, the contrary is the case.

Anticipated developments – such as faster jet planes, more powerful lasers, increased automation, bigger computers, holography, space travel, more diabolic weapons and a growing assortment of push-button devices – are at least as likely to make us more dull and robot-like than more lively and human. Indeed, for reasons to be discussed in Chapter 36, we should not be surprised to observe a continuation of the postwar trend towards increasing obscenity and violence.

Chapter 13

Science as Man's Servant: The Growthman's View

Among the forces that shape and direct economic growth, the most powerful in the modern world is science or, rather, applied science or technology. Like economic growth itself, science is alleged to be neutral. The enormous powers it confers on man cannot be associated with good or evil attributes. For science is the servant of man. It cannot therefore destroy except at the bidding of man. So runs the popular refrain.

Talking of man in this context, however, tends to evoke an image of a transcendent god-like creature that spans history and knowledge: some singular embodiment of heroic qualities and universal achievement. In the mind of the dedicated scientist this mythical being, speaking for all men, is destined to meet all nature's challenges and overcome all obstacles to progress – ultimately to move among the stars and conquer the universe.

Such images serve a social purpose, as an anodyne to quell the edging apprehension of reality. For the control of science and technology is not, as it happens, in the hands of *man*; it is in the hands of *men* – men as they emerge from history, organised into nation states, ideologically in conflict, and in perpetual struggle for advantage. While recognising the unwavering integrity of some men, and the sterling qualities to be found in many of them, there is no lack of incident in history to illustrate also men's imprudence, folly, corruptibility and inhumanity. Yet it is to this world of imperfect creatures that science vouchsafes its discoveries, to be translated into technology according to prevailing fashions or exigencies. If, within such a dispensation, science emerges as a power for good, it emerges also as a power for evil.

In fact, the *potential* of science and technology for good is not the issue in this debate. Their actual effects in the past and their likely effects over the future are what matter. Of course, it goes without saying that every scientist is under temptation to stress the 'good' uses of the knowledge that may be uncovered by his experiments. Even in so frightening a field as the study of RNA and DNA (the acid substances that store and pass on as heredity the blueprint for the production of proteins by the cell), further research will continue to be rationalised by the allegation that only in this way can scientists learn about the factors that produce abnormalities and, therefore, that only through such research can they hope to find ways of correcting them. The possibility of genetic controls for other less laudable purposes, perhaps serving the sinister ends of some fanatic government, is not dwelt on. Nor yet is the possibility of accidental escape from the laboratory of some new mutation of bacteria that could threaten man's survival.[6]

If we are seriously interested in the growth debate, we cannot then avoid the need to debate, also, the direction of modern science, its translation into technology by the industrial nations, and the influences it exerts on society at large. Intelligent conjecture about the future, however, presupposes some knowledge of the existing power and reach of modern science, and also some idea of the scientific developments over the future, from which we can speculate about the likelier consequences on our lives and character – always bearing in mind the avarice and myopia of men, and the limitations of their political and economic institutions.

Chapter 14

Man Will Learn to Adapt to the Future

As science and technology transform the world, men have no choice but to alter their habits of work and play, and the schedules and structure of their lives. The fact that men do have to adjust in order to 'keep up with the times' is not in question, and the certainty that they will continue to do so offers little consolation. If, for example, urban environments become yet noisier, the citizen may adjust in part by soundproof buildings, in part by the use of ear mufflers and in part by some loss of hearing. Even those who declare themselves untroubled by the persistent din may succumb eventually to any one or several of a variety of nervous disorders, or else may come to depend heavily on tranquillisers or other sedatives which expose them to malignant side effects. Again, people can, over time, become so innured to the foul stench of a neighbourhood as to become quite unaware of it. Yet it can affect their physical and emotional state, and thus their enjoyment of life.

Unless, then, we are interested primarily in the continued advance of science and industry, regarding them as prior ends of society, the pertinent question is surely whether this process of adjusting ourselves to the vicissitudes of 'the machine' – this process, that is, of somehow coming to terms with the changing physical environment and with the flow of technological hardware produced by the growth economy – will, in fact, make men happier, or bring them closer to a sense of fulfilment. Certainly, we are not to assume that adaptation *per se* implies fulfilment.

To illustrate, let us suppose that men can adapt equally well to a number of diverse conditions, A, B, C and D. Indeed, so as to avoid controversy on transitional problems of adjustment, we shall suppose that men can be born into these different conditions of society.

Would it not then be absurd to conclude, from the fact that men could adapt as well to one condition as any other – in the sense that they could, apparently, cope in each case with the tasks required of them – that they must all be equally felicitous?

Nor is the speed of their adaptation to any of the conditions a guide to its desirability. It has been observed by some students of the Nazi regime in Germany that after a few weeks of savage shocks most of the inmates of concentration camps became wholly adapted to their vile condition. As Stanley Elkins (1968) observes, they even looked up to their persecutors much in the way that children do to benevolent but stern parents.

Nor, for that matter, is either the wish or the reluctance to adapt to a particular style of life altogether decisive. Let state A be a more satisfactory life than the existing state B. But without actual experience of the A state, and without the time necessary to adjust himself to it, a man may continue to look with disfavour on state A and so work actively to defeat any proposal that would tend to move him in the direction of state A. If, however, as a result, say, of some emergency, he had to submit to living in the A state for some time, he would later, reviewing his life, freely acknowledge the A state to be the happier of the two.

I submit this rather trite observation only because, although people generally agree that the young do not always know 'what is best for them', they resist extending the remark to adults also. They fear, perhaps, that any acknowledgment of what is, after all, only common experience implies tacit agreement that others, the 'authorities' say, should disregard their overt political wishes and, indeed, should make all personal decisions for them. The only valid implication of this common fact of life for the growth debate that I can discern, however, is that, in any interchange of views on the subject, our vision of the good life, or of the better life, should not be constrained by the declared preferences of majorities of people whose values and pursuits and tastes have been shaped from birth by the technological society.

Chapter 15

Antigrowth as an Elitist Fad

According to the statements of some growthmen, those growth-sceptics who today wish to 'opt out' of the growth society are those who have already made successful use of the growth society. In effect, they are selfish hypocrites who, though only now, would gladly dismantle this wonderful economic growth machinery, thereby depriving currently underprivileged groups of opportunities for 'making it', in order to safeguard their own status and privileges.

To mention only the more common metaphors employed, the no-growthmen who have 'made it' now want to 'kick down the ladder of opportunity behind them', in order, ostensibly, to prevent their less fortunate countrymen from swarming up after them, eager as they are 'to share in the good things of life'. Again, these selfish no-growthmen are depicted as exclaiming: 'Stop the world, I want to get off! ' Heedless of the plight of the have-nots, they seek only to safeguard their environmental privileges.

It is hard to refrain from satirising such naive righteousness which misleads with respect both to the arguments and to the motives of those concerned with the quality of life. Those golden opportunities for sharing in 'the good things of life', which farther economic growth, it is imagined, will confer on all other people lower down on the scale of affluence, turn out to be very tenuous things.

First, in earlier ages, when only a few had the means necessary to travel widely, and those few were wealthy and aristocratic, the impact of travel on the physical environment was inconsequential. Like a magnificent garden, the natural beauty of a country can be kept attractive and tidy only so long as it remains the preserve of a few. Once the masses, eager for the same privileges, swarm into the garden and, encouraged by the commercial fanfare, begin to grab the flowers and deposit their litter everywhere, the garden will be turned into a wasteland. The result will be that, whereas once a few enjoyed the garden, and others might have hoped to, there is now no garden left to be enjoyed by anyone.

Although the rapid diminution of the world's stock of natural beauty has come about largely in response to the increase in sheer numbers of travellers, the change from patrician to plebian played an auxiliary role. There will always be exceptions, but it is a reasonable presumption that those nurtured in a tradition of *noblesse oblige* are likely to be more sensitive and long-sighted in such matters than are today's urban blue and white collar workers tutored by a commercial ethos to clutch at whatever brief pleasures the market makes available heedless of the morrow.

Of course, the issue does not depend crucially upon the social composition of the numbers involved and, if I mention it in passing, it is simply because people today choose to overlook the historic fact of the greater care and forethought of the aristocracy in deference to prevailing democratic passion. In the main, the environmentalist's argument turns, as indicated earlier, on the number of people relative to limited natural resources. Given the existing numbers within a country or within the world at large, to say nothing of the continuing increase in the world's population, the remaining areas of natural beauty are being overexploited and rapidly eroded. And the more people rush about trying to enjoy them, the more rapidly they erode. This, then, is one of 'the good things in life', once the preserve of the few, which it is impossible both to share among the masses and to preserve for the future. Indeed, the attempt since World War II to share it with the masses has issued in the greatest holocaust of natural beauty in the history of mankind.

In the event, current environmental concern may be expressed as follows: if the standards of 'the masses' have to be raised, either domestically or internationally, much thought must be given to raising them in ways that do not debase the environment further. Providing these 'masses' with yesterday's status symbols – with more motorised recreations, with more transistors and air travel, which have the effect of accelerating and intensifying the destruction of scarce environmental resources – is not the best way of enriching their lives – in particular, if any concern is felt for their children, their grandchildren, and for generations yet to come.

I might add in passing that one does not have to part from orthodox economics, with its many restrictive simplifications, in order to reach such a conclusion. Unchecked mass tourism may, quite clearly, generate spillover effects, in addition to current traffic congestion, in consideration of which the modern economist would be impelled to conclude that the existing volume of tourists exceeds some defined ideal or 'optimal' volume. Not all economists, however, are imaginative enough in identifying the various forms of irreversible destruction involved in mass tourism, or in extending the range of spillovers to include the impact of mass tourism on the character and the ultimate contentment of the inhabitants of the host countries.

Secondly, and placing the argument in a broader context, the metaphor of clambering on to the plateau of privilege and kicking down the ladder afterwards lest others follow is singularly inept. A more apt analogy for appreciating the social effects of economic growth is that of an endless moving staircase along which people are scattered. The average rate of economic growth is the rate at which the staircase is moving. While some people will be walking up the moving staircase, passing others who are either stationary or ascending more slowly, others will be descending the moving staircase. For a number of reasons that make no essential difference to the argument, these changes of position take place only within certain limits. Thus, the bulk of the population tends to assume much the same position between the highest and lowest individuals or families, the broad distribution remaining roughly unchanged in structure for decades despite the ingenuity of reformers and the efforts of welfare agencies. The tenor of my remarks, however, would not be altered if, instead, there were a distinct tendency for the limits of the distribution to draw closer over time.

Pressing the analogy further, the options to be considered are two: (a) the speed of movement of the staircase, and (b) the cluster, or spread, of the population along it.

If people are all eager for more speed, if all of them simply want the staircase to move faster irrespective of their position along it, they would, indeed, be justified in calling for more economic growth. Whether this is true of Western nations is, of course, one of the questions in the debate, the other being whether they would in fact benefit from continued economic growth, assuming it to be possible.

On this first question, however, there is some evidence to suggest that the bulk of populations in the Western nations are increasingly interested in economic status, or position in the pay structure of society, rather than in real income for itself. If this be the case, their aspirations cannot be met simply by having the staircase continue to move upwards or move upwards faster. There cannot, in the nature of things, be a mass improvement in status; the members of a community cannot all be made better off *relative* to others. What is more, it is highly unlikely that the continued movement of the staircase will itself – independently, that is, of government intervention – cause a shift forward of any significant proportion of those on the lowest steps to higher steps where the bulk of the families is concentrated.

From the growthman's point of view such a fact of economic life is most opportune. By reference to the plight of those on the lowest steps of the moving staircase he can, he believes, justify the call for more, and faster, economic growth – in the sure knowledge that, no matter how fast the staircase can be made to move, there will always be enough families left on the lowest steps to justify yet farther calls for more economic growth. Assuming economic growth continues, the 'underprivileged' families will, of course, become materially better off over time. Yet this group will always be designated as *relatively* impoverished and, therefore, *relatively* underprivileged.

This evergreen rationalisation for more economic growth clearly implies a rejection of any real, or absolute, standard of living as a goal of economic policy. A goal that would satisfy the quality-of-life proponents, and possibly also the bulk of humanity – that is, the goal of some currently agreed real standard of comfort for everyone – is therefore not on the agenda of growthmen. It would, perhaps, be mischievous to suggest that their preoccupation with *relative* poverty is no more than a cover under which they promote the material interests of the well-to-do. But it is certain that economic growth, *per se,* never hurt the rich, and that, indeed, the Establishment of bureaucrats, technocrats and businessmen stands to gain from it.

Of course, there are also some growth economists who are currently preoccupied with (b), with the idea of equalising incomes through taxation. But there are many more who shun the idea of radical redistributions of income or wealth, believing them, in any case to be politically unfeasible. In contrast, the so-called elitists – the environmentalists, the zero-economic-growth (ZEG) advocates, the quality-of-life exponents – are, all of them, entirely agreeable to the idea of a more equal sharing of the domestic aggregate product than is contemplated by existing governments.

Chapter 16

Economic Growth as a Perpetual Charity Ball

Allegation of a need to maintain the momentum of economic growth in order to enable us to do good, finds a reception in the guilty consciences of many of the well-to-do in the West. The good we are supposed to do includes helping the poor and ailing in all countries, promoting culture and expanding higher education.

It is to be noticed that this argument for continued growth is quite distinct from the arguments which turn on social welfare, for it might win ethical support even if it were believed that such growth would, on balance, reduce social welfare. Indeed, nineteenth-century political economists approved the expansion of industry, despite its manifest social disruption, in the belief that it would free the masses from poverty and thus enable them to participate more fully in the cultural benefits of civilisation.

However, if we confine our attention, for the moment, to the domestic economy of the highly industrialised nations, the fact is that such worthy objectives can all be realised without sustained economic growth. If it is a question of giving more to the indigenous poor in a variety of ways, or of promoting the arts or of expanding adult education, we ought first to ask about the magnitude of the sums envisaged. For the United States, for example, we might ask whether a capital sum of $100 billion per annum (at 1975 prices) would suffice. But the latter figure is, today (1975), less than three years' growth of GNP, at an annual average of 3 per cent. Thus, without making any one in the country worse off, if would be possible in three years' time to distribute an additional $100 billion each year among these good causes. If we really want to be munificent, we might be able to justify another six years or so of growth at current rates, but hardly more on this argument.

But for such laudable purposes do we really have to raise current levels of GNP at all? After all, if we allow that items such as higher education, job training, welfare programmes and cultural activities be included under the economic denomination of 'merit goods', on the grounds that people generally approve of them,[7] regard to symmetry would require the converse concept of a 'demerit good'. And with the abundance of 'demerit goods' in the West everywhere in evidence – with so much on the market that is trivial, inane, obscene and inimical – using up resources that could instead be transferred to the production of these more meritorious goods, there is no need for further economic growth.

If, on the other hand, the good deeds we are to perform as we become richer include that of helping the 'have-nots' in the economically backward two-thirds of the world, we are surely deluding ourselves. For one thing, the means by which funds are currently made available to poorer countries have uncertain effects on their economic development. Indeed, some economists have been persuaded that, on balance, foreign aid has had adverse effects on the economy of these countries. Professor Peter Bauer, for instance, has long maintained that foreign aid has actually inhibited economic development, promoted political corruption and encouraged economic parasitism. He observes (1974) that those poor countries that are able to make efficient use of foreign aid are also those that are, in any case, able to raise domestic funds and attract commercial capital from abroad.[8] However, even supporters of foreign aid programmes agree that a lot of it goes to waste.

No less significant is the fact that the magnitude of the foreign aid since World War II is not such as to inspire confidence in the frequent contention that we in the West must maintain, nay increase, our growth rates for their sake. The amount of foreign aid given by the United States, in absolute terms the largest donor, is less than one-half of 1 per cent of its GNP. If we supposed that on balance it does more good than harm, we should have to admit that it is just a shade better than nothing at all. Besides which, it is always a comfort to believe that while you are munching your lunch the crumbs are not entirely going to waste. I should not wish to exclude a reconsideration of the contribution foreign aid might make to improving living standards in the poorer countries if ever the West decided to donate a sizeable proportion of its income to them under conditions calculated to encourage its efficacious use. In that event, however, the crucial magnitude, at least for some time, would be the *proportion* of our income being gifted to them rather than its rate of growth.

In this connection, the possibility of a moral dilemma's arising later should not be excluded. For it may be that further economic growth in the West is bad for us but good for the poor countries.

Some modest hopes have been put on foreign trade rather than, or in addition to, foreign aid, the argument being that continued economic growth in the West will provide expanding markets for the foodstuffs, raw materials and simple manufactures of the poor countries. These hopes have not been fulfilled however. The post-war record reveals, not surprisingly perhaps, that, whenever the exports of manufactures from the poorer countries threaten profits and employment in the domestic industries of the rich countries, trade restrictions are invoked. (At the time of writing (end of 1975) additional protection against 'cheap foreign competition' has been extended to the British textile industry.) As for their raw materials, long before the formation of the Arab oil cartel in 1973 the industrial nations have persevered, not without success, in their endeavours to produce synthetic substitutes for them.

Chapter 17

The No-growth Pains Suffered by the Modern Economy

In so far as environmental economists and ecologists reject the notion of continuing economic growth as a desirable social goal for the industrial countries, they are insistently reminded by businessmen, economists and others of the problems that arise when, in fact, the modern economy does *not* grow. In each of the short-lived periods of stagnation of the American economy since 1900, for instance, there have been an appreciable rise in the number of unemployed, a decline in labour's share of the national income (except during the prolonged depression of the 1930s), a frustration of people's expectations, increased conflict among the working classes, and particular hardships borne by the poorest segment of the population.[9]

But these typical characteristics of a modern recession have no real bearing on the issue. They are particular to a growth-bound economy, one in which a spell of no-growth, or of a decline in growth, arises from 'market failures' or from allegedly inadequate monetary and fiscal policies. As such, they are necessarily accompanied by unemployment, stagnation and, therefore, increased discontent and resentment.

Those who are concerned primarily with the quality of life, however, have never proposed the deliberate creation of stagnation and unemployment in the modern growth economy as a means of diminishing the pace of economic growth. They seek rather to persuade the public to abandon the pursuit of economic growth in favour of something akin to a steady state economy. The actual means whereby a steady state is to be brought into being – the rationing of raw materials, the controls on technology, the desired level of affluence and its distribution – are, indeed, critical issues and should be the subject of prolonged public debate. Just now, however, they are premature. The immediate business of the environmentalist is that of inspiring the revolution of thought and feeling that is necessary if men's aspirations towards the good life are ever to be realised.

In other words, the current aim of the environmentalist is *not* a no-growth economy *per se*, much less a recession in a growing economy. It is that of persuading the public at large to accept a steady state economy as a desirable norm of social policy. More generally, it is to promote a public awareness of the extent of the crises facing humanity; to persuade people to foresake their faith in traditional economic criteria in favour of a radical reconsideration of the variety of factors that enhance the quality of life.

Chapter 18

The Appeal to the 'Political Parameters' of the System

We have already insisted on the need for gauging the likelihood of particular occurrences – for example, the likelihood of being able to check or reduce specific pollutants in the near future – in the light of prevailing institutions. It would seem to follow that the allegation made earlier, that some of the claims made for economic growth (such as the claim that it improves the lot of the poor) could in fact be realised without economic growth, ought properly to face the question of political realism also.

We may well ask whether it is likely that people in the United States would today agree to an additional internal transfer of some $50 billion, a sum that should more than suffice to remove all hard core poverty in that country. Although such a sum amounts to little more than the annual average rate of growth of the economy, the answer to our question is almost certainly no. Accepting, then, the existing attitudes and institutions – the 'political parameters' of the system – orthodox economists might conclude, in effect, that we can do more for the poor, via the growth process, only by doing more for all of us, which includes the wealthy, the middle class and the working classes, as well as the poor. On such attractive terms, it is not surprising that businessmen and technocrats are glad to 'help the poor'.

But if income transfers of this magnitude are politically unpopular today, the fact cannot be used to justify the continued pursuit of economic growth. Let the reader recall an earlier *caveat*: that in a critical assessment of economic growth, mention of any undesirable feature of modern society is to count only in so far as it arises from, or in connection with, the processes of economic growth. The undesirable feature in this instance – the fact that, even while there is, everywhere, evidence of overindulgence and almost criminal waste by many, the citizens of the affluent society cannot collectively agree to curb the general extravagance in order to alleviate the sheer poverty of a small minority of their countrymen – is surely related to the process of economic growth. If we agree that this unfortunate 'institutional constraint' or 'political parameter' springs from an ethos that is favourable to, indeed, brought about by, economic growth – if, that is, economic growth over the years has been maintained, and will continue to be maintained, by the self-seeking of individuals and enterprises, a self-seeking that is intensified by commercial pressures in the West – then such constraints or 'parameters' have to be included among the less desirable products of economic growth.

One might go further. The very readiness of social scientists to accept these current attitudes, the legitimate offspring of economic growth, as constraints or 'parameters' of the system, is itself an unfortunate consequence of the institutionalised pursuit of economic growth.

NOTES FOR PART III

Chapter 8

1 Many instances of this favourite ruse of modern growthmen are to be found in Wilfred Beckerman's *In Defense of Economic Growth* (1974), which I reviewed in 1975.

Chapter 9

2 Norman Podhoretz (1971).

Chapter 11

3 Wherever 'people's revolutions' are betrayed, there are always those imperishable 'enemies of the revolution' to fall back upon. What the purist socialist finds hard to explain is just why, if all preceding revolutions were betrayed or taken over by ruthless power elites, the new revolution that he himself wishes to bring about will fare any better.

4 The theme that economic feasibility is not enough and has not, in fact, prevailed against commercial and political interests, has been developed recently in connection with water pollution in the United States in an article by Albert Freeman and Robert Haveman (1972).

The full extent of the evasion by business of environmental legislation is hard to assess. According to the *Wall Street Journal* (5 November 1971): 'A new report by the non-profit Council on Economic Priorities – a privately financed self-proclaimed business watchdog group – accuses some of the nation's larger corporations of jumping on the environmental bandwagon with advertising that ranges from the blatantly false to the subtly deceptive. The cost of such advertising, the report says, in some cases may far exceed the amount of money the companies are spending directly to reduce pollution. . . .'

Again, according to the *New York Times* (5 November 1971): 'Of 289 pages of advertising costing about $6 million in 1970 issues of *Time, Newsweek* and *Business Week,* researchers found that more than half was from the five industries pinpointed in independent studies as having the most pollution clean-up work to do – electric utilities, steel, oil, paper, and chemicals.'

5 Wherever the resources and determination of a lobby cannot be overcome by the rest of the community (because, say, of the greater risks and heavier costs involved in attempts to organise a dispersed body of citizens), the stubbornly optimistic economist might wish to describe the situation in formal terms as one in which the 'transactions costs' of making the change exceed the net gains to society at large of reducing the pollution or nuisance in question. In doing so, however, he tends to overlook the scope for introducing institutional changes calculated to diminish such transactions costs. More important, he overlooks an important implication of this form of reasoning: namely, that, as a result of irreducibly large transactions costs, the net welfare to society at large (as measured by the conventional 'Pareto criterion') can decline with the introduction of such innovations.

Chapter 13

6 It is gratifying to come across signs of unrest among groups in the scientific community who are alert to the risks involved either in new technologies or in particular areas of research. A striking instance of the latter is a formal request by the American National Academy of Sciences' eleven-man Committee on 'Recombinant DNA Molecules' in July 1974 that their fellow scientists join them in suspending certain lines of research into gene manipulation and DNA transplantation until the hazards of pursuing those lines of research are fully investigated. A debate is beginning among scientists which is not likely to be settled for some time, if at all.

For an account of this unusual event, see Garrett Hardin (1975).

Chapter 16

7 An economic formalisation of the concept of a 'merit good' would require that its quantity enter positively into the utility of many individuals who do not themselves expect to enjoy the good directly, or participate directly in the approved activity. *Per contra,* a 'demerit good' is one that enters negatively into the utility functions of non-participants.

Clearly the concept of a 'merit good' is of a piece with what environmental economists sometimes call 'non-participant demand', which arises as a result of people's placing a value on some good – for example, a national park or the preservation of some species threatened with extinction – even though they do not expect ever to enjoy the good themselves.

8 An excellent summary of Peter Bauer's research and reflections on the subject can be found in his article 'The myth of foreign aid' (1974).

Chapter 17

9 This is the theme of many a popular article, often cast in the rhetorical form, 'Can we afford not to grow!' A recent specimen of this genre is the article by Rudolph Klein, 'The trouble with zero economic growth' (1974).

Part IV

Fading Hopes for Economic Growth

Chapter 19

More and Better Goods

Those who continue actively to support economic growth believe some or all of the following propositions.

(1) That environmental pollution is relatively easy and inexpensive to control.
(2) That the earth will be able to support a population several, or many, times that of the existing four billion inhabitants at tolerable living standards.
(3) That when it comes to natural resources, we have barely scratched the earth's surface.
(4) That the poor countries of Asia, Africa and South America will eventually follow the path of economic growth trodden by the West.

I place these beliefs in order of decreasing plausibility, even though there is no convincing evidence for any of them. Indeed, in view of some earlier remarks (Chapter 2), the first of them (1) is highly optimistic even where it is restricted, as it generally is, to air, water and soil pollution. Concerning the plausibility of (2) above, we have only to reflect that the existing population of some four billion cannot yet be supported at anything like tolerable standards; at least one-third of that number suffer from malnutrition on any official criterion. As for (3), it is literally true that we have barely scratched the surface of the earth since the deepest mines reach only to a few hundred feet. Estimates of the wealth of mineral resources buried in the layers of earth up to one mile beneath its surface tend to excite technologists no end. Economists, to their credit, become less excited at the thought; cost-conscious calculations suggest that only miracles of technological innovation could retard the onset of rapidly diminishing returns as we dig further into the earth. As for the fourth belief (4), it may charitably be interpreted as the persistence of the complacent postwar myth that a flood of exhortation, a steady stream of technicians, plus a trickle of aid, would suffice to overcome the social and economic problems of overpopulated and impoverished continents and, somehow, to launch them into the growth orbit. Despite all evidence to the contrary, this myth continues to appease the conscience of Western growthmen, though not without the connivance also of the governments of those countries in which millions live on the threshold of subsistence. Indeed, the myth is sanctified in diplomatic documents, and complacency is suffused over the globe, by referring to these destitute and sometimes desperate countries by the fatuous nomenclature of 'developing nations'.

However, even if all of these propositions are accepted as being substantially true, the case for continued economic growth has to be argued not simply on grounds of its physical possibility. It has also to be argued, as growthmen have begun to realise, on grounds of social desirability. In consequence, since about 1970, pro-growth economists, in addition to reiterating their belief in the technical potential for perpetual growth, have been energetic in attacking the growth-sceptics. Much of this counterattack has been feeble, and much of it misdirected – some evidence and arguments for this allegation being contained in Part II.

For the rest, their counterattack has made but little impact. The gist of all their arguments, in fact, reflects a belief that a continuation of those developments most closely associated with economic growth must culminate in a better life for the affluent citizen. The developments in question are: more and better goods, particularly more travel, more income equality, more education, more information and more scientific progress and innovation. All of these developments invite sceptical examination, and we shall consider them in the order given beginning with more and better goods.

In order to enhance the plausibility of the belief that a continuing rise in 'consumption standards' will have beneficial effects on social welfare, mention is invariably made of the wretched poverty that still lingers in the wealthier countries of the world – and sometimes, also, of the widespread destitution in the so-called Third World. The facts are not controversial, although their relevance is, as indicated earlier, in Chapter 16. Within affluent countries, at least, there is no economic obstacle to the removal of all 'absolute' poverty. Arguments built on the notion of 'relative' poverty are no more convincing. For, by definition, 'relative' poverty exists wherever there is any income inequality, even though everyone happens to enjoy a luxurious standard of living. We shall, therefore, free our minds from distributional considerations until Chapter 32, the better to attend to the welfare effects of more and better goods. For this purpose we shall suppose, in the remainder of this chapter, that the aggregate net product of the affluent economy is satisfactorily distributed among its members.

Now, if producing more goods and new varieties of goods have no effects other than gratifying existing desires, no matter how these desires came into being, most economists would concede the likelihood of diminishing satisfaction from additional increments of such goods. Although the question, whether the awakening or stimulating of appetites, and the creating of new desires, are good things in themselves irrespective of whether or not they can be fulfilled, or whether, instead, they are good things *only* if they are fulfilled – satisfaction depending in some way on the measure of the gap between desires and their fulfilment – is a philosophical question that we need not resolve here. It cannot, in any event, be resolved without factual judgments about the nature of man, and without information about the sorts of wants and desires that are being created in the wealthier countries of the world. However, as the reader may recall, we subjected the view that further economic growth is needed to satisfy man's complex nature to some cold scrutiny in Chapter 12. As for the specific sorts of wants and goods being created in affluent societies, we concluded there, and elsewhere, that they appeared to have little relish of salvation, or elevation, in them. Looking, then, at the proliferation of actual goods being created by the affluent consumer society, the best that may be said of a prospective expansion in the per capita consumption of such stuff is that social satisfaction is likely to lag behind the growth of measured output.

I might add, in passing, that in so far as the 'expansion of the area of choice' – to use a favoured image of the economist – takes the form of an increase in the number of brands and models there can be no presumption at all of an increase in social welfare. As observed in my earlier books, *The Costs of Economic Growth* (1967), the operation of competitive markets cannot be counted on to produce an optimum, or ideal, variety of goods. Brief reflection on the existing variety of transistors, recorders, detergents, furniture, breakfast cereals and so on certainly suggests that, for a large number of items, the optimal variety has long been surpassed. In order, today, to make a judicious choice, time, patience, effort and money are increasingly required, even where consumer information is available. Most people do not, of course, spend the time necessary to make this judicious choice, and, in consequence, are more likely to experience bewilderment and frustration, and to suffer annoyances and disappointments.

Returning to the anticipation of a rising tide of consumer goods, exception has always to be made for the oft-mentioned spillover effects arising either in the use, or in the production, of goods; an exception that dissipates the welfare presumption in favour of economic growth. In respect of the better-known pollutants, the economist rather fancies his techniques for prescribing solutions – although, owing to the absence of information and political will, he may have precious few opportunities for implementing them. The least economic, albeit politically the easiest, solution is that of installing plant and equipment in order to reduce however much air or water pollution is churned out by firms and individuals below socially prescribed tolerance levels. Although estimates of the costs involved run into tens of $ billions for a country such as the United States, pro-growth economists such as Wilfred Beckerman (1974) calculate them as a small proportion of current and future GNP. More sobering estimates have been put forward recently by Allen Kneese and Charles Schultze (1975), who also point out the too-often neglected difficulty of reducing any one kind of pollution without increasing, or creating, some other kind. For example, Beckerman asserts that the environmental impact of the pollutants emitted from high chimneys is 'often virtually zero'. But the informed layman must then be wondering what to make of the evidence and the repeated complaints from Norway and Sweden, that the acid rain which damages their fisheries and forests is caused by the sulphur dioxide from high factory chimneys in Britain and Germany. As for the sort of pollution that is technically easy to reduce, say noise pollution, the costs of making a noticeable improvement in the environment in this respect are so prohibitive that noise pollution receives only sporadic attention despite mounting evidence of the ill effects of a variety of machine-caused noises on the nervous system.

Moreover, further consideration of the problem of large scale pollution yields two arguments, both of which are continually evaded by pro-growth economists, and both of which go far to undermine the optimistic view that, notwithstanding the incidence of pollutants, net social benefits would continue to accrue – or, at least, could be made to accrue – if the happy day should ever dawn on which politicians gave economists a free hand in legislating for pollution controls.

The first is the distinct possibility that the actual amounts of particular goods produced by competitive markets, along with the pollutants generated, leave society worse off (on strictly economic criteria). It is interesting to discover that, in such cases, the existence of a law prohibiting all pollutants unless and until all sufferers were adequately compensated, could not result in the production of positive outputs of the goods in question. Although empirical studies of such cases have not yet been undertaken, a brief survey of these possibilities can be found in my 1971 digest of the pollution literature in economics. Noise pollution, I should think, fits into this category.

The second argument is yet more important. The costs of pollution to society, even where narrowly defined, are imperfectly known. The problem is not one of simple measurement; of transforming known data on physical damage into money costs. The fact is that knowledge of the effects of a vast range of pollutants, and potential pollutants, on human health and the environment generally comes to light slowly and haltingly. If growthmen propose – as often they do – that no action be taken to control production of an item until evidence of deleterious effects has been established, the evidence may come too late to avert a disaster. As indicated in Chapter 45, decades must pass before the ecological and genetic side effects of many thousands of new chemicals, drugs and food additives are understood. So long as society's response to innovations is largely that of 'business as usual' until firm evidence of harm is established, there is no presumption whatsoever that rising levels of GNP will increase society's wellbeing.

Finally, two other considerations tell against the affluent growth economy even when we ignore entirely the problems of pollution.

The desire to command more purchasing power *relative* to others, or to others in comparable occupations, has been relegated by economists to the category of spillovers. Yet it deserves special mention, if only because it is a spillover for which the economist can propose no remedy consistent with continued economic growth. This modern attitude to economic status has been dignified by the appellation of the *'relative income hypothesis'*, though it is now bandied about in the profession as the 'Joneses effect' (that is, the keeping-up-with-the-Joneses effect). The implications of the concept follow.

In an affluent society people's satisfaction, as Thorstein Veblen (1928) observed, depends not only on the innate or perceived utility of the goods they come to possess, but also on the status value associated with their possession. A more general way of putting the matter is to state that the satisfaction a person derives from his current expenditure depends not only on the goods that he buys, but also on the goods bought by others. In a high consumption society, for instance, it is not only a person's absolute income that counts; his *relative* income also counts – his position, that is, in the structure of incomes. According to this hypothesis, for which there is ample evidence, relative income matters more as affluence increases.[1] At some point, a man would prefer a 5 per cent *reduction* of his income accompanied by, say, a 10 per cent reduction in the incomes of others, to a 10 per cent increase in his income along with a 10 per cent increase in the incomes of others.

The more this attitude prevails – and the ethos of our society actively promotes it – the more futile is the pursuit of economic growth for society as a whole. For it is obvious that it is not possible to make everybody *relatively* better off over time. The economist has no means of measuring this source of welfare loss. But in recognition of its growing strength, estimates of the increase of 'real' income over the last few decades have to be rejected as wholly misleading.[2]

The second consideration is the attitude to things summarised in the term 'the throwaway society'. Whether it is regarded as a reflection of the diminishing marginal utility of goods, or whether it carries other psychological connotations, is an issue which we broach later (Chapter 28). Growthmen naturally favour the simpler explanation, and assert that the plethora of material goods tends to make people less materialistic; people, that is, come to spurn mere things, and turn their minds to higher matters. Since the decline in material greed has not been one of the more salient characteristics of the affluent societies over the last century, it is obvious that there must be other forces at work. We are bound to acknowledge, then, that the desire to command more purchasing power, or more purchasing power relative to others, irrespective of the assortment of goods available on the market, appears to be entirely consistent with the attaching of slight value to any item.

In a traditional society, ordinary goods and chattels were themselves a source of gratification, not only in appreciation of their individual workmanship but also because of their real scarcity. In consequence, a person's possessions generally accompanied him through life, a link with the past, and a fond reminder of events, personages and places. Thus, in an age when a child could not hope for more than one doll, she was overjoyed to receive it, and treated it with loving care. Today, she can expect about a dozen and will, at best, treat them as items in a collection. Gifts must lose their power as people come to have 'everything', and when incomes are such that no sacrifice is incurred in giving them.

The experience of universal plenty, of rapid obsolescence and rapid replacement, cannot but breed a throwaway attitude towards man-made manufactures irrespective of the materials or quality. There is no time to grow fond of anything, no matter how well it serves; and, in any case, it will soon be superseded by another model. Everything bought or received comes to be regarded as potential garbage. The 'more and better' that further growth offers can mean less, or worse, in terms of human welfare.

Chapter 20

More Mobility

Mobility, in the geographical as well as the social sense, has long been accepted as an index of progress. Travel, it was commonly supposed, broadens the mind. Not only do travellers enjoy the rich variety of the world, but also frequent exposure to customs and cultures different from their own acts to enlarge their sympathy and tolerance. The international movement of people, moreover, has long been regarded as a powerful factor in the promotion of mutual understanding between different nations, a condition that makes for a more harmonious and peaceful world.

World Wars I and II did little to shatter these common beliefs, beliefs that could be elaborated, though to no purpose. For it is no longer a question of pitting such beliefs against opposing considerations. The beliefs themselves are today manifestly untrue – as untrue as the once-popular belief that improved standards of living and the spread of education would go far to reduce the incidence of crime. Among determined growthmen, all the myths about the ameliorative powers of economic growth die hard, if they die at all. Counterevidence of the most glaring kind – for instance, the incredible rise, over the last decade, in the incidence of theft: in burglary, street robbery, embezzlement and, above all, shoplifting – is invariably dismissed as inconclusive; as an indication merely that economic growth is not fast enough to overcome other and exogenous forces. This sort of circular form of reasoning is as impervious to the facts as that of primitive tribes which continue to believe in the power of ritual sacrifice to induce rain: for if it does rain, the belief is once again vindicated; if it does not rain, the gods must be displeased, and therefore more sacrifices are called for.

Returning to the specific belief in the mind-enriching powers of travel, since an index of mind enrichment has not been formulated and accepted, there is perhaps some excuse for the tenacity of this belief among growthmen. But others, who are willing to reflect on the known facts about modern travel, are likely to be sceptical of it. For international travel today is almost entirely mass travel. And the mode of travel, the organisation of travel and the very scale of travel produce far-reaching effects also on the characteristics of the host country, both environmental and social.

It is not possible, moreover, to assess the range of consequences of the mode and scale of modern travel unless we give thought also to the twin instruments without which they could not be sustained: the automobile and the airliner.

The private automobile is, surely, one of the greatest, if not *the* greatest, disasters that ever befell the human race. For sheer irresistable destructive power, no other creation of man – save, perhaps the airliner – can compete with it. Almost every principle of architectural harmony has been perverted in the vain struggle to keep the mounting volume of motorised traffic moving through our cities, towns, resorts and hamlets, and, of course, through our distended suburbs. Clamour, dust, fume, congestion and visual distraction are the predominant features in all built-up areas. Even where styles of architecture differ between cities – and they differ less from year to year – these traffic spillovers impinge so blatantly and so persistently on the senses as to submerge any other impression. Whether we are in Chicago, Paris, Tokyo, Düsseldorf, Milan or Manchester, it is the choking din and the endless movement of motorised traffic that dominate the scene and rivet our awareness. The automobile has multiplied like the locust and swarmed with noise and stench through every street and alley, with the consequence that all the mingling of the crowds, all the gaiety in the streets, once associated with Paris, Vienna, London, Buenos Aires and other great cities of the world, have become things of the past.

We need hardly dwell on our psychological dependence on the automobile, since it is the very staple of automobile advertisements to depict it as a thing throbbing with sex appeal, as a thing of sheer beauty, as an irresistible status and virility symbol. And as the automobile population has grown, along with industrial empires needed to fuel and maintain the momentum, and the sales of new cars have become a separate indicator of the nation's 'prosperity', we have mesmerised ourselves into the belief that we are economically dependent upon automobile sales.

Our physical dependence upon this vehicle today is, of course, the direct result of its universal adoption. Our cities and suburbs have, in consequence, expanded without pause for the last quarter-century, and promoted a demand for massive and often-convoluted road-building projects that encourage the flow of traffic which, in turn, promotes the demand for more traffic projects. Since it is believed that the motorist has a right to see everything worthwhile from the seat of his motor car, beauty spots have a fatal attraction for highway builders. Indeed, the motorist is enjoined by advertisements to 'get away from it all' – along with a few million others. And the highway builder, in the unceasing attempt to provide him with the means to do so, must succeed ultimately in ensuring that it is virtually impossible to get away at all.

Yet, by the same token, it becomes ever more necessary for people somehow to 'get away from it all'. The one economic activity showing really impressive postwar growth is the creation of places, the result of highway builders' efforts, that almost everybody wants to get away from. Speeding along multilaned highways hour after hour, the American motorist sees nothing but thousands of other motor cars, vast hoardings, garages, motels and outsize 'drive-ins' – the commercial paraphernalia of an uprooted society, ever in transit.

One could go on, for the extent of its destructive powers is awesome to contemplate. Criminal success, especially of robbery and violence, has come to depend heavily on the fast get-away car. And, of course, motorists innocently kill off other people at the rate of about 150,000 a year (some 55,000 a year in the United States alone), and each year permanently maim about a million. Through its annual emission of millions of tons of foul gases, the automobile's contribution to sickness and death from cancer and bronchial disorders is just beginning to be understood (see Lester Lave and Eugene Seskin, 1975). What is already fully understood, however, is the connection between air and automobile travel on the one hand, and, on the other, the greatest holocaust of natural beauty since the beginning of history – though, for commercial reasons, very little has yet been done about it.

For, in addition to plunging us into an era of shrieking skies from which it is becoming virtually impossible to escape (short of dwelling in isolation in some remote part of the earth), the airliner has conspired with the automobile to create a tourist explosion that, within a few years, has irrevocably destroyed the once-famed beauty spots of the Mediterranean coastline. Indeed, it was enough to realise that a beach, a lake district or an inland resort was a scenic treasure for it to be doomed to 'development'. The chief loss will fall, as things go, on generations yet to come; on our children and grandchildren who will inherit from us a world almost wholly bereft of its once-natural grandeur and pristine loveliness.

In sum, the unchecked scale of modern travel, in response to the technical means and the affluence of the postwar era, has meant that in the very act of tasting the world's variety and richness the masses have also, unavoidably, destroyed it, or most of it. There is less and less for anybody to enjoy. The mass of tourists, in the absence of better places at the price, might still go on flights to Spain or Italy or Greece, to spend their week or fortnight at any one of 10,000 similar cement hotels. They still may seek a small space on some noisy and polluted beach in order to acquire a suntan, and jostle in smoky tourist-appointed nightspots. But it is too painfully obvious that they can never enjoy what the few once enjoyed, since practically nothing is left of it. They are increasingly regarded by the inhabitants of the host country as herds of gullible cattle to be milked of their currency. They are hardly in a position to imbibe culture or learn much of the vanishing differences in customs and traditions. They are not even 'getting away' in any sense other than a purely geographical one.

•

The transport revolution has had other consequences. The average time a person spends commuting has been rising for decades. Indeed, since the turn of the century, automobile transport has transformed our conception of living. We think today of the physical environment about us, whether urban or suburban, largely in terms of traffic. We live, eat, work and sleep in the midst of it. Time and distance, road conditions, highway routes, peak traffic hours, short cuts, traffic lights, freeways, tolls, road signs, parking, drinking, auto-repairs, fuel bills, car prices – all these along with the perpetual din and danger, have become the everyday stuff of our lives. Each city, each town, has, or soon will have, its own airport, more often than not a hastily erected structure, provisional and nondescript. Each city, each town, becomes more of a venue for arrivals and departures, a place of perpetual transit, sprouting innumerable car towers – one more noisome node in a network of roads, and freeways, and junctions, and beltways.

According to Vance Packard (1972), 40 million Americans change their 'homes' each year. In a fully motorised urban society, the fact itself is hardly surprising. But it means that the old idea of home, the family home, the place to which one returns in fact or in memory, is now obsolescent. Through song and verse and parable we may, for a while longer, show some nostalgic response to the word. But for a growing number, the word 'home' has been pared down to mean no more than their current residence, bungalow, apartment, motel or caravan.

For all that, no one will deny the growthmen's pet observation: that a man will gladly get into his car for any number of reasons, and would grieve if he were deprived of the opportunity. But this reaction proves nothing more than the obvious fact that he is a victim of circumstances. A prisoner of war in Asia would also lament if his bowl of rice were snatched from him, though not because he liked rice above all other foods he can imagine. In his situation he has no choice; it is either rice or death by starvation. To an increasing number of people, the choice has become automobile transport or immobility (in a world where he cannot earn or spend without mobility) or, alternatively, sometimes, hopelessly inadequate public transport.

If there is one thing that economists can agree on today it is that Adam Smith's doctrine of the invisible hand does not apply to the production and use of motor vehicles. Let our imaginations run, then, to visions of an alternative world, one that indeed might have come into being with smaller towns and cities unravaged by motorised traffic, their streets thronging with people, not cars. In such a world, the concept and the means of transport would be wholly subordinate to the goals of environmental amenity – to the creation of a physical environment from which there would be no need or desire 'to get away'.

As things turned out, however, the transmogrification of our towns and cities and of our homes and our lives in the endeavour to accommodate our outlandish traffic, ground and air, is the product of nothing more elevating than socially unwarranted commercial efforts to sell more cars and more flight tickets. The resulting growth in mobility we have experienced since the turn of the century has been anything but enriching or 'life-enhancing'.

Chapter 21

More Income Equality

The ideal of equal sharing of wordly goods has history that goes back to Antiquity. The doctrine has an honoured place in different religions and ideologies, and in the various political movements they gave rise to. But apart from primitive tribes, or small devoted communities, the practice of equal sharing has always lagged behind its lip service. Since the seventeenth century, the egalitarian ideal, in Britain at least, has wavered, waned and gradually waxed strong. With the advent of the welfare state, made effective by technical advances especially in the development of communications, there is a growing animus towards equality arising, in the main, from an increasing resentment of 'privilege', both economic and social. As I remark later in Chapter 40, in connection with the loss of personal freedom, the idea which is gaining ascendancy is that everything, everywhere, ought to be available and accessible to the multitude, from entrance to the elite universities to access to exclusive clubs, from participation in managerial decisions and privileges to a share in the plums of political office.

The current intellectual concern with income equality is, in part, the result of equating it with social justice; indeed, of treating it as if it were the greater part of social justice. As for the social preoccupation with it, as indicated above, it springs from that sense of resentment which is prevalent in any society whose economic life is activated chiefly by greed and envy. But even if it were widely acclaimed as a desirable social goal, income equality is hardly feasible in a community as large as the modern nation state. Bearing in mind the ineradicable differences of health, beauty, strength, talents, character and intelligence, in any large population, perfect equality of income between persons, assuming it could be initially implemented, would be as difficult to maintain as it would be to reconcile with any ideal state of affairs. Indeed, it would not be possible to maintain such a distribution without recourse to Draconian measures; without an intolerable degree of surveillance and coercion.

However, in a wealthy society, the urgency for achieving a greater degree of equality is not self-evident – even though some economists make a career of contriving ever-more sophisticated measures of income inequality, both over time and between countries, while others court popularity by calling for sterner measures to reduce existing differentials. Indeed, economist Arthur Okun (1975), in an otherwise interesting monograph, goes so far as to regard inequalities of material wealth beyond a factor of five as positively 'obscene'. Yet an effective appeal to the sense of justice cannot be made by reference alone to any index of inequality. There must be reference also to absolute standards of living.

A community in which some men consumed ten times as much as some others would indeed be morally repugnant if those in the latter category were slowly dying of malnutrition – and it were known, also, that distributional measures enabling everybody to live comfortably were entirely feasible. One's judgment about the propriety of the same disparities would be entirely different if, instead, the lowest income stratum of the population already lived in circumstances of material comfort. The architecture of social compassion should attend primarily to a 'floor' of minimal material comfort below which nobody in the community should be allowed to sink. The height of the 'ceiling' is a secondary matter, one in which the political power conferred by great wealth is the more pertinent consideration.

To put it basically, it is enough that no one should starve while others eat well. Beyond that maxim, we should move cautiously. To hold it to be indecent that some men have incomes which are ten times, nay fifty times, as large as some others, when, in fact, nobody in the community suffers any deprivation, strikes me as being no more than a political posture for which no persuasive moral arguments can be mustered. Adherence to such postures, moreover, tends to sanction the sophism of 'relative deprivation', that providential widow's cruse of the pro-growth battalions. For in the absence of something close to income equality, the existence of 'relative deprivation' can always be claimed, even though every family in the land is chocking in the products and byproducts of the affluent society.

For the wealthier nations, then, it is reasonable to believe that the scope for improved social wellbeing through further diminution of income differences is very limited. Where there is real poverty – and there are still pockets of it even in the wealthiest country – there is clear cause for concern. And where wealth, amassed in the hands of a few, is used to exert political influence, there is again cause for concern. But there is not much justification for concern over the existences of income disparities *per se*. Political preoccupation with them tends to arouse nothing more worthy than envy and resentment.

Finally, and bearing in mind that the fundamental and unalterable inequalities spring from genetic inheritance, especially the inequalities in the capacity for enjoyment, any sensitive regard to social welfare would seek rather to alter our philosophy of life than to alter income differences. For in those countries where no one need go hungry, there would be no cause for social discontent if people learned to accept differences in inherited wealth and talent as the capricious decrees of fate; and for the rest turned their eyes from self-inflicted temptations, striving instead to live their lives joyously within the limits of their capacity. But so simple and sane an attitude, though a precondition of the good life, runs counter to the ethos of the consumer society.

Chapter 22

More Education

Towards the end of the nineteenth century, a well-known politician confessed that, when he could think of nothing else to say at a public meeting, he simply said 'Gladstone', and the crowd always cheered. When all else fails, the growthman says 'education', and a respectful silence ensues. We shall not follow the convention here. In fact, as the following remarks will suggest, agnosticism is the more appropriate response to this evocation.

In the first place, it is arguable that there is much too much elementary education in the affluent West, at least if efficiency of learning is the criterion. It may be surpassingly convenient for young parents to have their children kept busy and out of the house during weekdays. It may also be a boon to elementary school teachers who enjoy the occupation and the community status. And though far from certain, it is possible also that the children themselves prefer to go to school rather than to undertake forms of employment suitable to their years. Yet if their formal education began, say, at the age of 11, rather than at the age of 5, as at present, it is far from imaginative to suppose that by the age of 15, or thereabout, they would have learned as much as they learn today and, to boot, would be more eager to learn and more receptive to instruction.

It is also reasonable to argue that if the overwhelming majority of children left school at the age of 14 or 15 to take up adult employment, many of the psychological problems we have come to associate with 'teenagers' since World War II would disappear. For a high-technology growth economy, however, this latter policy may not be thought feasible. As observed in Chapter 2, education, especially higher education, is properly regarded as a form of continuing investment necessary to keep the economic machinery of society in motion. Whether the numbers of young people preparing to enter the institutions of higher learning currently exceed the numbers necessary to keep all the parts of the machinery moving is debatable, though I am inclined to think that they do. The fact that unemployment among many types of graduate is not markedly greater than that among non-graduates cannot be construed as evidence against the view that there is too much higher education. The reader should bear in mind that a large number will, in any case, be employed in government offices by bureaucrats always anxious to expand their empires, and also that commerce and industry can be induced to employ them if their market price is low enough. And, in as much as higher education is heavily subsidised in the West – to the extent, in Britain at least, that is is virtually a free good for all students – the starting salaries of graduates in a large number of subjects are not much different from those of non-graduates. In fact, over their working lifetimes, their average earnings are such as to yield a rate of return on society's investment in their training that is well below the expected rate of return to industry, and sometimes close to zero.[3]

More to the point, however, is the recognition that this higher education we are talking of is predominantly vocational and technical. It is not education in the classical sense. It is not education in the humanities; it has no connection with the graces of civilised living. The nineteenth-century liberal idea of education in both 'science' and 'the arts' as being a part of every civilised man's attainment, though it lingers on fitfully in our time, is wholly impractical at a time when the average scientist in one narrow field has only the remotest idea of what is going on in other fields. Each person within one of the broader disciplines is able to master but a fragment of the growing literature, and, over time, as contributions continue to pour into the journals, his fragment becomes a tinier part of the total.

The liberally educated man today is a figment; at best he has some sort of *Readers Digest* notion of the broad outlines of some aspects of several chosen subjects, and therefore perhaps becomes a fluent conversationalist. But in the old-fashioned sense, nobody can any longer be 'educated'. He may be literate. He may be 'well-read' in a popular book-review sense. But he can be learned only over a minute segment of the spectrum of knowledge which he studied at the university or, rather, the multiversity – the highly organised centre of what cynics now call 'the knowledge industry'. For its main function today is to churn out the armies of specialists needed to keep the increasingly complex machine in motion.

In brief, the educational system is not geared today to produce educated men, men of cultivated intelligence and learning. It is geared to produce technicians. In fact, modern methods of education tend to reduce all disciplines to a set of techniques which, with persistent application, can be learned by students without any intellectual pretensions. The hyper-refined specialisation involved in postgraduate work, which cramps the spirit and warps the judgment, is indeed the antithesis of intellectual accomplishment.

Another development has added to the confusion over the implications of higher education. With the extension of the curriculum, in response to postwar expansionist policies, to cover a welter of practical subjects, many universities in this country have been tranformed into universal trade schools, while a number of technical colleges have been given the status of universities. In America these 'democratising' influences have gone much further; ice-cream making, basket weaving and a large number of other modest trades, along with agricultural skills, have become respectable parts of the curriculum of many a large university. More recently, 'Black studies' were introduced into a number of universities in popular protest against alleged 'white domination', and no one should be surprised if, next year, 'female studies' are introduced as a part of the strategy to liberate women from 'male domination'. Finally, to move from the absurd to the pernicious, a number of state universities have begun to forsake what academic standards they once sought to maintain, in the novel endeavour – in response to official policies and political pressures – to choose the racial composition of their staff and students so as faithfully to reflect the racial composition of the American population at large.

Were it not for the growing populist sentiment to give prizes to everybody, irrespective of merit, and for the desire of so many young people to enjoy (at little or no economic sacrifice) the privileges and social facilities provided by the university, and to postpone the day of reckoning, it would be clearly recognised that the bulk of our students would be better employed in industry and commerce, there to learn their trade as apprentices, than instead to be occupying space and using up resources at a university.

Be that as it may, in consequence of this sort of expansion and transformation, the idea of the university as a community of scholars, or as the guardian of civilised values, has become an anachronism. Developments since the war have made it abundantly evident that the university can no longer be thought of as a sort of secular cathedral conductive to detached reflection or eclectic debate. The expanded university is tending to become a microcosm of the real world. Into it are imported all the political passions and prejudices, the fashionable aberrations and the 'trendy' deviant movements, of the outer world – though often on so distorted a scale as to give certain universities a reputation for being a hot-house of intellectual intolerance or a seminary of weird cults. It is sad to reflect that, on so many occasions over the last decade, the one place where a controversial issue could *not* be debated in the liberal democracies of the West was the university.

Thus, far from being a community of disinterested scholars exerting an independent and civilising influence on society, the modern university is, at best, a rather muddled reflection of society at large, its chief function being to supply society's needs, real or imaginary, for trained personnel in the attempt to maintain the momentum of economic growth. At worst, since so many of the students today see themselves as transients, passing through the university but not of it, they tend to regard it as a permissive rather than a liberal institution. In consequence, the fashionable vulgarities and excesses that are taking hold in the affluent society find all-too-ready a reception on the campus. If postwar experience in higher education has shown anything, it has shown that 'more is worse'.

Chapter 23

More Information

With the development since World War II of low cost computers and related data-processing equipment, hopes have been expressed that the increasing adoption of facilities for the gathering and processing of information will enable us to discover and meet people's wants more effectively.

For a limited range of wants, such devices may appear auspicious. More dependable information on packaging and design of commercial products, from leather belts to bungalows, will add something to what economists respectfully refer to as 'consumer satisfaction'. One may anticipate also, in response to the growth of environmental disruption, the production of quantitative data on what are called 'trade-offs' between such scarce environmental goods as quiet, space, clean air, accessibility, etc. on the one hand, and man-made or market goods on the other; in effect, the production of improved estimates of the value to society of environmental goods. Such data could come to modify the development schemes of planners and bureaucrats; at least, it would raise the level of debate between environmentalists and technocrats. Again, better and more detailed information on public attitudes than the information provided by existing public opinion polls can be expected, and should have obvious political uses. And, for that matter, information on people's changing tastes for commercial products, say for pornography and violence, will be found useful in guiding private enterprise – or, as economists would nicely put it, in 'improving market performance'.

Thus, according to the extent and rapidity of commercial and administrative adjustments in response to more accurate and detailed information, some economic improvement from the current situation may be anticipated. Yet there can be no general presumption of net advantage. For there are few outstanding technological innovations that do not also give rise to social problems and, therefore, to a demand for new institutions and technology. Avoiding specifics for the moment, one of the outcomes of a sustained period of technological growth is the creation of an urban environment (an aspect of which was described in Chapter 20 on travel), which acts to increase loneliness, restlessness and anomie – for which maladies technology provides remedies in the form of sedatives, tranquillisers and other drugs, plus new forms of psychotherapy and a wide variety of books, magazines and tapes on self-analysis and treatment.

What is hard to envisage is how the massive increase of information that is anticipated can help us very much to realise the good life. It might, of course, be thought that surveys could be conducted and data acquired on people's ideas of the good life, or on what they believe is important for their happiness. And it might be thought that such data could be processed to discover whether a clear pattern emerges, or whether a number of distinct patterns emerge having, however, certain features in common. But the features of a good life on which there is likely to be broad agreement are largely environmental ones. For other features of society, it is doubtful whether much of value could be salvaged from such surveys. What, at any moment of time, a person believes to be important, or highly desirable, depends upon his age, on his pecuniary circumstances, on his idiosyncracies and enthusiasms, on the constraints imposed on him by society, on the currents of fashion and on the prevailing ethos. Ask an Indian peasant, a Yorkshire miner, a mid-western American farmer and a city tycoon what is important for happiness, and we should expect to receive quite different answers. Or go back in time, and ask a Greek slave of the fifth century BC, a Roman soldier of the first century AD, a serf in the twelfth century, an English yeoman of the sixteenth century, a European liberal of the nineteenth century, a member of the Hitler youth in 1940 and a British trade unionist in 1970 the same question, and we should expect to receive vastly different answers. Information of this sort, of the response of people to such questions, is not likely to be of much use in shaping broad social goals or providing guideposts to the good life.

It is more likely that, as a result of improved techniques for determining the public's attitudes in greater detail on a wide range of specific questions, more reflective and articulate political debate will be displaced in favour of the expressed mood of the public at the given moment of time. The political process will become, in consequence, increasingly responsive to the immediate impulse, or 'gut reaction', of the public. And this development will be taking place during a period when, because of the hazards of more complex technology, and the scale of its application, political decisions should be more sober and deliberate.

Even if, after mases of information had been unearthed and the issues debated *ad nauseam*, the public began to realise that the constituents of the good life were like those to be suggested in Parts V and VI, not much would come of it. For the constituents of the good life would then appear clearly to be at variance with the features of society taking shape under the inexorable advance of science and technology. And recognition of this fact would not, of itself, act to bring about the desired consummation. For each person, each group, each stratum of society or segment of the economy is, at the moment, impelled by pressing interests, by active anticipations of gains and by fearful apprehensions of loss. A collective initiative to forgo immediate and tangible benefits, or to sustain immediate and tangible losses, in order to creat for everyone a more wholesome and radically simpler style of life, or to forgo the familiar range of creature comforts and labour-saving devices in the quest for sources of more enduring satisfaction, entails a momentous social decision to abandon the whole system of presuppositions that has guided our thought and our endeavours over the past two centuries. It requires wisdom and courage of a high order, attributes not likely to be found in a society reared so long on the pap of hedonism.

Finally, the hope that more accurate and detailed information of people's wants will enable significant improvements in welfare to be made is one that is unlikely to be fulfilled for more ordinary reasons. With respect to market goods, it is unreasonable to believe that, in already affluent societies, more and better information, any more than more and better goods, can make a significant contribution to individual wellbeing. We have currently far more information about products and services than we can be troubled to use. There would seem to be more scope for increasing satisfactions by reducing the number of brands and models on the market.

As for the more important things in our lives, objective information may avail us little. Our immediate desires are warped by the pervasive pressures of consumerism, and our aspirations by the fevered expansionism that characterises modern society. They bear little relation to our deeper psychic needs. It is a commonplace of experience that even when our fondest desires are realised they seldom bring us the joy or pleasure we expected. A good part of our fantasy is used up in unwishing the things we chose to do in the past – the engagements we entered into, the places we went to, and the things we purchased. Indeed, as Somerset Maugham observed, people never know when they are happy. They only know when they *were* happy. We should be ill-advised, then, to repose any hope in the idea that improved information and communication services will bring us much closer to human fulfilment.

Chapter 24

Science and Innovation

Few phrases can sound more impressive to the innocent layman's ear than 'the free and unchecked spirit of inquiry' or, more poetic perhaps, 'the questing spirit of man'; phrases by which the diverse and highly specialised activities of scores of thousands of scientists are blithely sanctified irrespective of the social consequences of such activities. Since some of the resulting hazards that currently beset humanity have been mentioned in several places in this volume (in particular in Chapters 4 and 45), I shall restrict myself here to two cynical comments.

When anyone talks of *man* in these perorative phrases, he means the scientific fraternity only. These joys of 'free inquiry' are, in fact, the preserve only of the few. It may be suspected, by now, that they are treading the Faustian path to perdition. And if so, their fate, alas, will be shared fully by the rest of mankind.

Historically speaking, the scientific life is a new way of life, one that is shaped today by the specialised techniques the scientist learns to master and, compulsively, to employ. Problem solving has also become the opiate of the scientist, his refuge from the brawling world. His research and publications are not only the sources of his livelihood, but also the sources of his self-esteem. The kudos include travel to conferences, public addresses, press quotations, professional, and possibly political, recognition, a place in the pecking order, public respect and the prospect of public honours. There can be no stronger vested interests and, accordingly, the tendency of the scientist to rationalise his labours in terms of potential benefit to society is all but irresistable. There are not many cases, on record, in which a scientist opposed some path of investigation simply because no apparent purpose would be served by moving along it ('How can he know! '), or simply because his discoveries might give rise to dangerous situations.

Secondly, the increasing risk posed today by continued scientific progress is the result both of the continuing fragmentation of existing branches and sub-branches of science and of the increasing complexity of the products being created and substances discovered. The former, the multiplication of the already specialised divisions of a branch of science, is an inevitable process in view of the sheer accumulation of knowledge over the years. But it acts to diminish the responsibility of the individual scientist in advising officials. For no matter how narrowly the issue is defined, there will be side effects and social consequences that lie outside the area of his interest and competence. As for the latter trend, the increasing complexity of the products of scientific discovery, the full range of the genetic, ecological and social side effects is likely to take far longer to uncover – and this at a time when their applications, fostered by both commercial and technological interests, are proceeding apace. Bearing in mind the unhappy experience of a number of sedatives and chemicals which were widely marketed in recent years (see Chapter 45), and the number of near-catastrophes from nuclear accidents (described by John Fuller, 1975); bearing in mind, also, the increasing evidence of reluctance to abandon expensive projects even when they are known to be both uneconomic and dangerous, or to withdraw suspect synthetics and drugs until the case against them is established beyond reasonable doubt, one has to be exceptionally sanguine to believe that we shall be able, over the future, to contain the effects of the disasters that may emerge. Let us turn now to a consideration of the actual innovations that result from the application of scientific discoveries.

Every innovation, whether of a gadget or a service, whether arising from a new design or combination, initially promises some novelty of sensation or experience. The minor question is whether a sequence of these innovations, in so far as they are passed on to the consumer, do more than punctuate the tedium of the consumer society; whether, after the first twinge of exhilaration, or after the novelty has worn off, and it becomes another bit of the trivia of a throwaway society, there remains any access of enduring satisfaction.

However, in as much as innovations are also far from being neutral in their effect on the ultimate contentment, and on the tone, the character and the morality of society, the major question concerns their effect in these regards.

Any responses to these questions are better made with specific innovations in mind, both those in existence and those anticipated with varying degrees of confidence and enthusiasm. Within both categories we can usefully distinguish between process innovation and product innovation. New industrial processes, whether introduced to lower the costs of staple goods or to produce consumer novelties, will, more often than not, also produce one or more environmental spillover effects. Bearing in mind the political difficulties of controlling such spillovers, the true answer to the question whether the net contribution to society (by conventional economic criteria) is positive or negative will vary from one new process to another. In fact, we shall not often know the true answer, so that, on balance, the magnitude and direction of the cumulative net effects of a succession of such new processes remain unsettled questions.

As for some of the stuff that has recently emerged from the efforts and ingenuity of industrialists – inane novelties such as 'nothing boxes'; expendable novelties such as retractable headlights or electric saw-knives or exhibitionist attire; beads, bangles and trinkets by the bushel; everything imaginable in the way of freakishness and titillation; plus the usual cornucopia of new streamlined models of existing machines – the best that might be said of them is that they seem innocuous, although they throw an embarrassing light on the pathetic quality of the rise in 'real' standards of living as measured by economists.

Turning to innovations in existing consumer 'durables' – faster private planes, sexier-looking automobiles, three-dimensional televisions, air conditioning in a variety of sounds and odours (sea, mountain or desert air!) – there will undoubtedly be some moments of excitement before they, too, become commonplace; part of the essential equipment of every dwelling unit and hotel room. Yet this will act also to aggravate some lamentable trends that are discussed below.

Weapons innovations have obvious drawbacks, and also some less obvious implications which are mentioned in Chapters 46 and 47. The dangers of 'breakthroughs' in medicine is the subject of Chapter 43. As for the anticipations of more potent pain-killing drugs and, wistfully perhaps, more euphoric or 'mind-expanding' drugs, one cannot, again, rule out the possibility of irrevocable side effects.

One can extend the list of anticipated innovations in this somewhat cynical way without necessarily establishing a strong presumption of their adverse effects on human welfare – though a glance through Herman Kahn and A. J. Wiener's (1967) list of the 100 most likely innovations by the year 2000 should be enough to damp the optimism of most readers.

Any residual optimism, however, may be dispelled by the more serious considerations which emerge from a brief review of the social consequences of those consumer innovations that have transformed the lives of ordinary people in the twentieth century. We shall allow, of course, that in a purely functional sense, the innovations fulfil, with varying degrees of efficiency, the purposes for which they were designed. Their direct contributions to immediate consumer satisfaction, in fact, lend themselves, in principle, to economic measurement, usually in the form of dollar increments of 'consumer surplus'. Their long term effects, however, are less tangible but more powerful.

Already, in Chapter 20 on mobility, we have depicted a number of extensive consequences arising from society's adoption of the automobile and, later, the airliner. The social effects of the spread of television since the middle of the century also deserve some attention. Usually acclaimed as having limitless potential for education, television has proved to have, in addition, a limitless potential for holding people inert for hours. It is true that the ordinary television viewer can now behold panels of eminent personages and troops of specialists addressing themselves to problems in politics, science, economics, crime, housing, literature, gardening, history, sex, music, cooking, health, art and babycare. We need not descant here, on the alleged advantages of such a dispensation; we need only listen to the conversation of the ordinary person after two decades of exposure to it. There are, nonetheless, three consequences we might wish to think on.

First, that this daily parade of 'expert opinion' on every aspect of life must surely inhibit the range of men's speculation and discourse. A century ago, the civilised man would hold forth confidently on any subject under the sun. Today his spirit is muted in deference to an establishment of experts.

Secondly, the alleged tolerance that a man acquires from being silent witness to continual re-examinations of fundamental questions about religion, politics, psychology, manners and morals, is the product of uncertainty rather than of enlightenment. The distinctions between good and bad, truth and falsehood, vice and virtue, and sickness and health are blurred and reblurred through the efforts of an unending succession of savants and specialists, themselves victims of the current erosion of the moral, aesthetic and intellectual consensus on which Western civilisation was raised. Inevitably, the confidence of intelligent people in their own judgment and sense of propriety begins to ebb. The social tolerance they come to possess is the result, largely, of moral paralysis.

Thirdly, there is the effect of the medium on language. The repeated attempts to compel the viewer's attention on matters both large and small issue sometimes in a veritable frenzy of verbiage. Words are misused, abused, overused, pounded together, broken up and incongruously combined. And the sheer volume and interminable repetition are themselves destructive of the beauty of language.

Words of delicate sentiment lose their fragrance. Phrases, once stately or solemn, poignant or poetic, to be unveiled only on rare occasions, get dragged about in the dust of sales campaigns, rolled in with crude imperatives, until they become stale and sullied, shorn of the joys of evocation. Even obscene remarks, once held in reserve for infuriating circumstances, have become so common as to lose their power to shock or amuse.

Let us now broaden our approach a little to comprehend some of the social consequences of the innovations most acclaimed by growthmen: those designed to release us from physical drudgery. The most critical of these consequences, perhaps, is that relating to human intercourse, which is the subject of Chapter 31. Here, we confine ourselves to some ancillary considerations.

First, 'freedom from drudgery' is a phrase that rings in the modern ear as sweetly as any basic human right. The wording of modern advertisements, with their appeal to 'save time' and to 'take the irksomeness out of living', clearly implies that physical effort is obsolete, something to be shunned by a civilised person. The use of the word 'drudgery' by those who conceive themselves to be in the van of progress is, in fact, calculated to bias judgment about the value of physical work; their use of it suggests that work that is strenuous, repetitive or prolonged is necessarily tedious, depressing and even degrading. Through modern eyes, the day-to-day work of ordinary men and women in ages gone by is believed to have been of this enslaving nature; and not only the work of servants or labourers or farmers, but also that of the working population generally, and, to a large extent, that of shopkeepers and tradesmen also.

This notion of drudgery, as being the common lot of mankind in the past, seems to have come in the wake of the 'Industrial Revolution'. Economists of the first half of the nineteenth century, impressed by the plight of the workers flocking into the new industrial towns, ascribed it to the niggardliness of nature. Hope for a more comfortable life for the masses lay in population checks, hard work, better machines and the spread of industry. Yet, apart from some of these grimmer periods of history, there is no evidence to suggest that the greater proportion of working men and women thought of themselves as leading lives of great hardship and tedium. Indeed, until the close of the eighteenth century, the discipline and tyranny of the power-driven factory were unknown, and the wonders of the division of labour were just beginning to be rediscovered (for division of labour was not uncommon also in the Ancient world). A farmer's life was hard by our standards, except during the winter months. Yet it was a varied and healthy life. And instead of today's or yesterday's factory operator, there was the craftsman whose task it was to work the raw material – clay, wood, metal, stone, glass or leather – into the finished article.

Secondly, as far as 'drudgery' refers to repetitive muscular effort, there is less reason today to regard it askance. Technological progress is creating for Western man a life so sedentary that 'weight-watching' among adults, and even among children, forms one of our more popular anxieties – one which, incidentally, provides remunerative opportunities for physicians, writers, chemists, food manufacturers, and the manufacturers of gymnastic equipment, sports gear and slimming apparatus. It follows that men and women today would be physically fitter if a select number of labour-saving devises were banned from society.

Let us turn next to the alleged drudgery in the kitchen. Prior to the availability of prepared foodstuffs and an assortment of 'instant' concoctions, and prior also to the production of low-priced cookers, refrigerators and dishwashers, fresh vegetables and meats could not be stored for long, especially in summer. Moreover, preparing a meal over the fire, or in an old-fashioned oven, was an arduous task. One of the consequences, however, was that the meal had to be eaten by all members of the family together at the time it was cooked. Mealtimes were therefore also times of family gathering; something, indeed, of a ritual. With the advent of modern domestic conveniences, then, one of the ties of family is made that much the looser. Each parent, each child, can now come home at any time; pick out a snack from the refrigerator; heat it in next to no time; ingest it in even less; and move on to any other activity – if he does not, first, succumb to the mesmerising flicker of the ubiquitous television screen. As for drudgery in the home generally, true, when there was no central heating, a fire would have to be made in the living room or parlour. And glad the family was, on a cold evening, to sit around it together and – since there was no radio or television – read or converse for hours.

Indeed, it was the very absence of domestic labour-saving machines that made the mother the central figure in the home. Seen through the eyes of a society aspiring to a push-button utopia, the lot of the housewife before the coming of the twentieth century must seem a hard one. But, again, we must not suppose that, over the span of centuries and milennia, the duties of a housewife were thought to be so arduous as to tax strength or patience. We must not suppose either that she did not derive satisfaction from the work, or that she took no pride in it. For we should bear in mind, also, that her senses were not assailed daily by the ubiquitous media with their compelling visions of the joys of travel and romance, and of the wonderful things that were happening in the world outside her home. She was not, then, tempted daily into resentments induced by the uneasy conviction that she was being deprived of her share of 'the good things of life'. She was not told in so many words that she was 'vegetating' to no purpose; that smarter women were out there winging their way to fame and adventure. In this sense, the world of yesterday's housewife was a more parochial affair. But she was spared these continual pricks of vexation to which the modern housewife is exposed, and the consequent restlessness and mortification. It never occurred to her to doubt the importance of her vocation.

She was also spared the modern crisis about which Keynes wrote in 1930 (see E. Johnson (1971) and Chapter 28), arising from too little to do. Keynes indeed was directing his thoughts to the plight of the wealthier English and American housewives. But with the universal ownership of modern domestic devices, his remarks may be extended today to all housewives in the industrial countries. They too have become nervous and restless, and, indeed, defensive. Too many live in tiny dwellings or apartments, cooped up with all their 'mod cons', fretting as the days slip by, virtually a prisoner. It is not surprising that, in increasing numbers, they wish to break out of this 'woman's pen' into industry.

The vocation of housewife and mother has, thus, been made obsolete by the remorseless advance of technology. And with the collapse of her role, the institution of the family, of which she was the central pillar, has begun to collapse also. No one can fortell the momentous social consequences of this historical migration of women from the home to industry. Those for whom the family is the organic cell from which civilisations are built have reason to fear the future. For the rest of us, we may echo the plaintive sentiment that a home without a mother in it is no longer a home.

Needless to remark, I do not, at this stage, seek to establish a net social advantage or disadvantage for any particular innovation or small group of innovations; I seek simply to point up some of their longer term effects on social welfare that economists and others are apt to overlook, or to underemphasise, when totting up the benefits of GNP growth or of economic progress generally. Indeed, it would be futile to argue about the net advantages or disadvantages of a single innovation or small group of innovations at a time when our lifestyle, which is the outcome of all these innovations and the institutions they have led to, has come to depend upon their continuing availability – so much so, that the aspirations we espouse, whether old or young, have come to depend on their increased availability and improvement over time.

It is for such reasons that I propose we stand far back from our immediate hopes and desires, indeed from our conventional social indicators and social goals, in order to gain the perspective necessary in the endeavour to distinguish the chief ingredients of the good life, and to assess the extent of their compatibility with the pursuit of continued economic growth.

NOTES FOR PART IV

Chapter 19

1 The thesis that what comes to matter most in an affluent society is status as measured by one's position in the income structure, or in the professional hierarchy, has been described in somewhat different terms by other economists. Writing in 1958, Harrod referred to an unbridgeable gulf between what he called 'democratic wealth' on the one hand and, on the other, 'oligarchic wealth'. The former comprises goods that are available to everybody and which increase with the general level of productivity. Oligarchic wealth, in contrast, can be enjoyed only by the few, since such wealth consists of such things as servants and goods that are absolutely scarce (such as land or masterpieces).

These two categories are translated by Hirsch (1976) into a 'material economy' and a 'positional economy' respectively; for the former has reference to goods that are capable of being multiplied by industrial progress whereas the 'positional economy' relates to goods, or to work or social position, that are limited in an absolute sense – or else to goods that are 'subject to congestion or crowding through more extensive use'. According to Hirsch, it is the competition to possess these 'positional goods', which over time bids up their prices, that contributes to economic progress.

Although such distinctions serve to add force to the thesis described above, they are subordinate to it. The relative income hypothesis or 'Joneses effect' (first propounded by Dusenberry in 1949) – interpreted as above, as a growing concern with position in the structure of incomes – is, by itself, a sufficient explanation of the apparent failure of continuing economic growth in industrialised countries to raise the level of social well-being, even in the absence of environmental spillovers and other unforeseen side effects of the growth process. The more dominant is this effect, the more the growth process becomes a 'zero sum game', one in which the gains to one party entail equal losses to another party.

The concept of 'positional goods' then – at least those that are not also bought as a defence against environmental spillovers, especially 'congestion or crowding', which are better treated separately (as they are in the following chapter) – can be said to add some interest to the relative income effect by way of a slight extension of Veblen's conspicuous consumption of the wealthier classes to their consumption also of privileged goods. Thus the satisfaction derived from status itself, or relative income as an index of status (Dusenberry), can be augmented by expenditures designed to display one's wealth (Veblen) or to perpetuate family privilege (Hirsch). And the fact that some of Hirsch's 'positional goods' – land, art treasures, though not servants – are finite in supply is incidental in this context. The essential point is that both conspicuous and positional goods, whether yachts, luxury travel, Rembrandts, exclusive clubs or troops of servants, are *relatively* costly and are, therefore, available only to a wealthy minority.

We should remind ourselves, in conclusion, that the thesis in question is valid only for societies possessed by the economic growth ethos, expressed in individual ambition for advancement and, consequently, in dissatisfaction with one's present economic status. In a traditional society, or one in which one's position in the hierarchy is believed to be preordained, one's position, no matter how humble, is not, of itself, an active source of dissatisfaction.

2 Wilfred Beckerman (1974) has seized on the Joneses effect in the attempt to exorcise the problem of environmental pollution. If a person's welfare is entirely a matter of his *relative* income position, he argues, then additional pollution can be of no importance to society as a whole (since everyone will be worse off to about the same extent).

I cannot tell whether Beckerman regards this as a serious argument or whether he is being sly and provocative. But it should be stated, for the record, that the argument misconceives (inadvertently perhaps) the relative income hypothesis, which has it that what matters to a person is his income, or purchasing power, relative to others, where only *market* goods enter the calculation. Pollutants, however, are *not* market goods, or rather not market 'bads', as they would be if nobody need absorb any unless he were compensated for his loss of welfare. Thus, each person in a community could have all the market goods he wanted, to the point of satiation. The only purpose of going beyond that point would be to flout his wealth before his neighbours. But with respect to the 'public bads', such as pollutants, there is no market in which to dispose of them. Far from being able to dispose of them to the point of 'satiation', he will suffer their incidence along with everyone else. Consequently, he will also benefit with others when the pollution is reduced.

In sum, then, only if all pollutants were *market* 'bads', which, in the nature of the universe is not possible, would Beckerman's argument be correct.

Chapter 22

3 For a discussion of the economics of existing methods of financing higher education, and related questions, the reader might wish to consult my article, 'Heretical thoughts on university reform' (1969).

BOOK 2

Economic Growth and the Good Life: Fundamental Disharmonies

Part V

Constituents of the Good Life

Chapter 25

Food and Shelter

In this Part and Part VI I make tentative remarks about the constituents of the good life, or at least *a* good life, that are likely to command general support, even in these fragmented times, among the population at large. Bearing in mind earlier remarks about man's innate nature, and paying particular attention to his complex psyche and seemingly contradictory urges, the good life that we seek is one that, broadly speaking, manages to bring him into tolerable harmony with himself in order, also, to bring him into harmony with others. Such a life, then, will arise from the establishment of an external order that does no violence to a man's internal order; one in which his vital instincts find vent, and range without harm to others or to himself. In order to endure, it must not simply cater to the aspirations of an elite, either cultural or professional; it must also make ample provision for the needs and pleasures of ordinary men and women.

In the chapters that follow, the headings and subheadings may be regarded as covering a minimum programme in any blueprint for the good society; one that should outlast the flux of events, and the changes of fashion, custom and culture, that occur with the passage of time. Within the chapters, the reader's attention is continually directed to those current trends, and likely developments, emerging from modern economic growth in the attempt to assess its compatibility with the chief constituents of the good life.

FOOD

Life cannot be enjoyed by the ordinary person unless his diet, which exceeds some minimum in nutritious value, is supplemented by some minimum variety. The same remark applies also to adequate shelter in the form of clothing and housing.

Clearly, a large proportion of mankind, perhaps as much as

half, lack these minimal requirements even today. But for the overwhelming mass of the populations in the industrial countries, they have long been surpassed and, given the political will, could easily be extended to the less fortunate minorities living there. Indeed, such minimum standards were available to the bulk of the people in the richer countries before the turn of the twentieth century, and also in some earlier civilisations.

Nobody will deny that there are still pockets of degrading poverty even in the wealthiest countries. But it is exceedingly doubtful whether further economic growth of itself will remove them. As indicated in Part IV, however, it is technically (though not politically) feasible to remedy this situation by direct transfers or by other, and perhaps more efficacious, schemes of redistribution.

It may, of course, be remarked that the sorts of foodstuffs consumed in the richer countries are not particularly healthy, and that many people there tend to overeat – or, for that matter, to overdress and 'overshelter'. Nonetheless, the important fact is that the conditions, at least, for a good life in these basic respects have already been attained in these countries. Indeed, with a growing public awareness of nutritional requirements and the value of organic foods, a better balanced diet for the mass of people might well be anticipated, ignoring the possibility of worldwide food shortages over the future – a possibility which, however, cannot be excluded at the time of writing.[1]

There is, however, a countervailing consideration. Allowing that economic growth in the West is not interrupted by worldwide famine, increased per capita expenditures on food consumption in the wealthier countries will come about as a result largely of innovations in packaging, preserving, food blending, etc., which activities currently occupy troops of specialists and admen. But the satisfaction that society obtains from this process cannot be other than slight and ephemeral. Whatever it be, it is likely to be more than offset by the ill effects on health of the use of an increasing variety of chemical food additives.

CLOTHING

Remarks similar to those in the preceding paragraphs apply to clothing. It is not often that we read of people in the West dying from exposure owing to inadequate clothing. And, again, distributional measures could have prevented distress as a result of inadequate clothing before World War I. For the bulk of the population today, however, there is a surfeit of clothing, the predominant concern being no longer with protection from the elements but with adornment. There cannot, for example, be many individuals in the United States, men, women or children, who do not, at any one time, possess at least half a dozen complete changes of clothing. Most women will have more than a dozen different outer garments, and quite an assortment of nightclothes, underwear, boots, shoes and sandals. The recent fashion, among the middle class young at least, for carefully designed bottom-tight jeans, frayed, patched and nicely faded, and for an incongruous assortment of styles from a variety of countries and occupations, is itself a symptom of the growing sense of surfeit and, perhaps also, one of many futile gestures of protest against middle class values and the (notional) Establishment. In the circumstances, it would be idle to pretend that further economic growth will realise significant increases of welfare in virtue of the additional resources it can make available for more and fancier costumes. Already, the gallery of fashion, domestic and foreign, past and present, is being ransacked in a desperate bid, it seems, to maintain the momentum of the industry.

HOUSING

It may be thought that further economic growth is required to enable us to expand and improve the stock of housing in the nation. But we are to bear in mind that one of the sources of dissatisfaction with what housing we have is to be found in its location; too much of it is in clamorous conurbations. Again, the increased mobility and the smaller size of families in the postwar period, both developments also attributable to economic growth, have aggravated the apparent shortage. So also have the exaggerated expectations generated in a growth economy by politicians, technocrats and social reformers.

What is at least as significant in this connection is the fact that – if we were prepared, as a nation, simply to curb our more extravagant consumption of 'demerit goods' (see Chapter 16) for two or three years – we could, with our existing economic potential, provide all deprived families with adequate housing by present standards.

Of course, without this 'sacrifice', continued economic growth may bring about more and better housing over time. But since continued economic growth is likely also to degrade the urban and surburban environment, it is far from certain that people will become more content with their future stock of housing.

In conclusion: although comfortable dwellings have to be included among the tangible ingredients of the good life, we need not look to economic growth to provide them. Indeed, since homes cannot be comfortable unless the environment in which they are placed is also agreeable, economic growth *per se* does not answer.

Chapter 26

Health

A man may achieve great things even though he suffers from chronic ill health. Yet no man will deny that one can enjoy life a lot more if he is healthy than if he is continually sick.

In what ways are people healthier today than they were in the recent past or in other ages? And is it plausible to believe they will become healthier over the next few decades? An overall indicator of good health is not yet available to us. Perforce we have to fall back on general impressions and particular facts. People are taller and heavier today than they were fifty years ago, though possibly, also, less hardy. Longevity is greater, though it has not increased noticeably over the past two decades. In some countries, the United States for instance, it appears to have declined a little since 1960. Again, a number of diseases common for centuries in the Western world appeared to have been brought under control in the last century, while others – pulmonary, carcinogous, coronary and some 'stress' diseases – have grown over the postwar period.[2] I use the words 'appeared to have been brought under control' advisedly, for with the postwar popularity of air travel and the growth of mass tourism – regarded by many as among the tangible benefits of technological advance – the West seems to be becoming more vulnerable to traditional epidemics such as cholera, diphtheria, typhus, smallpox and influenza, and to tropical diseases also.

Turning to innovations in the field of medicine, broadly defined, some of the more promising developments are also those that make us more uneasy. Mechanical aids, substitute limbs and artificial organs are surely to be welcome – unless we are morbid enough to imagine a future in which a quasi-human is made up largely of interchangeable parts, and natural reproduction is no longer necessary. Electronic or chemical stimulation of specific brain areas, whether for pleasure or for increased mental capacity, though fascinating to contemplate, carries with it sinister possibilities in an age of totalitarian states and expanding bureaucracies. Similar misgivings arise in connection with developments in microbiology and genetics, referred to briefly in Part IV. Again, Herman Kahn and A. J. Wiener's (1967) 'Item 39', consisting of more reliable drugs for the control of fatigue, mood, personality, perceptions, fantasies and other psychological states,[3] is hardly reassuring. The possibility that the greater part of the civilian population of the West will come to live in a state of more or less permanent sedation, each person's judgment and perception muffled in a blanket of mild euphoria, all critical faculties blunted, is all too reminiscent of the emotional cretins that inhabited Aldous Huxley's Brave New World.

As for the publicity given to the more spectacular developments in modern medicine – cosmetic surgery, organ transplantation, psychosurgery, among others – it conveys a wholly misleading picture of the state and the progress of the art. The numbers who benefit from these glamorous and expensive techniques form a negligible proportion of the population. For the incomparably larger numbers who suffer the more pedestrian ailments – rheumatims, arthritis, migraine, even the common cold – no relief is yet in sight. Indeed, in many cases, more virulent strains of germs are evolving in response to the indiscriminate application of powerful drugs. What is more, the medical profession has begun to acknowledge maladies previously unknown, the side effects of antibiotics and other drugs that are today so liberally prescribed by physicians.[4]

The unyielding pace of modern life in congested and media-soaked urban environments may reasonably be held responsible for the rising trend of stress diseases. Although one can only conjecture about the impact of so unnatural an environment on the harassed citizen – exposed as he also is to a deluge of newsprint and of day-to-day, hour-to-hour radio and television coverage of global news and views, to bursts of entertainment and snap-fast comedy – it is impossible not to link such developments with the increase in psychic disorders, or with their expression as neo-pagan practices such as weird and primitive rituals, witchcraft, wantonness, exhibitionism, obscenity and violence.

At any rate, in so far as these psychic disorders do arise from some of the common characteristics of affluent societies, is it reasonable to expect that continued economic growth of itself will bring about their diminution? We might well ask whether the pursuit of economic growth in the West is compatible with a reduction of stress diseases. Perhaps the best the growthman can hope for is the discovery of yet more powerful tranquillisers – provided their side effects will not prove too dangerous or dehumanising.[5]

Chapter 27

Nature

Awareness of nature, and of himself as part of nature, is commonly believed to have been a source of enduring satisfaction to man. If we go along with this belief, the good life would require that society be so organised that people are not, as many are today, far removed from the immediate sight and sound and rhythms of nature.

Two aspects of economic growth act to weaken men's contact with nature. First, large-scale or capital-intensive farming drastically reduces the proportion of the population living in farm areas. It is true, of course, that with growing affluence, and with the increased availability of rail, road and air travel, the urban dweller has new opportunities to visit places of natural beauty all over the world. But the other aspect which weakens men's contact with nature arises just from these developments. Considerable efforts and costs are today necessary to avoid finding oneself caught in a multitude of a 100,000 other individuals, each with his automobile, camera and transistor, in the same resort or national park. Thus, from the point of view of space, the world's growing population is problem enough. But the problem is intensified by people's motorised mobility. The United Kingdom, for instance, seems to be vastly more crowded than it was before World War II, or even before 1950. Yet the population of these isles is only about 10 per cent greater. It is the coming of the automobile as a way of life that has spread the traffic through the land and caused the suburbs to invade the countryside. Within a generation, it has become all but impossible really to get away, not only from the endless built-up areas, but also from motorised noises, whether of cars and airliners or of farm and garden implements.

The pressure of human population is, then, like the pressure of a gas: the product of the number of molecules within a given volume and their speed of movement. At present, both the number of humans on this finite earth and their speed of movement are rising rapidly, for governments are either unwilling or unable to slow down the growth of people or their speed of travel.

Special mention is to be made here of 'peace and quiet', by which I mean freedom from unwanted noise. Unwanted noise includes both motorised noises from automobiles, aircraft, motor-boats, snowmobiles, skimobiles, chainsaws, lawn-mowers, and all oil-powered or electric-powered vehicles and implements, and also (as a result of technical improvements in amplification) the noise from other people's record players, transistors, and hi-fi and stereo sets.

Freedom from unwanted noise is surely something that people will agree is a 'good thing' to the extent of regarding it as a prerequisite of the good life; something that should qualify for enactment as a universal right. For many people, quiet is not only necessary to good health; quiet is beautiful.

Yet the hope of checking the increasing scale of 'noise pollution' is slight. The continuing growth of travel at home and abroad, the tourist development of resorts in mountain areas, and along coasts and lakes, serves to 'spread' the noise uniformly over the face of the earth. It may be true, as is repeatedly alleged, that automobile and aircraft engines will one day be less noisy than they are now, but their numbers are expected to increase. Continuation of present trends point to a future in which there will be fewer places on earth, perhaps none at all, where a sensitive person can escape the continual disturbance of engine noises, yet not live in isolation.

Indeed, quite apart from the near-impossibility of escaping entirely from noise and effluent of the ubiquitous internal combustion engine, the growth of affluence and travel technology has succeded already in removing from this seemingly tiny planet almost every area of unmarred natural beauty or grandeur. According to a new Worldwatch monograph (1976):

'International hotels are springing up in isolated places like Machu Picchu, the lost city of the Incas. A real estate firm has begun selling off some of the world's few remaining uninhabited islands through advertisements in London newspapers. So many trekkers have come to the Himalayas that they are exacerbating the firewood shortage as well as littering the lower slopes of the mountains with discarded gear. The growth of luxurious tourist hotels near Mount Everest has required the installation of special landing strips and water systems, both jeopardising a fragile environment.'

The best that can be hoped for just now is some belated international agreement to leave some of the remaining areas of natural beauty free of development and traffic. But though such legislation may contain the spread of tourism and development it could not, in our lifetime, restore to the world the beauty of things that were. As for the domestic environment, only the strictest controls and regulations would enable us to reshape our urban and rural areas so as to afford easy access to natural surroundings for the mass of people. Certainly quiet could be enforced and the level of fume reduced, so that once again people might be able to hear the rustle of leaves and smell the bracing salt of the sea. Yet the sheer size of today's populations must, at least, produce crowdedness in any area that is both accessible and desirable.[6]

This last remark is a reminder of man's need for space. Experiments on rats, rabbits, deer and other animals have shown clearly that crowdedness produces the most disastrous effects on their behaviour. For instance, even when food, temperature and other factors are maintained at optimal levels, an increase beyond a certain point of the number of rats within a given space leads to a disruption of nesting patterns and a breakdown of normal behaviour. Male rats cease defending their nests. Female rats cease caring for their young. And the incidence of violence, rape and sexual deviancy escalates. Juvenile delinquency, disorientation, miscarriages and abnormal births ensue.

There is no reason to believe that man alone is immune from the ill effects of prolonged crowding, and there is no evidence whatever to suggest that he is. Indeed, since his nervous system is more complex, his reactions to living in cramped conditions are likely to be more complex.

The space requirements of a person or family depend upon a number of factors. A group of families can live together in reasonable harmony in small houses that are huddled together if, as in a quiet village, they are surrounded by open country. The average houseroom per family may be much larger in a modern metropolitan area but, since the inhabitants are deprived of natural surroundings or easy access to them, the sense of crowdedness is greater. And it is aggravated by the perpetual din and fume, by the streams of congested traffic, by the jostle of the crowds, and by the general impatience and nervousness, features that have arisen chiefly from developments in transport and industry.

It is perhaps unnecessary to observe at this juncture that man is not so much a rational as a rationalising animal. Recent trends, particularly in the larger cities, towards increased delinquent and deviant behaviour, which can be understood in terms of psychological stress, are interpreted by the victims in terms of emancipation from cramping conventions. The new 'permissiveness', that in historical perspective can be recognised as a symptom of social disintegration, appears to the participants as a belated extension of liberty to experiment in new 'lifestyles'.

Chapter 28

Leisure

Among people of the most diverse views there is general agreement that leisure is a necessary ingredient of the good life. This is not surprising since the amount of it is unspecified, and the word itself carries commendable overtones. Indeed, unless we define it more closely, we cannot say whether it has increased or decreased for different classes of people over the last half-century,[7] or in the modern world as compared with the medieval.

Thinking in terms of the good life, it is useful to think of leisure-time, not as the time remaining after hours of paid work have been subtracted, but rather as the time available to the individual for his immediate enjoyment. In the latter sense, his leisure time has no purpose other than the direct satisfaction he associates with the activity or inactivity itself. Clearly, the ability to enjoy leisure in this sense presupposes a state of mind, arising from a sense of ease and unhurriedness, which allows a person to immerse himself fully in the here and now. It is a state of mind more easily attained by children, by some primitive peoples, or by groups whose role in life is set by an unchangeable hierarchical order, than by, say, the modern executive or professional.

It is common knowledge that the business executive tends to choose his forms and places of recreation and entertainment with an eye to advancing his promotion or the interests of the company. The ambitious company man, for example, soon discovers that there is very little of his office-free hours that cannot be put to some advantageous use. Though the accepted phrase is 'mixing business with pleasure', what in fact he is doing is the selecting of 'pleasures' with the express aim of promoting his material prospects, a stratagem which is likely to impair his enjoyment of life if only by gradually corrupting his character.

As for professionals and academics, it is certain that, as a class, they work harder today than they did in any earlier period of history. With new and more specialised journals each year adding to the annual flow, with knowledge (in impressionist terms) accumulating at an exponential rate, the continuing struggle of the professional man to keep abreast of developments within his chosen field leaves him little time or spirit to enjoy leisure in the sense described. With the postwar expansion of academia, moreover, there has emerged, unavoidably perhaps, a pecking order in each of the disciplines to which all tend to pay court, and which, for all too many, also influences their manner towards colleagues and their choice of friends.

Less widely acknowledged is the fact that skilled and semiskilled workers are today becoming subject to similar pressures. In the words of a prominent orthodox Labour economist: 'As the supply of educated labour increases, individuals find that they must improve their educational level simply to defend their current income positions. If they don't, others will and they will find their current jobs no longer open to them. . . . The larger the class of educated labour and the more rapidly it grows, the more such defensive expeditures become imperative.'[8]

Apart from these large categories of workers, like tendencies are discernible among the rest of the adult population. A good part of the spare time of the relatively unskilled, of office workers and of housewives is currently spent in 'self-improvement' pursuits; in reading 'approved' books, in enrolling in courses, in attending popular lectures, or in otherwise using such time 'profitably'. Thus, although new trends can be detected (Chapter 50), the demands of a technological society combine with the remnants of a Puritan ethic in tempting large numbers of people to postpone immediate gratifications for the later rewards of improved earnings, status or social acceptability.

Notwithstanding this tendency, there are still many people (apart from 'drop-outs' and vagrants) who are not, as yet, prone to these psychological compulsions. If economic growth continues, the unpre-empted leisure of this class is likely to increase over the future. The problem they will face is a different one and, for society, far more unsettling – a contingency that was foreseen, among others, by John Maynard Keynes (1963).

Writing in 1930, Keynes foresaw the possibility of solving the economic problem within a hundred years, at least within the industrialised nations. But he recognised also the danger for a society in which, for the first time in history, the imperative to work would vanish – at least, for masses of people. He thought 'with dread of the readjustment of the habits and instincts of the ordinary man, bred into him for countless generations, which he may be asked to discard within a few decades'.

'Must we not', asked Keynes, 'expect a general "nervous breakdown"?'[9]

Other writers, including Herman Kahn and A. J. Wiener (1967), have also pointed out that men continue to derive satisfaction from their daily work. The actual work done may not always be congenial. It may consist of no more than performing a few routine movements on a machine. Yet however tedious it is, the job is their chief connection with reality. They have a place in the busy world; a role to perform. Through it they come into contact with others, and experience a sense of comradeship. Should the dreams of youthful reformers ever come true, and ordinary men and women become 'forever freed from drudgery', and their services no longer really necessary, some profound psychological revolution will be needed if they are not to feel useless and unwanted. For while it is wonderfully stirring to hear young would-be revolutionaries talk of emancipating the masses from toil and of setting free their creative powers, experience of the world reveals that ordinary people will all too soon become uncomfortably aware of their creative and artistic limitations. Without the imperative of the daily routine, their lives lose order and structure, their senses become clogged, and they tend to drift about aimlessly and resentfully. Add to this deprivation of economic role and status the mortifying knowledge that they are, in effect, wholly expendable – mere parasites in a complex world controlled by scientists, technocrats and computers – and their despair might come to release destructive impulses.

Even if we do not look quite so far ahead – if, instead, we consider only that further economic growth may be such as to warrant a shorter working week, say, ten to twenty hours on the average, or, alternatively, vacations of between three and six months – the psychological problems of adjustment may be insurmountable. Although serious thinkers today regard this prospect with satisfaction, as enabling the fruits of continued economic growth to be taken out in the form of increased leisure, so economising on the use of scarce natural resources, they do not reckon on human limitations. If the experiments could be made, we might well discover that a working week of less than, say, thirty hours, or vacations of more than six weeks, would tend to leave ordinary men and women in their prime in a state of restlessness, indecision and anxiety. Indeed, there is already overwhelming evidence pointing to the difficulties in modern societies of adjustment to retirement and even to part-time work. As indicated earlier, the fact has to be faced that there are limits to the length of vacations that people can enjoy, to the hobbies they can practise, to the art they can create, and to the culture they can imbibe.

A solution to the modern tedium of work could more profitably be sought, not in shorter hours, but in work that is more agreeable; work in which the man is the master of the material he is shaping as was the case with the artisans and craftsmen of old. Yet this is not a solution that is compatible with sustained economic growth as conventionally measured.

In the absence of this solution, however, mankind faces a dilemma. If working hours for the masses are substantially shortened, we run into the psychological problems mentioned above which have disquieting and possibly dangerous consequences.

If, on the other hand, the trend over the last few decades persists, and the average reduction of working hours in industrial countries continues to be less, proportionally, than the average increase in productivity, then sustained economic growth, although it may reduce official working hours, is apt also to reduce unpre-empted leisure or leisureliness, not only for the reason mentioned above (that, in a technological society, it is necessary to devote non-work time to keeping abreast of new knowledge and developments), but also for another important reason.

Consumption of the plethora of consumer goods, churned out by affluent economies, is itself a time-absorbing activity. Thus, even a person who is unskilled, who has neither ambition for better status nor fear of a worse one, is perforce subject, in an industrial growth economy, to mounting pressures on his spare time. The continuing growth of finished output per capita over the years must itself entail a reduction of the time in which each of the consumption items can be enjoyed. Put otherwise, the universal attempt in affluent economies to cram increasing amounts of consumption into a fixed twenty-four-hour day is a central explanatory factor in understanding the increasing frenzy of modern life.

The observed bustle and agitation of modern life, therefore, may be viewed as the struggle of the individual to cope with an increasing flow of new goods by 'cutting corners', by curtailing the time spent on various consumption activities and, by extension, also on social activities.[10] In response to the problem, of course, the market economy directs research into the production of more efficient and time-saving consumer goods.

Moreover, there are two factors that aggravate this development and also act to check the desire to reduce hours of work as 'real' income rises. The first is the growing importance of 'recreational goods' in affluent countries having the object, presumably, of enabling the citizen to extract more exhilaration from his spare time. As Staffan Linder (1970) observes, Americans in particular tend to accumulate more sports gear and domestic gadgetry than they have the time, or inclination even, to use. Not surprisingly, in an innovative economy, all sports and pastimes, old and new, become increasingly expensive. It is not only that the sports equipment itself, from tennis rackets and golf clubs to sailing boats and monoplanes, is today made with new materials and synthetics, and is more distinctively designed. One has also to pay for the fashionable apparel and for the fashionable facilities necessary to enjoy the sport in question (which sometimes require joining an expensive club), and also to defray the costs of travel and other associated expenses.

Thus, sports and pastimes that were once the preserve of the well-to-do filter down to the lower strata of society. Not only do they become fashion goods for an increasing proportion of the public; but also participation in them is deemed necessary in order to 'meet people', in order not to be 'left out', an attitude carefully nurtured by commercial interests. However, since expenditures come to form a large proportion of a person's income – and there are social inducements to increase them, linked as they often are with the display of hospitality – there is little incentive, individual or institutional, to reduce the working week.

The second factor follows from the first. The rapid growth in the demand for costlier forms of fashionable recreation can be met only by the provision of more facilities, both recreational and travel. Owing, however, to lags in their supply and to natural scarcities, there has been increasing pressure on currently available facilities; a prolonged state of disequilibrium, in effect, that has taken the form of congested highways, delayed flights, lengthening queues for tennis courts, golf links, ski lifts, etc., and long waits to become a member of a popular sports club. The consequent frustration naturally creates impatience, resentment and occasionally outbursts and acts of fury – more especially in the affluent society where time is felt to be so precious.

The obvious way of escaping the frustration is to move to a wealthier neighbourhood, to own or share recreational facilities, and to join only the most exclusive clubs; in other words, to adopt a relatively expensive style of social life, an aim that cannot generally be realised except by devoting more time and thought to pecuniary matters.

To conclude, then: a simpliste view may suggest that, in a society of increasing material abundance, the members would want to avail themselves of opportunities for shorter working hours and increased leisure – if only because of the diminishing marginal utility of goods. Yet, for reasons indicated above, there is, in the affluent society, evidence of countervailing, indeed of contrary, forces at work.

Chapter 29

Instinctual Enjoyment

It is possible to conceive of a good society without opportunities for instinctual gratification; for example, a good life could be lived by small groups of men dedicating their lives to some holy cause or some high purpose. But for ordinary mortals, such feats of spiritual power and self-abnegation are not reasonably to be looked for. Even if they were possible, the good society would be a more joyful society if opportunities for instinctual enjoyment could be fitted comfortably into the established pattern of living.

What is at issue here is a social balance between, on the one hand, the freedom of the individual to enjoy his instincts and, on the other, the need for society to place curbs on its exercise in order to survive. The checks to the individual's freedom in this respect are enforced by repressive institutions and repressive mechanisms; that is, by the outer repression exercised by the community on the aggressive and sexual drives of the individual, on the one hand, and, on the other, by the inner repressions of the individual's own psyche. Put otherwise, restrictions on the free expression of an individual's desires are shared between the community and the individual, taking shape respectively as custom and taboo – the outer forces of repression that, on occasion, may be skirted – and as infant prohibitions that become 'introjected' or imbedded, so to speak, in the psychic plasma and which cannot by any means be flouted.

The growth over historical time of individual inhibitions on the expression of aggressive and sexual impulses is, as observed by Sigmund Freud (1930) in his *Civilisation and its Discontents,* inextricably connected with the rise of civilisations. In particular, the discipline entailed in sustaining a modern technical civilisation takes the form of 'sublimation' – habitual denial of immediate gratification of instinct in the interests of pursuits that accord with the requirements and approval of the civilised society. The Protestant ethic, regarded as eminently congenial to the rise of modern capitalism, is the most quoted example of social incentive for sublimation. It imbued men with the vision of the hard-working, thrifty, God-fearing individual, enjoying the Lord's blessing, made manifest in his growing prosperity. Nor was there any lack of intellectual justification for a man's growing devotion to material aggrandisement. According to the doctrine of 'the invisible hand', the general interest was best served by each man's following his own private business interests.

The middle classes associated in the eighteenth and nineteenth centuries with the rise of commerce and industry, Marx's bourgeoisie, became the 'inner-directed' men. And their children were reared strictly in order to enable them to follow in the steps of their successful fathers. Early in life, then, they learned to renounce their natural impulses for approved forms of satisfaction. They developed self-control and farsightedness, useful assets in an expanding capitalism.

Deploying the concepts of id, ego and superego, in connection with these historical developments, the import of Freud's view, as I understand it, is that these inner controls inculcated in the child, in its early years, become powerful enough to check the full expression of instinctual enjoyments. Thus, in moulding his personality to the requirements of the new capitalist civilisation, in learning to withhold immediate gratification of impulses, a man's more animal feelings of joy, or anger, or carnal gusto become somewhat muted. Both their full expression and the release from them become somehow incomplete. This inability fully to 'let oneself go', to experience the full meed of instinctual gratification, is part of the price that modern civilisation exacts, first of its protagonists, the hard-working middle classes who foster its growth, and, subsequently, of an increasing proportion of the working population. The latter become 'motivated' to subject themselves to years of disciplined training in order to acquire any one of the specialised skills needed by a technically complex economy; motivated also to spend their prime years in a continual search for improved prospects and status. Indeed, this form of sublimation is to some extent institutionalised by society through its educational system which absorbs twelve to twenty-five years of the individual's life, beginning from the age of 5 or thereabouts.

In so far as habits of instinct control are acquired in childhood, the resulting inhibition on sexual and related feelings continues to operate, though at a deep psychic level. Subsequent expressions of rebellion against parental or social restraints, do not dislodge it. Even resort to orgiastic indulgence, although they can be initially exciting and can gratify an urge for defiance, cannot enable the individual to recapture the pristine flavour of the physical sensations as the individual apprehends them through dreams and fantasies. The pleasures of instinct enjoyment are more accessible to populations living in a pre-industrial society; to people who do not habitually plan and live for the morrow; to people who live in the present, in the here and now; to those whose bodily passions are not tethered at their psychic roots and who are restrained in their exercise only by custom and prudence.[11]

Until the turn of the century, the peasantry and the working classes of Western Europe were less inhibited by infant training and less driven by ambition than the middle classes. To that extent, although their material condition was harder and, in some cases, close to destitution, their animal appetites were lustier and their enjoyment of them heartier.

It is a fact today that most people living in the richer countries believe themselves to belong to the middle classes. We need not trouble to define that category, for what is significant are the values implied by the term, values to which, by and large, assent is tacitly subscribed by the claimant to middle class status. During the twentieth century, at least the idea of worldly success, of material self-improvement, of raising one's position in the economic structure of society, has spread throughout and beyond the Western world – exception being made perhaps for a more recent, though limited and sporadic, reaction chiefly in the United States, in the form of drop-out movements.

Nor is the postwar upward trend in crime any exception to the achieving society. Crime is a 'subculture' of the achieving society. It seeks worldly success by illegal means. Within the underworld of crime, also, there is division of labour: a managerial class, technicians, a whole hierarchy of trades, and of 'firms'. And a continuing struggle for self-improvement, for status and power, is also to be found there.

If this Freudian view is correct, if the achieving society that we are wedded to is one that, even with attempts as 'enlightened parenthood', is designed to breed an 'inner-directed' individual, independent and self-reliant – perhaps all the more so, as the older type of community (what E. F. Schumacher (1973) calls the 'translucent society') vanishes, and society becomes increasingly anonymous, being composed largely of mobile nuclear families dwelling predominantly in metropolitan areas – then, whatever the claims to be made for the pleasures of the intellect, and for the satisfaction of worldly success by those who realise it, we have to recognise a concomitant decline, not in libidinous *pursuits*, but in libidinous *gratification*. Such a diminution of instinctual enjoyment, an inability to experience the full release of physical passion, can, once he is aware of it, impart a sense of frustration to the individual which he may seek to relieve through travel, through drugs and alcohol, through pornographic theatre, through explicit sexuality, or through attendance at bizarre cults. The scholar or scientist is apt to write off such a loss of 'animal feeling' as a small price to pay for the manifold blessings that science and civilisation confer on mankind. But for those thinking in terms of the ingredients of a good society, the matter should not be so summarily dismissed.

Although, admittedly, the evidence for it is not overwhelming, the prevailing view is that of a negative relation between the technical complexity of a civilisation and the individual's capacity for instinctual enjoyment. At any rate, an awareness of some deficiency in the immediate enjoyment of living seems to have grown over the years. It is borne out by the increasing popularity of psychotherapy, by the numbers being enrolled in classes and courses claiming to enhance the personality and to enlarge the capacity for enjoyment, and by movements, mystical and otherwise, that offer hope of joy and serenity – to say nothing of more deviant cults. This pervasive desire to escape from the repressions and vexations of our civilisation provides much of the inspiration of commercial advertisers who tend to associate their product or service, from deodorants to foreign travel, with an image of sublime fulfilment. Not that, in any particular instance, the public is completely taken in, of course. But people cannot help hoping that some new item, some new and revealing article in one of the scores of women's periodicals, some medical discovery or new drug or exotic plant, some miraculous scientific breakthrough, will enable them to revive the roots of sensation and to achieve the uttermost in fulfilment.

The crucial question here is whether this loss of 'libido', to use the Freudian term, is inherently inseparable from the movement towards a technically more complex civilisation. Is it possible, that is, to rear children who will eventually take their place in a technically complex civilisation, and withal remain as liberated as the pagan at the deepest psychic level?[12] And if it were somehow possible to rear children who, up to an early stage in their lives at least, were as capable as any primitive tribesman of surrendering to aggressive or carnal impulses, would not the habitual calculation, the habitual forethought, the routine planning and preparation required to cope with the exacting work patterns of a complex and rapidly changing civilisation, act, over time, to curb the spontaneity, to weaken the thrust and to dull the frenzy of a man's animal passions?

True, the way I have posed the question is partly rhetorical.

Although candour impels me to confess that I am not quite sure that the answer is yes, it is highly plausible to believe so. Perhaps we can conclude, provisionally, that some shift from inner restraints to outer restraints is desirable in order to allow men greater scope and intensity of their instinctual enjoyments. The need for this diminution of inner restraint, or inhibition, in order to free the flow of sensation, has been argued above. At the same time, an increase of outer restraints is also needed in order to curb recent excesses, and to keep norms of behaviour from transgressing limits beyond which the stability of society is endangered. The more effective checks to socially aberrant behaviour, however, are the pressures of custom and convention, backed by sanctions at the disposal of the small community.

Granted the desirability of such a change, it is difficult to see how it can come about without a drastic reduction of geographic mobility and without a changeover to a nation made up of smaller and more 'translucent' communities in which social disapproval again becomes an effective sanction in curbing misconduct. But, in the normal course of events, such a development cannot reasonably be anticipated in a modern growth economy.

Chapter 30

Security

A sense of security, without which the good life is not possible, implies safeguards against victimisation either by the state itself or by groups or by individuals within society. Protection of the individual against the power of the state need not be emphasised here, since we shall discuss the issue at length in Chapter 40 on personal freedom. It is the protection of individuals against the aggression of others that is the thesis of the present chapter.

It is true that the mills of justice grind slowly. Shakespeare included 'the law's delay' among the vexations suffered by mortals. But this is inevitable in a society where justice is given high priority. No matter how urgent his case is to him personally, each individual has to wait his turn. Due process requires evidence to be gathered, and to be examined and assured in open court according to formal and time-honoured procedures.

In lawless territories, or in times of social upheaval, such legal procedures are brushed aside in favour of rough justice. In such places, or at such times, a man may temporarily feel secure in following or shaping popular opinion. He may be elated in joining his voice to that of a mob, in denouncing the 'enemies of the people' and in crying out for their execution. Yet his complacency, or his predatory excitement, can be turned to dismay and terror if, by some quirk of fortune, he finds himself represented by others as a 'traitor to the cause', and stands in immediate danger of being dispatched himself in summary manner. Imagine, in the moment of shock at his predicament, how fervently he would wish once more for the slow process and ordered procedures of the law; for the presumption of his innocence until guilt was proven beyond reasonable doubt; for an explicit statement of the precise laws he is accused of violating; for legal representation of his own choice; for the right to object to the composition of the jury assembled to hear the evidence; for the right to cross-question all the witnesses; for the solemn interjection of an impartial judge and the unhurried deliberations of the jury; and, finally, in the event of an adverse judgment, for the right of appeal that his case may be heard again in a higher court. Without a defined body of law and legal procedure, without faith in the machinery of justice, and without freedom from the fear of arbitrary arrest and punishment, men cannot live at their ease and, therefore, cannot fully enjoy their lives.

As suggested in the first paragraph, however, the immediate threat today comes not from the state, but from the increasing power of law breakers. No matter what the opportunities for material comfort and enjoyment the economy offers to the citizen, life is a dismal and pathetic affair if a man must creep about in fear of his life, or in terror of physical assault and violence. Men are not generally apprehensive about unavoidable accidents or 'acts of God'. But they do become apprehensive in a society where either arbitrary arrest, or an attack on their person or property, is a common occurrence. Without determining a figure for the required incidence of each crime, or the required probability of its occurrence under given conditions, we may perhaps agree that in particular epochs, and in particular areas of the world, the fear of crimes of violence was such as effectively to mar the ordinary enjoyments of life. Over the last decade or so, the United States seems to be moving into this unhappy category. In and around the great American cities, families fear to stroll out of doors of an evening. Increasingly elaborate precautions are taken against intrusion and burglary. Parents live in a twilight of varying degrees of anxiety lest one of their children be kidnapped or murdered or mutilated. Surely, no accumulation of novel devices, no proliferation of consumer goods, no permissiveness of attire or wantonness in entertainment, can compensate for this one ugly fact that has come to blight the lives of millions of Americans and to turn to ashes their hopes of a better future.

The pertinent question is: how has this come about; in particular, whether, and in what ways, is the phenomenon connected with economic growth?

Generalising from the history of the eighteenth and nineteenth centuries, reformers were convinced that crime, especially crimes of robbery or violence, were the products of material deprivation and ignorance. But this simple belief is not borne out by historical evidence. Rising standards of living and education in all the richer countries have been accompanied, over the last two decades, by a rising incidence of crimes of violence, notably among the young.

Apparently, the fact that, in the West today, nobody need starve to death – indeed, the fact that a person can live without physical hardship on the welfare services provided by the state – affords little satisfaction in an increasingly anonymous and competitive society, within which men are ranked primarily according to wealth and professional status. True, being poor is not regarded as a violation of the law – even though, in some economists' models, the mere visibility of the poor is conceived to inflict a disamenity, or 'external diseconomy' on the rest of society. But there is still, in America especially, an unmistakable condescension which verges on impatience for those who 'do not make it'. Arnold Toynbee once remarked that America was the worst country in the world to be poor in.

As for the spread of educational opportunities, the great hopes once attracted by this prospect would seem to have been misplaced. The fact that educational opportunities have been vastly extended since World War II, and may be extended further, can mean only that more and more young persons will be encouraged to enter the race. It cannot ensure that all of them will emerge with prizes.

The unsuccessful individual may well feel more resentful towards a system that makes it evident to all when he fails in fair and open competition, than towards a system in which the bulk of the population has, in any case, no hope of, and little ambition for, a higher education. For though such a person will be envious of the good fortune of others, in either system, in the latter he does not, in addition, suffer from an ineradicable sense of mortification; he can, that is, plausibly attribute his humbler status and lower earnings to a lack of educational opportunity or to the neglect of Providence. By contrast, in the thorough-going 'meritocracy', which is a culmination and a justification of the pursuit of equal opportunity, there can be no retreat into these consoling reflections. Those unlucky enough to be born with very modest genetic endowments must, under a rigorously impartial system of universal opportunity, emerge eventually as the gammas and deltas of the economic hierarchy, their innate inferiority manifest to all.

If much of the crime in such a full-blown meritocracy were to be committed by those unavoidably relegated to the inferior tasks within a society devoted to economic efficiency, we should hardly be surprised. Since we are moving in that direction, though not rapidly enough to satisfy the aspirations of good socialists and liberals, we should not be surprised either that many of the crimes of violence are being committed today by failures and 'drop-outs'. In so far as we regard the movement towards a meritocratic society as a necessary feature of a rapid growth economy – necessary in that the pace of economic growth can be maintained only by improving the quality of human capital and by expanding the supply of scientific and technical skills – we have an additional reason for doubting whether the striving for faster economic growth can bring us closer to the good life.

Apart from the discontent, expressed in crime, of the indigenous have-nots, who are made increasingly aware of their lowly status in the West, there is another link between economic growth and rising crime: that arising from innovation that promotes or facilitates crime.

How much does modern crime depend upon the fast get-away car? How much of the increase in assault and robbery on the streets of American cities and suburbs can be attributed to the gradual disappearance of people from the streets, a result of the mass adoption of the motor car and, to some extent also, television? How far has the adoption of the private automobile also fostered a beggar-my-neighbour attitude, and encouraged each family and person to seek safety within the privacy and protection of his car or behind his own locked doors?[13]

The use of airliners both to commit crime and to escape justice is too obvious to mention. And the sheer sprawl of the metropolitan areas, the outcome of economic expansion and of new technology, offers irresistible facilities for wreaking havoc on vulnerable populations.

In the older and smaller communities, in contrast, far less coercion is needed to maintain law and order simply because the close physical and social interdependence itself exerts sanctions on behaviour. Criminal activity is harder to conceal since everyone knows everyone else's business, and effective community action is easy to organise. Admittedly, these comfortable features sometimes have another and less engaging side to them. The burden of social conformity lies more heavily on smaller communities than on larger ones, and the inhabitants of the former can become insular and intolerant. Yet not all small communities are necessarily repressive or benighted, and, given some freedom of movement, an individual need not suffer for long.

Finally, there is the relation between increasing affluence in the West and the increasing permissiveness with respect to sex and pornography, and with respect to violence and vandalism. Permissiveness in films, theatre and media entertainment, one of the consequences of competition for increased circulation and audiences, has gone far to implant the idea of physical violence as rugged, chic and sexy. It has acted also to encourage public tolerance of violent and antisocial behaviour, and contributed to a mood that has resulted in greater leniency in the treatment of offenders.

The modern views that crime is not so much wickedness as

rather a symptom of maladjustment,[14] and that far from wanting to punish the criminal society should seek to provide the treatment necessary to rehabilitate the unfortunate person, have gained ground since World War II. Punishments for the offender have become more lenient and, one may reasonably infer, the deterrent to a life of crime has become weaker.[15] But this trend towards a weakening of the sanctions against lawlessness is not compatible with the need for a sense of security that is a precondition of the good life. It is arguable that the detrimental effects on the social life of people in the West, arising from the growing fear of violence since World War II, far exceeds the conventional economic calculation of the damage sustained by them.

For it does not require very many crimes of violence on the streets to erode the trust between people and thus, over time, to destroy the traditional forms of propriety, civility and hospitality between men, which is the finest fruit of civilisation. When one considers that trust of strangers is an attitude that is slow to develop, and that only when it is established can a people begin to enjoy the amenities of civilisation – to stroll freely through the streets and the parks without fear of molestation, to exchange greetings with all, to extend hospitality to any one without fear of abuse – indeed, when one reflects on the contribution to our sense of wellbeing made by an atmosphere of social warmth and security, then, and only then, can we properly assess the iniquity of those crimes of violence against people.

The punishment currently meted out to those who assault their fellow beings would then seem slight when compared with the losses their predatory actions inflict on the community – a loss of ease and cordiality and dignity arising from the destruction of an environment of mutual trust and respect, an environment that is an essential ingredient of the good life. There is a strong case for punishments of street crimes far harsher than those currently contemplated.

Chapter 31

Love and Trust

A life without at least some hope of love would be almost intolerable. Indeed, the conviction that one has been cheated of love can lead to bitterness, to vindictiveness, to ruthlessness, to sadism and to crime. This being so, one can understand the importance to men of a belief in God conceived as a Deity that loves all his creatures and with whom communication is always possible. For not only can a man turn to God for love when alone and deserted by others, but, in addition, the faith that prompts him to surrender to the compassion of his Maker itself gives impulse to the flow of feeling that draws him closer to others in the vital experience of love. With the growth of the secular society, with the diffusion of the scientific attitude that is both the cause and consequence of industrial growth, this irreplaceable source of solace and inspiration is lost forever.

Turning now to social and economic considerations, can anything be said of the conditions under which love and affection take root and grow? In what sorts of civilisation, for example, should we expect love to flow more easily, whether romantic, fraternal or filial? To be more specific, is it reasonable to believe that closer personal relationships will be formed in the modern growth-bound society than in the more traditional society?

It can be, and has been, argued that in releasing the mass of people from drudgery and providing them with opportunities to move about and meet others, economic growth promotes personal contacts and improves personal relationships.

It is sad to record that otherwise able economists have reasoned thus (for a recent example, see Professor Wilfred Beckerman, 1973). Indeed, much of the reasoning of pro-growth economists, is marked by excessive abstraction and superficiality, and has scant regard to the facts. Along with liberals and socialists, many continue to believe that poverty and inequality are the chief causes of crime, in spite of the mounting crime wave over the past two decades, above all in the United States, the richest country the world has ever known. On the same simple reasoning, we should be led to anticipate that, with the spread of material prosperity, financial corruption and political chicanery in the United States and elsewhere would decline.

As Beckerman (1973) innocently surmises, the obsession with material wealth *should* be less important when there is more of it; after all, that is what follows from the concept of diminishing marginal utility! The same sort of logic would suggest decline in acquisitiveness, a growth in the sense of ease, a decline in the friction of human relationships, and an increase in cheerfulness, courtesy and family feeling, in all the rich industrial countries.

Such arguments are a reflection of the hopes of nineteenth-century reformers. They were superficial then. Today, they are manifestly spurious; they not only ignore theoretical developments in orthodox economics, but also give no thought to the actual direction being taken by consumer innovation. Four attributes of modern economic growth will serve to illustrate this criticism.

(1) The very pace of modern life does not lend itself to the cultivation of friendship. It is not only the case that the tight scheduling of a life directed chiefly by efficiency criteria makes us edgy and impatient, or that the deluge of news and views spewed forth by mass media seems to swamp what limited spare time we have. It is also the case that the very produce of the system acts to rob us of the sense of spaciousness. As indicated earlier, the consumer in the richer countries is becoming exhausted in the attempt to cram a growing assortment of goods, including 'leisure' and 'recreational' goods, into a fixed number of hours a week. A sense of the pressure of time, of lagging behind, of things undone and of much to be fitted in, is the common experience of citizens of the affluent society, especially among the professional classes. Clearly such a mood is uncongenial to the enjoyment of friendship. Freedom from the pressure of compulsion and anxieties is a precondition for the release and flow of joyous feeling.

Again, if long familiarity with personages and places is a source of deep gratification to men, and if only through long association can the bonds of trust and friendship be formed, if, indeed, slow months and years are involved in the experience, we cannot but conclude that the prospects for this form of human fulfilment in the modern world, one in the throes of rapid and perpetual change, are bleak. In particular, the advancing technology of transport transforms the environment and goads us into restlessness. Each year, as mentioned earlier, 40 million Americans change their homes.[16] This trend in mobility, which shows more people moving more frequently year by year from one city to another, from one country to another, does, of course, enable them to extend the number of their acquaintances by the score. But this does not meet the issue, any more than does the postwar tourist boom. A week in a mountain hotel, a package tour in the Mediterranean, a jet bargain enabling us to see 'seven countries in ten days' and to meet other 'beautiful people', each may offer some moments of elation, at least some pangs of anticipation to help us bear the insistent routine of daily life. But, in truth, there is time enough only to throw postures, to go through the conventional motions of revelry and, for the rest to hope that something or somebody will turn up. For the young, there is, of course, the flurry of excitement, the stylised infatuations, the hectic exchanges of personal data and confidences. But out of these jet age experiences one cannot hope to fashion the love that is the slow product of time and care.

Indeed, the sheer numbers of people we meet, the crowds we have to jostle our way through, induce a reaction similar to that produced by the proliferation of man-made goods. Masses of people, that is, begin to seem expendable too: items in the throwaway society. As the numbers of people we pass through, and the amounts of goods about us, continue to increase, in pursuance of economic growth, the quickness of our response to them diminishes. It becomes hard to dispel a sense of boredom, of exhaustion and sometimes of despair.

(2) Another attribute of modern life that weakens the formation of affectionate ties springs from the faith in the powers of science, more precisely in the power of techniques, to solve all problems, industrial, technical, social and personal. According to Jacques Ellul (1965), this faith in the power of modern technology is the distinctive feature of society today. Wherever some defect in the working of the system is detected, even if the defect is attributable to the use of a particular technology, the proposed remedy is, almost invariably, the application of some new technique.

Broadly defined as a form of systemisation of all activity, technique has begun to edge itself into every niche of what used to be a person's private life and feelings. Popular techniques for expanding a person's capacity for love, passion, surrender, repartee, laughter and fantasy are today imparted to the buyer of the booklet or tape, or to the enroller in the course. For the would-be lover – which, in this market, always means sexual lover – the precise movements, the breathing and rhythm, the timing of a variety of caresses, pinches, grunts, sighs and bites, are now elaborated in films and illustrated monographs.

No personal problem is so intimate that a technique cannot be fashioned to deal with it. Social science 'experts', for instance, have begun to introduce life adjustment courses as part of the student services of the university. In the year 1972–3, The American University Community Center, Washington, DC, offered its students a range of therapeutic services which included:

> *Encountertape Groups:* These are personal growth groups designed as structured, encounter experiences focussing on themes of trust building, giving and receiving feedback, direct communication, and sensory awareness. They will serve as an introduction . . . for well-functioning groups.
> *Interpersonal Skill Building Groups:* In these ten-session skill-focussed groups, students will be taught to monitor and master anxiety, using . . . improved social skills by learning to be appropriately assertive, and more direct empathic communication.

This pathetic exhibition of inept jargon is itself a corollary of the sanctification of a techniques approach that views the hapless human as an operationally defective machine in need of a standard overhaul. The widespread acceptance of the idea that emotions of trust and affection, which should come to us as naturally as breathing and sleeping, are now to be acquired by a course of instruction and drill is itself indicative of the sorry state of mind induced by our faith in technology. We might well marvel about the mental condition of a person who expects that by taking a selection of these popular courses he will learn to 'control and direct aggression' and to 'convey and receive empathy'. But the growth in the enrolment for such courses is a fact – one that is indicative more of the despair and gullibility of the patients than of the success of the treatment.

(3) The spread of the individualistic ethic which accompanies economic growth in the leading industrial countries is a third attribute, one related to the faith in technique discussed above. True, the seemingly inevitable replacement of economic services for personal ones in an increasingly complex economy – which (as observed in Chapter 3) acts, incidentally, to inflate

estimates of real national income and its growth – can also be described as a commercialisation of life. Indeed, this phenomenon has recently been referred to by Hirsch (1976) as 'the commercialisation effect'. However, it is more illuminating to interpret it as an extension of the individualistic ethic which is a primary feature not only of a market economy but also of any modern economy. For the term individualistic ethic comprehends not only calculated behaviour in production, a development often associated with the 'capitalist ethic', as a driving force of the economy. It also comprehends the self-regarding search by individuals to procure increasingly more of their satisfaction in life from the finished goods produced by the economic system – irrespective of whether such goods are produced by the market or by the government. In other words, the individualistic ethic is not an attribute only of an advanced capitalist society. It is an attribute also of any collectivist economy that seeks to increase output by offering individual incentives and, in the process, replaces personal services with economic goods.

The growth of the individualistic ethic is then, also, an apparently inevitable consequence of the growth of mass urbanisation, mass auto-mobility, and those labour-saving innovations mentioned in (4) which follows. For these things together have acted to destroy local communities and, therefore, also the sense of community loyalty and the personal interdependence and mutual obligation arising therefrom. As a result, the growth of affluence and urbanisation over the last century has brought with it not only a diminished personal dependence on the direct help and the company of others but also, as an immediate consequence, a diminished reliance upon, and therefore an erosion of, that mutual trust prevalent in pre-industrial societies manifest in the vital importance for them of propriety, custom, unwritten conventions and informal understandings. In their stead, as mutual trust between persons and between classes – between buyer and seller, landlord and tenant, employer and employee; more recently alas, between teacher and student and between doctor and patient also – has eroded over the years, we observe the growth everywhere of formal contracts with increasingly detailed provisions and of explicit quid-pro-quo agreements between the parties.

Ironically enough, it is this universal diffusion of the individualistic ethic, cherished by liberals, and its success in loosening the ties of personal obligation – in progressively isolating the individual from a real community and transforming him into a self-contained independent decision-making unit – that has also led to the expansion of the collective countervailing power which they deplore. For as he is cut off increasingly from the sources of comfort and assurance provided by a real community, the individual turns elsewhere for these things. His search for security from the threat of powerful economic and political forces in a world of rapid change, his search for guidance in a world of growing complexity, brings into being a market for the instruments of countervailing power in the familiar form of labour unions, employer and employee associations, consumer organisations, tenant associations, citizens' advisory councils, and so on.

No personal love or care or respect is involved however. We are now far removed from the smaller world of mutual obligation and trust. The individual simply pays his dues, fees or taxes, and obtains the service (or else, as a ward of the welfare state, he is entitled to it). Thus the growth of institutions of countervailing power adds to the variety of service organisations offering the individual protection and expertise as they take over ever more of that part of our lives that was once suffused with personal services and obligations.

There is, moreover, not only cause for regret. There is cause for alarm. For the decline in mutual trust and mutual obligation, associated with the rise of the individualistic ethic, inevitably produces a decline also in standards of personal integrity and public trust, qualities that are yet necessary for the efficient operation even of an impersonal economic system. Indeed, such qualities become important if the rapidly expanding public sectors of the wealthier economies are to be run with some tolerable degree of efficiency. It is, then, altogether possible that the decline in personal integrity resulting from the spread of the individualistic ethic has already gone so far as to impair the operation, even to undermine the viability, of the post-industrial economy.

(4) Fourthly, our attention should be directed also to the impact on our personal relations of the specific kinds of consumer innovation that are produced by economic growth. Nearly all of them come under the umbrella term 'labour-saving'; that is to say, they are rationalised as serving to reduce the vexations we are presumed to suffer from having to make physical effort – what the advertisements call 'drudgery'. The ultimate objective of consumer innovation is apparently, perhaps unavoidably, to create for us a push-button world in which all our whims can be gratified on the instant, and in which therefore we shall subsist in a continuous state of surfeit. In so far as we have come to suppose that the time and effort

needed to perform ordinary physical tasks are a drain on our enjoyment of life, technology can boast a modest success: most Western households today are continually ahum with electric devices that enable their occupants to lead the sedentary lives which are the main support of the medical profession.

Although technology has been less successful in enabling us to overcome psychological frustrations, speculation in this respect may draw on some of the characteristics of Aldous Huxley's Brave New World. The reader may recall that the denizens of this synthetic utopia were raised in test-tubes and continued to fill the occupations they were to follow. There were happily no sexual taboos, no doubts and no apprehensions. Any incipient anxiety was dispelled by swallowing a euphoric tablet called 'soma'. Indeed, since the inhabitants and this new world were designed to fit together perfectly, Huxley's mock utopia can be interpreted as the nemesis of today's fuzzy-minded progressive, with his touching faith in salvation by science, and with his outraged rejection of the notion of sin, or of the value of human sacrifice or suffering. For in this beautifully tailored civilisation, prescribed over by a benevolent dictator, the concepts of good and evil were indeed obsolete. Where all activity, economic and social, was guided by an elite of technocrats, nothing was left to chance or choice. Consequently, there could be neither vice nor virtue. The only relevant categories for such a dispensation were health and sickness, these being associated, respectively, with efficiency and inefficiency.

And what are the consequences for humanity of achieving so ideal a state of adjustment? Imagine a potential Juliet of this Brave New World stumbling into the arms of a potential Romeo. The first flicker of desire would be quenched by instant fornication. And if, for some perverse reason, Romeo vacillated, Juliet could be counted on to console herself at once with a couple of soma tablets.

In a world without frustration – in a world, that is, of instant gratification – there can be no sublimation, and therefore there can be no romantic love. In such a world there can be no conflict, and therefore there can be no drama. In such a world there can be no suffering, and therefore there can be no tragedy. In such a world there can be no sacrifice, and therefore there can be no heroism. Neither can there be passion. Nor can there be poetry. And, it goes without saying, there can be no transcendental emotion and no abiding affection.

Assuming then that we manage to survive the gauntlet of hazards, ecological and social, that arise on all sides from the growing scale of technology, the future that faces humanity is not inviting. For if the conscientious endeavours of science, directed as they are towards realising the dreams of countless reformers to free mankind from the frictions and frustrations of this world, finally bear fruit, how can the resultant civilisation be different from Huxley's colourless and unheroic society of emotional cretins?

The contemplation of so ignominious a destiny is premature, however. Let us consider, instead, the more immediate threat to human intercourse posed by the propensity to produce labour-saving innovations in the industrial economies of the world. Inevitably such innovations act over time to reduce the direct dependence of people on other people, and to transfer this dependence to the machine. Yet the fact of physical human interdependence is – or, rather, was – one of the main viaducts along which friendliness and affection have habitually flowed.

Children's television programmes have made the bedtime story obsolete. But does not the child who rests warmly in his mother's arms, attentive to her voice as the tale is gently unfolded, enjoy a richer experience? At the flick of a finger, any room in the house can be flooded with orchestral music that is perfectly executed – and a delight to the ear were it not so available on such easy terms that it serves us now as background noise against which we eat, talk, read or do odd chores. But, before the end of the century, when the music a man could enjoy depended largely on his own musical talent, on his wife's proficiency with the piano, or on his daughter's singing, did not these domestic performances also release some spring of joy between them?

These forms of mutual enjoyment and personal contact necessarily decline with the growth of push-button entertainment and labour-saving gadgets. They have already declined with the spread of supermarkets, cafeterias and vending machines, and with the spread of transistors, television sets and, of course, the automobile. And they will continue to decline with the trend towards increasing automation in factories and computerisation in offices, with the trend towards patient-monitoring machines and computer diagnosis in hospitals, and with the trend towards closed-television instruction, language laboratories, teaching machines and automated libraries.

It follows that opportunities for meeting directly and personally the needs of other people, opportunities for the exchange of sentiments, opportunities for cultivating friendship that arise from the exigencies of life, are all on the wane in a technological civilisation in which machines are being designed to provide us with everything. It is hard then to avoid the conclusion that the compulsive search for efficiency – embodied, in the main, in innovations designed to save time, effort, and any human intermediary –

will continue to produce for us yet more elegant instruments for our mutual estrangement.

The inevitable consequence of this trend in technology would seem to be, therefore, a drying up of the direct flow of sympathy and affectionate communication between people. However the increase in the material conveniences of life is valued, they are slight compensation for the concomitant diminution of opportunities to enjoy the vital experience of love.

Chapter 32

Self-esteem

Life cannot be satisfactory, and society itself cannot be stable, if the citizen is lacking in self-esteem. In times gone by, a man could perhaps take pride in the belief that he walked erect in the sight of the Lord. There are not many of that breed left today in the Western world. In the modern, competitive, highly mobile society, self-esteem has come to depend predominantly on worldly success. Put crudely, money has become the measure of a man – even though it is one that is supplemented by professional status.

The powerful movement towards equality of opportunity in the affluent democracies must bring about a social ranking that is no more inherently just than a hierarchy based on inheritance or, indeed, any principle besides efficiency. Within the higher ranks of the meritocracy towards which we move will be those fortunate enough to be born into a rich genetical inheritance. They will be the winners in a perpetual competition for which, at any one time, there are only a limited number of worthwhile prizes. And while the young have their hopes and high spirits to keep them running, most of the older members of society will, sooner or later, have to face the fact that they are not of the stuff from which winners are made. It behoves them to rationalise accordingly if they are not to feel morose or resentful.

Some of them may be able to convince themselves that their lack of success is due to some particular stroke of ill luck. Some may continue to plod on in the faith that hard work and long hours must bring eventual rewards. Some accept their failure, yet carry on doggedly in the hope that the achievement of their children will ultimately vindicate their self-esteem. Yet others nourish their fragile self-regard on the unfailing stream of newsbits that testify to the corruption or unworthiness of others, or translate their resentment into militance against social injustices of the system. For the remainder, for the honest but unphilosophical, it becomes a losing battle against the encroachment of despair.

In the past, a man's self-respect was linked to his specific place and role in the community's life, the products of his close association with the church, with the municipality or self-supporting village, perhaps also with the craft or merchant guilds or trading companies. There are, to be sure, remnants of the older tradition to be found in modern societies in the form of local activities which act to diminish the strains of the individual's continuous struggle for self-betterment, and yield him some measure of local pride and satisfaction. Yet of those and other older institutions that served to allocate to every honest man a place and a rôle in the community, only the family survives today, and then in a more loosely knit form than hitherto. The family is supplemented by modern economic institutions that are both less demanding and less embracing, such as the trade unions and trade associations, also local political associations and social clubs, which – though of only ancillary concern in a world of instant communication, one attentive primarily to national figures and national politics – still offer some recognition to many who might otherwise sink without a trace into an ocean of anonymity.

Nevertheless, in a civilisation that is dedicated to the goal of increased efficiency through the diffusion of higher education and economic opportunity, the influence of local activities in strengthening the self-respect of scores of millions of citizens is sure to recede over time. For this reason, it is worth pondering on the sort of community usually associated with an older tradition, a community held together by an intricate web of customs, rights, duties and privileges. In the five chapters that follow, on kith and kin, on customs and mores, on role and place, on the moral code, and on the great myths, conceptions that pervade traditional societies, we shall have occasion also to consider other connections between a person's self-esteem and his role in the community.

Chapter 33

Kith and Kin

A pervasive and enduring sense of security, in the broadest interpretation of the term, is a fundamental prerequisite of any good society. The importance of security against physical attack by others has been discussed in Chapter 30. In the preceding chapter we touched on the self-esteem of the citizen, which is part of the psychological sense of security. We have now to consider the need for security against apprehensions of social disintegration, something that can arise from a number of causes, though also from a separate malaise against which society must guard itself: namely, the doubts about the larger purposes, and value, of life on this planet.

This chapter, and the four which follow, address themselves to the issues arising from a consideration of this last sense of security. Although these five chapter titles refer to concepts or features of society which together produce that social and psychological state of security which is part of the prerequisite of a good society, there is expositional convenience in separating the issues under these chapter titles rather than treating them under subheadings of an outsize chapter entitled 'Social and Psychological Security'.

The term 'family', regarded as a human institution, can be understood to refer to what we now call the nuclear family – man and wife, plus children, if any – or to the extended family, in the sense either of additional relations (such as grandparents, uncles and aunts, nephews and nieces) living and sharing together as one household, or else of a group of closely related families living in neighbourly proximity and in continuous communication. The demise of the family, nuclear or extended, would not preclude the formation of informal relationships between two or more persons based on mutual convenience and affection, nor, therefore, the formation also of larger groups which choose to live for some time as a closed community according to agreed rules or conventions. The difference between these informal associations and families, then, is that the former have no settled and enduring structure of relationships, one sanctified by law and custom, traditionally held together by mutual privileges and obligations, and about which much of the community's social and economic life is organised.

The possibility of a good life for humanity in the absence of the family cannot be dismissed as innately impossible. But since sporadic experiments in group living, both past and present – including 'disintegrative' family innovations such as spouse sharing – have not exercised any lasting influence on the mass of mankind, there is no evidence to support arguments for a dissolution of the institution. Indeed, since there is no record of any civilisation's existing without the family, it is unreasonable to deny a presumption in its favour. The burden of proof, that is, must rest on those who would convince us of the balance of advantages that would accrue to humanity from its abolition.[17]

I find it difficult to sympathise with the objection to family life on the argument that it tends, today, to constrict the sexual liberty of the adult. The postwar experiments in 'swinging' (spouse swopping and sharing) should, of course, be taken seriously, but no more seriously than any of a number of fashionable abberations, from the uttering of obscenities in common discourse and popular entertainment to the spread of witch covens and devil worship, from blatant exhibitionism and public pornography to homosexual conferences and demonstrations. All such licentious developments, which find shelter under the umbrella term 'permissiveness' are largely traumatic in origin. Although, on a partisan view, they are rationalised as exciting experiments in extending the range of sensation, they can plausibly be explained, as indicated in Chapter 27, in terms of reactions to the growing stress and strain of a society that is in the throes of rapid technological change.

Rather arbitrarily, then, I shall consider none of these permissive experiments as offering any viable opportunity for human betterment. Although indulging in such permissive practices may indeed conflict with the enjoyment of family life, there is no case for resolving the conflict in favour of permissiveness. I shall, therefore, assume that the emotional need to belong to a family is not at issue. What is at issue, and what calls for more reflection, is whether life can be more enjoyable in a society of nuclear families or in a society of extended families. As already indicated, members of the extended family may occupy a single dwelling or they may occupy a cluster of contiguous dwellings. But whatever the living arrangements, members of the extended family are deemed to be in continual and frequent communication with one another.

If society were more stable than in fact it is, the nuclear family might be thought to foster more intense affection between husband and wife, between them and their children, and between the children themselves. And the eventual desire of the son or daughter of such a union to share such a home with a single partner would perpetuate this close emotional dependence. Nuclear family life, then, could produce greater extremes of joy or misery than those experienced by persons reared in an extended family circle. For the latter extend their love and trust to many, and are consequently less vulnerable to the mood and behaviour of any one member of the extended family. To that extent they will feel more protected and secure. The manifest fear of 'emotional involvement' voiced today by men and women (an attitude discussed at greater length in Chapter 50), and the trend in preferences for a larger number of more superficial love affairs, may sometimes be traced to unhappy childhood experiences which are more intensely felt in the nuclear family.

It is reasonable to suppose that the extended family tends to generate a greater sense of security and equability, the more so if relatives live together, or come together frequently, either from force of custom or for ceremonial occasions. There are, in addition, some obvious but by no means negligible advantages: those that arise from opportunities the younger members have of learning from the experience of the older ones about domestic, marital or infant-rearing matters, and also the assurance everyone has of ready help from some of the others when an emergency strikes or an important occasion occurs. After all allowance has been made for any reduction in privacy, the extended family would seem to offer a more emotionally satisfying arrangement than does the nuclear family.

However, if it is true that the extended family is likelier to produce a greater sense of emotional security and more stable personalities, it is undeniable that the rising trend in both occupational and spatial mobility, which is directly associated with economic growth, favours the nuclear family. Furthermore, the popular innovations that free us from physical dependence upon others and those also that free us from social dependence on others – enabling each one of us to generate his own privately chosen entertainment programme simply by pressing a button or turning a knob – act to undermine the rationale of the extended family.

A final reflection. Since personal servants were once a part of the household of all but the poorest classes, and could, in the circumstances, be regarded as an extension of the family, a word or two about their role and place in the home need not be thought of as a digression.

Following World War II, the servant class in the West, after being an institution for hundreds of years, has all but vanished. Whether their lot, working along with others in a large household, was less secure and less happy than that of the millions who today inhabit small rooms and commute daily to the town or city centre, to a routine job in a shop or office, is an interesting question. The answer to it depends, to a large extent, on the attitude of acceptance or rejection of one's existing role. The further back we move in time, the more common it was for a person to accept his position in the economic and social structure, whatever it be, and for the rest to avail himself without reserve of whatever joy or amusement was offered. Today, it is the general rule to accept one's present status on sufferance only; to be striving continually for self-betterment, prodded along by up-to-date statistics which enable one to make invidious comparisons between the earnings of one's own occupational group and those of others. For large numbers of people, in short, modern psychological stress succeeds old-fashioned physical strain.

Be this as it may, there is another consideration. The institution of household servants had, on the whole, a salutary and civilising effect, despite inevitable abuses and occasional vice and disorderliness. In the richer households a miniature hierarchy was established; duties and privileges were allocated, and codes of behaviour were enforced. The routine and regularity of a well-run servant home exerted an influence on the family and held it together. The very presence of servants, and the desire to keep them respectful, also acted to instil prudence and responsibility in the adult members of the family. In consequence, the tone of family discourse was necessarily more moderate and its manners more restrained.[18]

Chapter 34

Customs and Mores

Under this heading I should include the persistence and general acceptance in a society of norms of propriety: all those customs, conventions, rituals and forms of address which shape the character of a people. Admittedly, there is some enjoyment to be had in occasionally dispensing with the formalities, or some excitement from flouting time-honoured customs. But placed beside the great convenience and satisfaction derived by society from the daily affirmation of its customs and mores, the occasional complacency in cutting a convention or the exhilaration of defying a tradition is of slight consequence.

It is not to be denied, of course, that the custom and mores that mark a particular age can be inappropriate and, indeed, oppressive. But we must not cast the net of speculation too wide. Except perhaps on some elusive Marcusian definition, the cloak of custom and tradition that envelopes the body of Western civilisation never looked more flimsy and threadbare than it does today. We may then address ourselves to this rather disconcerting development.

A disintegration of the norms of priority is invariably accompanied by a decline in the level of personal communication, and some increase therefore in vexation, contention and misunderstanding. Basically, people become unsure of the interpretation of the address and behaviour of others. Psychological signals are misinterpreted, expectations are thwarted, and, instead of a smooth flow of communication and feeling, there often is a jarring and a fumbling and a tenseness.

Known ways of deportment in all routine situations, set forms of address and of communicating approval or disapproval, help us to move more smoothly through the day. The signals are understood, and there are only a limited number of acceptable responses to any overture. The psychological demands of human intercourse are lighter, and one feels more at ease in society.

This description contrasts with the trend since World War II of increasing informality of deportment and discourse, a trend that is commonly approved of as being less hypocritical or more natural and honest. However we interpret these words, it is certain that the affection of informality can be burdensome – especially as one becomes unsure of the nature of the formalities that are to be avoided. Guided only by what seems at the moment to be 'natural', or by the hope of appearing original, it is hard to avoid some degree of apprehension about being misunderstood or being outmanoeuvred. Indeed, the freer society seeks to become of established forms of behaviour, the higher is the individual's self-consciousness in social intercourse and the greater is the strain he has to bear.

Obviously, formalities can be carried to excess. But this platitude does not argue against the advantages of a nice system of formalities in human intercourse, extending from the minor forms of politeness, such as the seemingly quaint custom of men's raising their hats to the ladies, to the proper forms of deference to the elderly, or from a set style of introducing friends to established etiquette in table manners and in conducting conversation.

Far from being onerous, as is sometimes alleged, these forms and procedures can soon be turned over to the effortless custody of habit. Thus, while doing the socially approved thing from force of habit, one's mind is free to take stock of the situation. Indeed, once the forms of behaviour are established, no one is precluded by his station, or by his lack of natural gifts, from excelling in these respects and from gaining, thereby, some modest reputation for his politeness, an accomplishment which affords some satisfaction and pride to those having no other claim to distinction.

However, as suggested, by far the greater advantage of living in a community held together by a firm framework of custom and etiquette is that of relieving its members of effort and anxiety in a wide variety of social situations. Phrases, actions, gestures even, follow time-worn patterns, while our thoughts and feelings are free to take shape. It is, then, just because the directions we are to follow are so well known, just because the highways and byways of social intercourse are so familiar, that we move so easily in our intercourse with others, reserving our thoughts and feelings for more spontaneous experiences.

It is vain, however, to hope for a return to a strong framework of custom and propriety in the context of rapid economic growth. Indeed, economic growth, as we understand it today, could not have taken place without breaking the integument of traditional societies. The rise in living standards is accompanied by the neglect and gradual obsolescence of traditional forms. For one thing, there is 'not enough time', as indicated earlier (Chapter 28). For another, whatever customs and conventions are observed are increasingly ephemeral, the product not of a slow social process but of technological innovation and commercial fashion.

Chapter 35

Role and Place

In contrast to the large-scale complex technological society of today, the acceptance of one's role and station in life was fundamental to the stability of the small-scale traditional society centred on town and village. Although the transition period to the modern society was indeterminate, and could be measured in centuries rather than decades, Britain was largely a traditional society as late as the middle of the eighteenth century. If a member of the 'lower orders' then did not till the soil, he might be apprenticed to some trade, possibly to that of his father, and in time become a master of his craft. Though his position in the hierarchy was a humble one, as we go back in time the more likely he was to become a member of a guild or of a self-governing body of craftsmen or merchants that commanded social recognition and respect. Always aware of its responsibilities to the public, such a body set its own standards and regulations, and looked after the interests of its members and their families. Once initiated into 'the mysteries of the craft', the member acquired a distinct status, a place in the community, and a continuing assurance that the work at which he excelled was valued by the society of which he was part. Nothing further was expected of him in the shape of 'making his way in the world'. For he had served his apprenticeship. He had been accepted, both economically and socially. There were no social heights for him to scale, no moving belt of technology to keep up with. He was free to move at his own pace along an extended plateau that would end with his life. Thus, he was expected only to practise his craft or calling diligently, to strive for excellence, perhaps to participate in local government, and for the rest to avail himself of what amusements and diversions came his way: to enjoy the holidays and holy days, to partake in the rituals and ceremonies, and, sustained by the solace and satisfaction of family life, to bear with dignity the vagaries of misfortune – the occasional hardships, the natural sorrows, and the infirmities of age.

These older institutions, and the harvest feasts and churchgoing that went with them, acted to soften the harshness of the struggle against the niggardliness of nature. Their influence lingered on into the nineteenth century as a counter to the increasingly abrasive struggle between men. In bringing people together at the local level, in play and in prayer, in feast and in ceremony, they affirmed the fact of their direct interdependence and kept them aware of their common humanity.

Yet such institutions that, in the traditional society, assured men and women of a place and a role within an intimate community, could only hinder the growth of the modern industrialised economy. For sustained economic growth in the industrial economy is linked to a continuous struggle for self-betterment, a continuous struggle to maintain and improve one's position and status against the competition of others, and in the face of advancing knowledge and technology.

There can, of course, be countervailing arguments in favour of the competitive modern society – which arguments will, necessarily, appear more weighty in a civilisation that has succeded in imbuing its citizens with inordinate ambition and envy. But if a traditional society provides the institutions by which a person is assured of acceptance within his community – assured, that is, of a place and role both in its economy and in its social hierarchy – it has to be credited with the provision of a vital source of wellbeing that is no longer available in a modern society.

Again, any comparison of traditional and modern societies cannot overlook either the importance of the role of the sexes. Whether, in different periods of history and in different areas of the world, the lot of the man or of the woman was, on the whole, the more arduous – put otherwise, whether, taken in the round, the life of the one sex or the other was the more satisfying – is a difficult question to agree upon. It need not be resolved here, however. Even if the currently popular, though superficial, view – that, at least prior to the twentieth century, the woman had the rougher end of the partnership – were accepted, the belief would not affect the general proposition: that the distinct and complementary role of the sexes can be a source of immense satisfaction to both.

It is far from impossible that the differences between the sexes have been exaggerated in the past, although the tendency today is rather to underestimate them. Yet the exaggeration of these differences is, perhaps, evidence less of people's credulity than of their desire to make the most of them. Myth is always more satisfying to ordinary folk than naked truth, assuming we could uncover it. The belief that it needed a man and a woman to make a home together; the belief that while a man went out into the world as the family breadwinner, the woman kept the home tidy and attractive, kept it warm and cosy, looked after the children (alone or with the help of servants or relations), welcomed her husband's return with a good meal on the table, and, withal, took pride in, and derived satisfaction from, this role – this belief may today be anathema to militant feminists. But that such beliefs were widespread, and that they gave vent to pride and satisfaction in family life, are facts for all that. No doubt, had women in earlier times been long exposed to siren voices that sang of liberation from the pains of childbearing and the indignities of household chores, many of them might have come to despise the domestic role allotted to them. But being born earlier in history, they escaped such exposure and, therefore, continued in their sublime innocence to strive to excel in their womanly role and, often, to enjoy it.

The knowledge that for centuries, for milennia, little girls have played with dolls and, as they grew into women, helped with the housework, and learned to sew, knit and embroider, to arrange flowers, to cook and to mend clothes, has become a thorn of mortification to the feminist liberators of today. The fact that men got some keen pleasure from witnessing the performance of these womanly tasks would not be denied either; indeed, it would be a part of the feminists' heavy burden of resentment. Nor, for that matter, could they deny the equally humiliating fact that there were women who actually enjoyed being watched by men as they went about their work in the home. But, then, it is also true that these same women derived amusement and satisfaction in watching a man's fumbling attempts, occasionally, to do some woman's work. 'Just like a man!' they would exclaim with unconcealed complacency. On the other hand, if there was some heavy work to be done in the home, or some awkward business to attend to, there was no doubt but that it was 'a man's job'.

These continual affirmations of the belief in the inherent differences in the character and the abilities of the sexes, as evidenced by such commonplace remarks as 'Every inch a woman' or 'You know what men are', were always a dependable source of merriment and satisfaction between the sexes, one that lingers on even in these times of growing uncertainty as to how a woman should behave and what she should feel and think.

However, so long as society persists in regarding GNP as the measure of all things we must turn our backs on these innocent beliefs. For their existence can only retard the emergence of that unisex meritocracy we are straining to realise. And if progress, measured in such terms, requires that modest talent must not be left to enhance the personality but must search instead for its price on the market, and that the direct services performed by a wife or a mother for the persons she most cherishes must now be degraded to the category of domestic drudgery (in comparison, that is, with the services she might instead perform for an anonymous public, working in a factory, shop, bank or office), then, indeed, there is everything to be said for accelerating the movement of women from their homes into the wide world of industry – there to enjoy the ephemeral triumphs and to suffer the perennial anxieties, there to be subject to the inevitable stresses and vexations which impel all too many white collar workers to resort to some unholy mixture of stimulants and sedatives simply in order to 'keep going'.

Now, so long as we are hopelessly immersed in the restless status-seeking atmosphere of modern civilisation, I confess to sympathy with women who believe – sometimes correctly – that they receive less money than men do for the same work, or that, with the same qualifications as men, their economic opportunities in many fields are more circumscribed.[19] Indeed, if one believes that technological developments have, in effect, made women increasingly expendable if not (in a childless family) superfluous in the home, and that therefore there is no other respectable role for women other than in industry, then equality of opportunity and remuneration is clearly justified on grounds both of equity and of efficiency. But in determining the features of a good society, we cannot be bound in judgment to the constraints of the existing society in which we live. For if we had the wisdom to choose forms of technology most fitting to the good life, we might not choose the existing technology after due consideration of its likely effects on the all-important relationships between the sexes.

If, then, the good life we aspire to rejects the capitalist virtues of maximising and, therefore, of inordinate ambition; if, instead, our vision of it exhibits more co-operation, more feeling, more fun and more love and trust between people – then the question of sex is crucial to it. Not, of course, the carnal aspect which has become obsessive to the point of hysteria, but the aspect that concerns the distinct and proper roles of the sexes, from a recognition of which flows the mutual attraction between them.

With differences in architecture, in accent, in dress and in manner and customs everywhere giving way to the monotony of fashion and expedience, it may seem unavoidable that differences in sex should also be blurred and even negated until an expressed preference for bodily intimacy with one's own sex is hailed by crusaders for liberation as a mark of enlightenment. But it is hard to believe that such gratuitous 'breakthroughs', which destroy the belief in the mutual dependence of the sexes, will not also dissipate the attraction between them.

In the small scale and more stable society, which seems to lend itself more easily to the good life, the assigning of roles and the encouraging of variety is of the essence even if the prevailing variety is not one that changes much over time. One aspect of this variety is, of course, the cultivation of differences between men and women with respect to role, dress, manners and accomplishments, all tending to accentuate their real and believed differences. This traditional emphasis on the distinctiveness of the sexes, and their complementarity, acts both to enhance the mystery of sex and to maintain the family as the centre and basis of the social order.[20]

To conclude, the modern movements for women's liberation, supported as they are by the blessings and perfunctory endeavours of economic liberals, are, when viewed in historical perspective, patently instrumental to the forces of economic growth and technology. They extend the capitalist ethic to women, luring them out of their homes into the hurly-burly of the marketplace. What is more, in so far as the forces making for sustained economic growth continue unabated, there is not likely to be any let-up of this social pressure on women. For, as indicated earlier (Chapter 24), such pressure has been generated by that minor technological revolution of the last half-century directed to perfecting domestic labour-saving appliances – vacuum-cleaners, refrigerators, washing machines, electric mixers, and so on – which (when supplemented by childcaring services) diminishes the manifest need for women in the home for the first time in history.

Soon, though not soon enough for the militants, they will all be economically as 'independent' as men; as free to compete for jobs on the open market, or to collect unemployment pay; as free to acquire skills through present sacrifices, and to enter the professions on equal terms with men. Whether they will be any happier than they were once the process of their assimilation into the workforce is completed, and no vestige of female privilege is left to them, remains to be seen. Needless to remark, the excitements that accompany the initial legislative and institutional victories of this seemingly inevitable movement cannot endure. Going to work each day, in factory, mine or office, whatever be the rates of pay, has not been regarded by men as a particularly exhilarating experience. Nor, as a whole, have they claimed to find, in their role of daily worker, that independence and fulfilment which the ardent advocates of more economic opportunity for women seem to anticipate. But this is by the way.

Chapter 36

The Moral Code

Since, under any form of social organisation, men are occasionally exposed to circumstances that prompt their darker impulses or, at least, tempt them to follow their immediate interests to the detriment of others, and since, also, no means of deterrence can be wholly or even largely effective, the security and welfare of society depend ultimately on the checks that individuals willingly impose on their own actions. In so far as these checks operate automatically, in that they arise from men's consciences, they are likely to be the expression of some moral code implanted into them at a tender age, even though they are reinforced at times by a desire for social approval or by a fear of social reprisal.

Not all moral codes, however, are equally effective. Nor are they all equally satisfactory. Some, for example, will so extend themselves in response to the dominant aspirations of an epoch as to be unduly repressive of spontaneous expression of one sort or another. At other times, the prevailing moral code may be so weak and uncertain as to leave society open to internal collapse or external conquest. Be that as it may, the main questions which come to the fore in connection with morality and the good society are that of private versus public morality, and that of secular versus religious morality.

The fashionable though insipid expression used today for a private morality that is also a selfish morality (if that is not a contradiction in terms) is the expression of a right 'to do one's own thing' – the belief in each individual's right to follow his own inclinations untroubled by social conventions or the opinions of others. Although the phrase passes as part of the legal tender of the so-called counterculture, and is properly understood as an attitude of modest defiance against established authority, it also has pretensions to affinity with uncompromising individualism especially when the pursuit of self-interest is extended to non-pecuniary ends. What is pertinent to our inquiry, however, are the social implications of this maxim of individual behaviour which, though obvious enough, have not been recognised – least of all by those who, anxious to be seen always in the van of progress, are now captivated by the antics and abberations of the young.

A community in which each person invariably did 'his own thing', whether or not his particular thing was inspired by deep conviction or by the whim of the moment, would not last long. No one need tax his imagination to realise that one person's thing can be another person's 'antithing'. Of course, where one's thing is no more than some harmless self-indulgence, such as a mustard bath three times a day or a daily breakfast of oysters and strawberries, no important issues arise. A liberal society does not proscribe personal eccentricities that have no direct and tangible effect on others. But, to move to the other extreme, if one's thing includes the occasional indulgence in rape or arson, or even the fun of driving on the wrong side of the road, its exercise is clearly incompatible with the wellbeing of society at large.[21]

To put the matter more generally, the smaller is the degree of consensus with respect to morals, the smaller is the likelihood of maintaining a viable society, much less a good one. Since one of the chief functions of a moral code is to protect the members of a society from the untoward consequences arising from the actions of any individual or group, such a code will inevitably seek also to establish acceptance of the golden rule of personal conduct or the liberal maxim of individual freedom.[22] Doing one's 'own thing' becomes socially defensible, then, only so long as the thing being done is socially trivial; so long, that is, as no one else in society is put to any discernible and unavoidable expense or inconvenience by the indulgence of any one in doing his 'own thing'.

We may now ask: what influence is exerted by economic growth on the moral code?

In as much as modern economic growth assumes rapid technological change which, in its turn, produces rapid institutional change, the young come to a different understanding of the world than their parents. Their feelings about the world are different. The natural conflict and impatience between generations are now reinforced by a new and formidable secular dimension. What is more, there is little consensus among the young generation themselves at this juncture in history. Many, indeed, are uncertain whether the traditional morality has any relevance to the world they live in. They are surrounded by fashionable escapist movements and organised licentiousness on an unprecedented scale, activities that are partly rationalised by youthful rejections of 'the whole rotten system'. They move also among lank-haired, unkempt, flower-children living in a grubby paradise atop the debris of the affluent society in a continuous daze of song and sentiment. And they meet militant activists and sexual deviants who affect to derive their animus from unfathomable depths of feeling – this source of inspiration being thought enough to justify any action no matter how barbarous or perverted. These motley social phenomena, along with a new stir of concern for the fate of our planet, have moved in to fill the void left by the decline of a traditional morality, a decline of morality that is the counterpart of the ascendancy of the scientific spirit.

There is, naturally enough, much talk today of 'moral relativism'. For in an age of rapid material change, it may be thought proper that the norms of society should also be in a state of perpetual change. No rule of conduct would, in such circumstances, be binding, and society would have to resign itself to expending much thought and energy in the task of revising the rules accordingly.

But a plastic morality, one continually remoulded to the apparent requirements of a society in the throes of technological and material change, is no part of our quest. Since the moral code, like other institutions of the good society, is to be designed for the satisfaction of men, it is pertinent to observe that an absolute morality has decided advantages over a relative one – and not only so on grounds of economy. For sure, society would prefer to be spared the anguish of continual self-examination, the exhaustion of redebating fundamental questions, and the effort and expense of readapting the altering institutions in the light of new developments.

Such a continual process of adaptation is, in any event, not likely to be successful. Can any moral system be effective, can it be accepted by members of society as binding, when it is openly acknowledged that all the rules are, in the last resort, no more than instruments of social expedience improvised by a thoughtful body of citizens expressly for the style of life that emerges from the existing, though transitional, stage in the development of science and technology?

It is more than just possible that only an absolute morality, one that, in essentials, transcends historical change, can provide people with that abiding sense of security they seek. Men by nature desire permanence and absolute truth, at least in the greater things. They become disillusioned, of course. But the amount of disillusion they can bear with is limited. Most men want a transcendental law, a permanent code of right and wrong, placed far above the realm of mortals, impervious to the flux of history and to the ebb and flow of events.

But whether my surmise is right, whether belief in a permanent code of ethics is imperative for the good society, the moral law we have inherited is not likely to survive our scientific age – an age in which social codes, customs and conventions are the subjects of detached scrutiny by troops of ambitious academics who invariably find in favour of historical relativity; an age in which matters once held sacred are now the stuff of popular television programmes, there to be pulled out and turned about in endless debate until every ounce of faith is wrung out of them.

Chapter 37

The Great Myths

A related question to the one posed near the end of the preceding chapter, whether belief in a permanent code of ethics is imperative for a good society, raises another question. Assuming the answer to be affirmative, can this permanent code of ethics endure within a wholly secular society?

In a small community of saints, or in a school of intellectuals dedicated to the pursuit of truth, disinterested adherence to an adopted code of behaviour is not impossible. But for the mass of ordinary people, the case is quite different. There has been no historical precedent for a code of ethics that is not embedded in an organised religion. And one cannot feel optimistic about any venture to sever an ethical code from the community's belief in the divine origin of that code. There will be times when some members of a community begin to have doubts on some points of doctrine, or regard the adopted religion partly as superstition. But if the moral law is ever explicitly recognised by all members, or even by a sizable minority, to rest ultimately on reason, then it may be expected that reasonable men, and, alas, not only reasonable men, will challenge its supremacy from time to time, so weakening its authority.

Worse still, it will be hard for any man, guided solely by the light of reason, to avoid the conclusion that it is generally in his own interests to disregard the moral law, if he can get away with it, whenever obedience to it conflicts with his immediate desires or interests. For the larger society is, the smaller will be the individual's impact on it. Thus, if in following the moral law, he sacrifices his own interests to the common good, his example will virtually be lost on society at large, whereas the material benefits he will reap from any selfless action are likely to be negligible. On the same reasoning, the adverse repercussions that he himself will suffer following any successful infringement of the moral code in pursuit of his own interests are also likely to be negligible. Thus, in the light of pure reason, the pursuit of enlightened self-interest alone in large and mobile societies would require that each individual disregard the moral code wherever he believed he might gain from doing so – even though it could be shown to be to the common advantage of all men to uphold it.[23]

No moral law, no matter how enlightened, will command the allegiance of men if it is known to be founded explicitly on considerations of social expediency. Instinctive submission to its precepts is ensured only if they are writ in lapidary on the inner layers of the conscience, distinct and inerasable, resistant alike to exemptions and concessions. In effect, it must trace its origin to a divine lawgiver, in consequence of which alterations to meet changing conditions are not to be thought of. Indeed, there are to be ritual deterrents against such thoughts. Hence, the Talmudic injunction to 'Build a fence around the Torah!'; that is, to set up strict rules of conduct so as to discourage trespass on more fundamental matters that lie closer to the centre of the holy law. It is true that religions have evolved over time or, rather, changed over time along with the rise and fall of civilisations. It is also true that there have been periods of acute conflict between competing religions, often enough when they were being used for worldly ends. But it does not follow from these facts that the mass of people in any historical age were aware of a relation between economic and political conditions, on the one hand, and the prevailing religion on the other. All past religions have been of divine origin. They have centred on personal gods, who were believed to be involved closely in the affairs of men. And whatever the religion adhered to at the time, it was held to be true for all time and for all conditions of men.

Religions in the past are then in clear contrast to 'private' religions, or to secular or humanist religions, with their faith either in some abstraction such as the 'universal spirit' or the 'life force', or else in Man himself or (what comes to the same thing) in Science.

In order to avoid misunderstanding, however, I should add that an unquestioned acceptance of the moral law does not imply a suspension of reason. There are questions of interpretation to be resolved, and questions of priority where different principles appear to conflict. Extenuating circumstances surrounding an offence have to be considered. Above all, judgment must be constrained by a recognition of human fallibility, and justice must be tempered with mercy. The essential point of the preceding paragraphs is simply this: that the core of the moral law has to be accepted as sacred, and beyond the will of men to alter; indeed, that any trespass into the area of religious injunction surrounding it is to be regarded as dangerous and exceptional.

It is far from implausible to believe that men should want to find God, a being placed in judgment above them, one to whom they can turn for love and comfort. As Sebastian de Grazia has cogently argued, men do seek an authority (a father figure as psychologists would say), a super-being who is a source of understanding and compassion. There is, apparently, a need to worship, if only because it serves to open the heart. But, with the growth of science and the spread of secular knowledge, the ordinary person in the West has lost his capacity to believe in an omnipresent and benevolent Deity. Lost innocence cannot be retreived. Once we have announced the fatal news, that God is dead, we cannot go back to the days when there was joy of belief and when there was hope beyond the grave.

This is sad enough in itself. But if, as I believe, a categorically imperative morality cannot long endure in separation from the belief in its divine origin, the liberal West may be passing through a twilight state, its social cohesion shored up only by the crumbling remains of its moral capital. In that case, only a new despotism will be able to check the trend to social disintegration.[24]

Chapter 38

Personal Freedom

A society in which public and private behaviour is strongly influenced by the society's acceptance of a moral code might seem, in these 'permissive' times, to be uncongenial to the enjoyment of personal freedom.

However, the notion of some irreconcilable conflict between personal freedom and the restraints imposed by strong traditions, between individual creativity, on the one hand, and the customs and conventions of society, on the other, does not stand up to inquiry.

The term 'liberty' or 'freedom' is, first of all, conceived differently by different political movements. There is, in particular, a divergence of views: by those who seek to conserve the existing constitutional forms of a libertarian society, and by those who seek a radical departure from them.

Since the rhetoric of freedom extends to all conceivable desiderata, I restrict the term 'personal freedom' to the conditional freedom to voice one's social and political views in public; to the freedom to engage in any legitimate activity, such as setting up a business or entering a profession or occupation, or to joining a club or society; to the freedom to travel or to migrate without being subject to state control, or regulation or pressure; and to freedom from arbitrary police powers of entry, search, arrest or detention. I do not intend the term to be understood in any of its popular extensions to indicate an absence of hardship or deprivation, as in the phrases 'freedom from want' or 'freedom from pain' or 'freedom from drudgery'; nor yet to indicate a state of permissiveness such as 'freedom to love' or 'freedom to do one's thing'.

The classical liberation conceives of liberty in terms of a constitution that extends to the individual the freedom to avail himself of opportunities for enjoyment and self-betterment so far as the exercise of that freedom does not result in any reduction of the welfare of others. This familiar conception of liberty is consistent with that expressed by John Stuart Mill, and it is comprehended by the more conservative maxim that the protection of society is the only legitimate consideration in any proposal to limit a person's freedom to act as he sees fit.

The phrase 'freedom of expression' is, of course, much misused. The phrase today is invoked as a rallying cry in connection with the trend towards increasing licence of pornographic entertainment or reading matter. And the pertinent issues are usually evaded by insisting that 'the public has a right to choose'.

Since once a thing is made legally available, it would be absurd to prevent people from availing themselves accordingly, the critical and prior question is whether the thing ought, or ought not to be, legally offered to the public. And a moment's reflection suggests that the public is apparently content that a number of marketable items should, in fact, be withheld from the market or else be offered there only in very special circumstances. Firearms and explosives, literature exhorting others to violence, and a wide variety of drugs and chemicals are at present among such items. The principle that justifies such restrictions is, broadly speaking, the protection of society from internal disruption – a grave consideration against which the advantages of free enterprise must contend.

Although freedom of expression takes precedence over freedom of enterprise, the former also is circumscribed in some respects (recourse in public to obscene language) or in some circumstances (calling out 'fire!' in a crowded theatre, or urging a mob to attack persons or property). Thus, all freedoms have to be justified in utilitarian terms, as serving the welfare of society, and proscribed or limited wherever they threaten society's welfare.

This principle is indeed repeatedly acknowledged in the classic justification of the lesser freedom – freedom of private enterprise – by Adam Smith in his famous *Wealth of Nations*. There it is justified by the argument that, under a given framework of laws, freedom of competitive enterprise will redound to the common good. A number of clear exceptions, however, are elaborated by Adam Smith, and many more have since been added by economists, all of them deriving their sanction, ultimately, from the welfare of society.

There are reasons enough for regarding free enterprise in pornographic entertainment as falling within that category of exceptions, in as much as the spread of its products raises considerable misgivings about the immediate and longer term effects on the character, the cohesion and the satisfaction of society. Public debate on the legitimation of private enterprise in pornographic materials conducted by reference to any other terms – those of personal freedom, for instance – is impertinent and futile.[25]

On this conception of the limits of freedom, for instance, there can be no constitutional right of unfettered free speech on all subjects. If the mere truth of a statement were the governing criterion, there would be difficulties enough in determining where it lay – which is one reason for allowing all opinions on social and political issues to be freely expressed. But even where the truth is believed to be certain, the broader principle of the social interest need not sanction its propagation. The law of libel, for instance, does not regard the truth of an accusation as sufficient reason for its publication; it must also be evident that it is in the public interest to know the facts in the case. The same considerations apply to a far graver threat which may arise from the dissemination of new ideas. Allowing them, always, to be closer to the truth than existing ideas, their absorption into society may well serve to diminish its sense of security and satisfaction.[26]

At all events, the fruits of liberty, on the classical view, cannot grow to maturity unless they are supported by a strong framework of law founded on a social consensus. The political nature of liberty, that is, requires constraints on the action of the individual, a view that is in stark contrast to the anarchic notion of liberty which would abandon all constraints on individual freedom. For unless the state of anarchy could be counted on soon to generate a moral renaissance, each family would live in fear of the liberties that others might wish to exercise. The unavoidable result of so insecure an existence would be the formation of pacts and alliances designed to reduce the dangers and fears besetting individuals in exchange for some necessary reduction in their liberties and for some specific obligations, a process of consolidation which, if continued, would culminate once more in the sovereign state. It is difficult, therefore, to imagine a state of anarchic liberty, save as a temporary phenomenon, the result of a breakdown of the prevailing social order.

Thus, when it is asserted that without a moral consensus on the limitations of individual freedom there cannot be any enduring liberty, the statement is made with the classical conception of liberty in mind, recognising that security is a precondition of the enjoyment of liberty. Put in its elemental form, then, the argument is that in order to enjoy some liberties, the members of society must collectively agree to sacrifice those particular liberties which, if exercised, jeopardise the wellbeing of others. Thus the renunciation of any right to engage in those actions that are intended, or likely to harm others becomes an integral part of the moral consensus of a civilised society, and one that is reinforced by penal law.

Moreover, in addition to a consensus that is embodied in law, there can be, as indicated earlier, a consensus covering a wide range of customs and conventions; indeed, covering all those forms of behaviour that, in a traditional society, regulate the terms of social intercourse. Of course, many of those who are, today, prey to the capricious gusts of fashion might affect to discern in such traditional forms no more than a web of conformity stifling to individual expression; the social sanction for them also stems from the same broad consideration invoked to protect members of the same community from hurt by others. Although it is clearly more urgent that society enforce sanctions against robbery, assault and murder, a code of behaviour that serves effectively to diminish the exposure of its members to embarrassment, abuse, scorn, insult or shock in their personal and social intercourse is surely also of inestimable value in enhancing wellbeing. Indeed, if we pondered for a while on the embroidery of custom and convention in a traditional society, we should soon convince ourselves that there are distinct advantages in knowing, without a shadow of doubt, just how to deport ourselves in a wide variety of social circumstances.

If, therefore, the prevailing customs and conventions are appropriate in that they foster good citizenship and promote social intercourse, no sensible man would find it onerous in complying with them while following his own inclinations in more intimate or creative matters. Some non-comformity of conventions may, of course, be tolerated in a stable society. Indeed, provided a man was not ostentatiously offensive, his eccentricities would be welcome as adding some local character to the neighbourhood in which he lived.

Accepting the proposition that the enjoyment of liberty is not possible without adherence to a moral code, and that social life can be enhanced by a far-reaching consensus on appropriate forms of behaviour – on what is right and wrong, what is proper and improper, and what is good taste and bad taste – then any dissolution of the moral code or the social consensus threatens the enjoyment of liberty and social life.

This dissolution of consensus is, however, one of the byproducts of continuing economic growth, at least in already affluent and liberal societies. For with the ascendancy of the scientific spirit and the diffusion of secular education, the belief in and the respect for the great religions are undermined. And when these crumble so also does the traditional basis of mankind's moral conduct.

Another familiar feature of modern society, the mass media, play its part in the process. Not only in making repeated, albeit unnecessary, attacks on a declining faith in the scriptures, but also, as mentioned in Chapter 24, in offering the public alternative and sceptical views on all aspects of morality, leaving the bewildered citizen without a principle to cling to.

There is certainly no lack of evidence today of increasing discrepancies within public opinion about what is proper and improper, and what is right and wrong. But whatever the outcome of these dissensions, we appear to be entering a stage of increasing uncertainty and apprehension concerning the purpose of life and the moral basis of our civilisation. The spread of such morbid doubts and obsessive self-examination hinders the enjoyment of liberty and is incompatible with the good society.

Be that as it may, economic growth also constricts the area of personal freedom in a more direct and less subtle way; as a result, that is, of technological innovations having specific social and political consequences. This thesis is of topical interest, for it poses a dilemma to growthmen who are just beginning to perceive a connection between the rise of technology and the decline of liberty. Since a chapter alone cannot do justice to the many facets of this thesis, the whole of Part VI is devoted to their illustration and analysis.

Before moving on to Part VI, however, it might be as well to guard against a possible misunderstanding. Repeatedly, in Part V, I have drawn attention to the ways in which the growth of science and technology has acted to dissipate moral consensus, patriotic sentiment and the myths on which they rest. Since such terms today evoke a variety of emotional responses, not all of them benign, I shall risk boring the reader by going over the meaning to be attached to them in the present context, and by setting bounds to their roles.

First, the moral consensus I speak of has reference to an accepted system of beliefs prevailing within a civilisation about what is good and evil, and what is right and wrong, for a wide range of behaviour, both public and private. It comprehends consensus on the fundamentals of the moral law, on the nature of civic virtue, on sexual mores, on propriety and custom, on what is decent and on what is fair. I have argued that the collapse of such a consensus breeds misunderstanding and anxiety, and results in increasing conflict and violence.

Secondly, the patriotic sentiment I mention is not to be interpreted as jingoism but rather as an expression of a people's pride in its past, in its institutions and traditions, and in its character and genius, without which pride the ideals of selfless public service, the readiness to make sacrifices for the common weal, must wither away. I have argued that where this source of pride and complaisancy has dried up, public morale is low, checks to self-seeking and hedonistic excesses are weak, and the nation is vulnerable to internecine conflict and external conquest.

Finally, the myths in question include not only the great monotheistic religions but also all the supernatural beliefs that guided and influenced the behaviours of societies large and small. And they include not only the sacred myths but also the secular ones – those sustaining beliefs held by a tribe, a folk, a race, a nation, about its heroes, and about its heroic origins and its heroic achievements.

The importance of the myths in imparting stability and cohesion to societies has been consistently underestimated, if not overlooked, by modern humanists and enlightened reformers. The view I take is that, without such myths, patriotic pride and social consensus cannot long endure. Once such myths are called into question, once they are exposed and disbelief sets in, the libertarian society begins to disintegrate. And since, indeed, popular belief in the great myths is manifestly on the wane this process of social disintegration has already begun – although, as indicated, the omens and portents are apt to be misinterpreted as instances of the new permissiveness, and therefore as an extension of personal freedoms.

However, and this is the point of this addendum, it must not be supposed by the reader that I am asserting that folk pride and moral consensus are among the highest goods on any ethical scale. They are to be regarded only as instrumental to social wellbeing. By themselves they are not enough either for contentment or for the good life we are concerned with.

I have taken the precaution, in developing my thesis, to restrict chronological comparisons to the last few decades. But I am not averse at this juncture to range farther over the past. I am ready to concede that even the most casual knowledge of history is sure to convince any one that the prevalence of patriotism and consensus within a society does not preclude the possibility of its engaging in acts of injustice and savagery. The historical age itself, and the stage of economic and moral development, should not be overlooked in any judgment of the darker side of a particular civilisation.

Thus, if religious or patriotic fervour in the past has been diverted into predatory wars – as, indeed, has been the fervour for liberty, fraternity or justice – it is not very surprising. In this sadly imperfect world of ours, of power-seeking groups and demonic personalities, there is no shortage of examples to illustrate the unresisted temptations to subvert powerful mass sentiments, both religious and ideological, to unworthy ends. Indeed, it would be hard on the historian to determine whether, over the centuries, more crimes against humanity have been committed in the name of justice, in the name of freedom or in the name of God.

However, my contention has been that patriotic sentiment and moral consensus are *necessary* for the cohesion, stability and contentment of a society. They are not by any means *sufficient*. But being necessary it follows that their continued erosion brings us closer to a day of reckoning. When the depletion of our inherited 'moral capital' has gone on a little longer we shall discover that there is no common sentiment, no common purpose, no common faith, left to hold together our so-called pluralist society. Only a rapid expansion of the repressive power of the state will then prevent a descent into the maelstrom.

NOTES FOR PART V

Chapter 25

1 For some reasons for believing there is likely to be a world famine, see Gordon Rattray Taylor (1975, ch. 12).

Chapter 26

2 The increased incidence of cancer and coronary diseases may be thought by some to overstate their danger since people who, in earlier times, would have died of smallpox or dysentry or diphtheria now live on, eventually to succumb to cancer or heart attacks. But not by much, bearing in mind that cancer is the leading cause of death today among children under 15.

3 This being the thirty-ninth item on the list of the 100 innovations believed likely to be adopted before the end of the twentieth century by Herman Kahn and A. J. Wiener (1967).

4 As Garrett Hardin (1972, p. 59) puts it:
'Science is an occupation in which most experiments fail. . . . Confronted with any new untried nostrum, a scientist, if called upon to place a bet, will bet that it won't work. Such is the conservative judgment.
The overwhelming probability is that any newly proposed remedy won't work. More: experience shows that there is an almost equally high probability that the new nostrum will cause actual harm.
The most intelligent way of dealing with the unknown is in terms of probability. Therefore we should assume that each remedy proposed will do positive harm, until the most exhaustive tests and carefully examined logic indicate otherwise'.

5 Gordon Rattray Taylor (1972) offers some evidence for the interesting hypothesis that every significant change in the pattern of a man's life, whether the change is favourable or unfavourable, has untoward effects on his health.

Chapter 27

6 The case for establishing separate areas for communities of people who would be glad to disencumber themselves of motorised conveniences in return for the resulting collective amenity is discussed at length in Chapter 3 of my *Making the World Safe for Pornography* (1973).

Chapter 28

7 The thesis that the intellectual classes have suffered from a reduction in leisure, regarded as the time available for intellectual activities, is argued in a fascinating article 'What price economic growth' by Anne and Tibor Scitovsky (reproduced in Tibor Scitovsky, 1964).

8 Professor Lester Thurow (1972).

9 The passage continues:
'. . . a nervous breakdown of the sort which is already common enough in England and the United States amongst the wives of the well-to-do classes, unfortunate women, many of them, who have been deprived by their wealth of their traditional tasks and occupations – who cannot find it sufficiently amusing, when deprived of the spur of economic necessity, to cook and clean and mend, yet are quite unable to find anything more amusing. . . . To those who sweat for their daily bread, leisure is a longed-for sweet – until they get it'.

The lines are taken from the chapter on 'Economic possibilities for our grandchildren', in E. Johnson (1971).

10 An amusing account of how this comes about can be found in Staffan Linder's well-written book, *The Harried Leisure Class* (1970), which also includes a mathematical appendix for the more fastidious reader.

Independently of Linder's work, the same ideas have been formalised by Gary Becker in an excellent article, 'A theory of the allocation of time' (1965). Both Linder and Becker introduced their theses by reference to the rise in real wages, the result of the growth in productivity. Since both their models assume (unrealistically) that each person is free to choose his hours of work, they infer also that time is equally scarce, at the margin, with respect both to work and to consumption activity.

Chapter 29

11 Philip Slater (1970), makes the interesting point that although the chaperoned girl of Mediterranean countries is compared, often scornfully, with the emancipated American girl who travels about the world on her own and knows 'how to look after herself', it is the former, who in the event, finds the sexual experience more enjoyable and less problematic than her American counterpart. The Mediterranean damsel has to be chaperoned simply because she is not inhibited. The modern American girl, in contrast, has in effect internalised her chaperone – and, to such an extent, that even when the conditions of sexual activity are acceptable to her, she is unable wholly to divest herself of its vigilance.

In this respect, the greater sexual permissiveness of today's young does not alter the situation. All it does is to underline their disenchantment with their parents' values, or what they imagine their parents' values to be, and their cynicism about the achievement-oriented society. But this reaction of itself can do little to erase the impress made on their unconscious minds by early childhood training for the disciplines of modern society.

12 Restricting his analysis of the revolting young to the United States, Philip Slater (1970) puts some of the blame for their indulgent but stifled upbringing by overfond parents, or by determined mothers, on the influence of Dr Spock's books, which, however, were less in vogue in Western Europe. In fact, Spock was writing for an achieving society in which 'enlightened' middle class parents (who, as indicated earlier, include a large proportion of the working class) were trying hard to throw off the Victorian heritage, as they imagined it, while at the same time trying to rear successful and creative children. Parental love and

indulgence became the order of the day. But they were lavished on the children not in order to encourage impulse enjoyment, but in order to encourage expressions of achievement.

Chapter 30

13 Gordon Rattray Taylor (1975, p. 87) mentions the Kitty Genovese episode, the girl who 'was stalked and murdered in New York, while more than twenty people looked on from their windows, without so much as telephoning the police'. He mentions a similar incident in Liverpool, and goes on to reflect: 'Perhaps, seen through a window in the cold illumination of street-lamps, Kitty Genovese appeared little different from the familiar images of violence on the television screen. Maybe watching television fosters a sense of remoteness and impersonality'.

But it is not only television or the motor car that fosters impersonality. As is indicated in Chapter 31, consumer innovation generally is guided by considerations that ultimately ensure this feature.

14 There is, seemingly, an imperitive need for many people today to regard themselves as enlightened and progressive. They must avow that retributive punishment is barbaric whether or not it has a deterrent effect, a position they support by effectively defining antisocial behaviour as a form of sickness. However, the full implications of this point of view often escapes them.

If a man who commits a crime is no more to blame than is a faulty machine, then a man who performs a good deed is not to be praised either. In both cases, the man's action is the product of forces beyond his control. But if, in fact, men do not really choose, if choice is but an illusion, there can be no good or evil in the usual meaning of the words. There can only be health and sickness; and diagnosis and therapy have to replace moral judgment and moral injunction. It must follow, also, that the great themes of art and literature, of legend and epic poetry, are misconceived. For if a man cannot choose, he cannot be responsible for his acts.

This view of man as, basically, a complex machine that can sometimes go wrong has appeal to the technocratic mind which thinks of solutions to social problems in terms of system controls. It would justify a Huxley-type Brave New World in which social stability was maintained by subjecting all humans to early conditioning and to massive doses of drugs in order to keep them in a state of permanent contentment.

15 Of course, there are people who continue stubbornly to believe that, *ceteris paribus*, the deterrent effect of punishment has no relation (or even an inverse relation) to its severity. In such cases the appeal to good sense is useless, though such people may be disturbed by a recent summary of the affirmative evidence reached by a number of recent statistical studies in an article by Gordon Tullock (1974).

Chapter 31

16 In this connection, see Vance Packard's (1972) account of postwar developments.

Chapter 33

17 An argument that is contrived to persuade us that some particular innovation – such as the abolition of the family and its replacement by some alternative organisation – would better meet the demands of a community that is being shaped by modern technological developments,

cannot be admitted. As I remind the reader from time to time, we are not engaged in a search for ways of adapting our lives in order to meet the demands of technology. We are seeking, rather, for the technologies, among other means, that best meet the demands of the good life.

18 It might be countered that in the more punctiliously regulated households the constraints on being able to express one's feelings were rather stifling. But the change in question is largely one of form only. Joy or anger, tenderness or resentment, can also be conveyed in ways that are less explicit and emphatic than are common today in servantless families. In altercations, for instance, the conventions were understood differently. And if, in the circumstances, the accent was more on articulation than on gesture and volume, there was no loss of communication and some saving of dignity.

Chapter 35

19 However, the extreme hostility that such apparent economic inequalities arouse in many women is a reaction peculiar to this day and age.

The wilder blasts of the trumpet against the iniquitous regiment of men, and the coarse language and more extreme tactics of a part of the feminist movement, express an almost uncontrollable vindictiveness which, although it can be explained by the individual psychology of the offenders, can be explained also as a social phenomenon. Thus, I would place it in the same category with other extremist movements and explain it in terms of a reaction to the growing frustrations and strains which, I argue, arise in our competitive and rapidly changing society; a society tending to produce innovations that effectively raise the level of apprehension and estrangement.

20 The importance of the family as the basic building block in a liberal democratic society is the main theme of Salvador de Madariaga (1958).

Chapter 36

21 Similar observations apply to prejudices on which people act. No one is much upset to discover that some people prefer brown bread and others prefer white. The market will provide for both. But in a multiracial society, one in which, say, the numbers of blacks or whites form a significant proportion of the total population (say, over 1 per cent), then racial preferences, or prejudices, can be translated into action. If, for example, 20 per cent of the black population hate the whites, and come to believe that they have a moral right to hate them, then only the strong arm of the law, everywhere in evidence attempting to enforce adherence to rigid principles of impartiality in social and economic affairs, can prevent racial antagonism from erupting into racial strife. Indeed, only an eventual consensus that racial prejudices, privately held, ought never to be allowed to inform policy, or to influence one's actions so as knowingly to cause harm to others, can release society from so burdensome a strain, both psychological and financial.

How to bring about such a consensus beginning with an unpromising situation is, of course, the besetting problem in the United States. It is unlikely, however, to be solved by the present policy of the 'race relations industry' there. For whatever else it merits, it is one that, in effect, never permits the black-white issue to sink for an instant from the consciousness of American citizens. On the contrary, the existing rift between the races is given prominence and made manifest at every turn and in every quarter. One's nose is so rubbed into the issue, that it is hard not to feel antagonised, whatever one's views.

Nothing strikes the casual visitor to the United States so much as the numbers game approach to black placation and, more recently, to feminist placation, a game that is sanctioned by the aspirational notion of 'participation'. A business corporation or government department having less than *x* per cent of its employees black, or less than *y* per cent of them women (where *x* and *y* are, respectively, the overall percentages of blacks and women in the American population), may, at any time, be charged with 'discrimination', and legal actions can be instigated against it. A university having fewer blacks than *x* per cent, or fewer women than *y* per cent, on its teaching staff, on its administrative staff, or on its student population, is also vulnerable to such charges, and also subjected to pressures somehow to generate the ideal mixture. The manifest absurdity of a university, a seat of learning's, being influenced or, worse, being guided, by so irrelevant a criterion in its selection of staff and students, and, indeed, the explicit recognition of the absurdity, have been unable to prevail against the pervasive and intimidating atmosphere created by the American race-relations industry.

Other achievements of this hard-working industry are more difficult to appraise. It is, for instance, difficult to find a poster, or package advertisement, or television commercial, in which more than three people are represented, but one of them must, conspicuously, be a black (unless, of course, they are depicted as 'baddies'). Presumably, this naive strategem, based on an interpretation of a Pavlov or a Skinner, is designed to condition people to accept a judicious mixture of black and white as the normal thing.

Whether it will act to prevent or reduce racial prejudice among the young is a debatable point. It must certainly annoy those already prejudiced. And it is hard to believe that even the most enlightened American citizen does not, occasionally, feel heartily sick of those omnipresent reminders that he must behave himself nicely in the race relations society.

There must surely be more subtle and effective ways of bringing about harmony between the races, without which the American society – or, the British society, for that matter – can never become a good society.

22 The golden rule, which bids us to 'do unto others that which you would have them do unto you' appears more 'positive' than the liberal maxim that would have the individual circumscribe his freedom whereever it infringed on the freedom of others. Some philosophers will be able to turn out a thesis from this difference. But the maxims are cognate in spirit and a person who is guided by one is likely to be guided by the other also.

Chapter 37

23 An analysis of such situations, and many revealing examples, are given in the classic work by Mancur Olson, *The Logic of Collective Action* (1965).

24 Evidence of incipient social disintegration is provided by Gordon Rattray Taylor (1975, Parts II and III).

For some reflections on the trend to despotism in the West, see Robert Heilbroner, *The Human Prospect* (1974).

Chapter 38

25 Some reflections on the social consequences of the new freedom to engage in pornographic enterprises can be found in the title essay of my volume, *Making the World Safe for Pornography* (1973).

See also: *The Public Interest* (1971); David Holbrook (1972); Victor Cline (1974); and my review of the latter (1976).

26 I have touched on this issue in Chapter 39, on the great myths, in connection with the spread of secular and scientific knowledge.

Part VI

On Technology and Freedom

Chapter 39

Capitalism and Freedom

Liberal economists or, less ambiguously, libertarian economists have long regarded a competitive private enterprise system not only as an economically efficient institution but also as one of the great bulwarks of liberty. This view has been eloquently argued by a number of outstanding economists in our own day. For instance, Frederick Hayek in his celebrated book, *The Road to Serfdom* (1944), quotes Adam Smith as follows:

'The statesman who should attempt to direct private people in what manner they ought to employ their capitals, would not only load himself with a most unnecessary attention, but assume an authority which could safely be trusted to no council whatever, and which would nowhere be so dangerous as in the hands of a man who had the folly and presumption to fancy himself fit to exercise it'.

Elaborating on the nature of this danger, Hayek goes on to remark:

'Once the communal sector, in which the state controls all the means, exceeds a certain proportion of the whole, the effects of its actions dominate the whole system. Although the state controls directly the use of only a large part of the available resources, the effects of its decisions on the remaining part of the economic system become so great that indirectly it controls almost everything. Where, as was for example true in Germany as early as 1928, the central and local authorities directly control the use of more than half the national income (according to an official German estimate then, 53 per cent) they control indirectly almost the whole economic life of the nation. There is, then, scarely an individual end which is not dependent for its achievement on the action of the state, and the 'social scale of values' which guides the state's action must embrace practically all individual ends.'

Hayek might well have carried the argument a stage further. For the beliefs, popular among socialists, that in a democracy the state itself is, in the last resort, controlled by the electorate, or that a free press ensures the existence of an 'open society', are less than half-truths. When one considers the sheer size of the modern nation state, the control exercised by the electorate over the full range of activities of a government that absorbs close to, or more than, 50 per cent of the entire national product is limited to broad direction only. Its control of detail is remote and ineffectual. The continuing concern of the politically minded citizen is, of necessity then, directed in the main to contemporary bread-and-butter issues, on which issues politicians and political parties base their bid for office.

Thus, a bureaucracy that has come to embrace about half the entire economy, whose tentacles are spread wide in all directions, is not easily reformed, or even influenced, by a political party's brief tenure of office. States grow within states. There are groups within subcommittees within committees within sections within departments, the activities of which, nay, the very existence of which, are unknown to the public and unsuspected by politicians. For example, under the general rubric of what is today known as 'research and development' or R & D (especially R & D associated with internal and external defence), projects are undertaken and experiments conducted which, were they known, would outrage the public. To quote an instance I came across at the time of writing, the *Sunday Times* (6 July 1975) reported the remarks of an American psychologist, Dr Thomas Narut, at a Nato conference held in Oslo, that convicted murderers were among those selected and trained for naval commando-type operations and also for serving as 'hitmen' in American embassies. Their training included the showing of films of violence designed to enable them to dissociate their feelings from the act of violence. Whether or not the report is true in substance, it is plausible enough, and only one of many reports that occasionally come to the surface, create a stir and then are forgotten.

Be that as it may, the good fight against the persistent tendency towards government expansion never falters from lack of support. Among the more outstanding economists today who, through their writings and speeches, have sought and continue to seek actively to arrest the growing encroachment of the power of the state on the diminishing private sector of the economy, perhaps the best-known is Milton Friedman, who would readily affirm today what he wrote in his *Capitalism and Freedom* in 1962: 'The kind of economic organisation that provides economic freedom directly, namely, competitive capitalism, also promotes political freedom because it separates economic power from political power and in this way enables the one to offset the other.'

Declaring that *economic* freedom (in the sense of individual freedom to choose man-made goods) is best realised through competitive markets, Friedman goes onto observe that: 'What the market does is to reduce greatly the range of issues that must be decided through political means, and thereby to minimise the extent to which governments need participate directly in the game. The characteristic feature of action through political channels is that it tends to require or enforce substantial conformity. The great advantage of the market, on the other hand is that it permits wide diversity.' Yet this same competitive private-enterprise system that extends economic freedom acts also, according to Friedman (1962), to promote *political* freedom. For:

'the fundamental threat to freedom is the power to coerce, be it in the hands of a monarch, a dictator, an oligarchy, or a momentary majority. The preservation of freedom requires the elimination of such concentration of power to the fullest possible extent and the dispersal and distribution of whatever power cannot be eliminated – a system of checks and balances. By removing the organisation of economic activity from the control of political authority, the market eliminates this source of coercive power. It enables economic strength to be a check to political power rather than a reinforcement.'

I confess that I am in sympathy with the broad sweep of this argument. Like most of my colleagues in the economics profession I am always ready to concede a presumption in favour of decentralised private enterprise and competitive markets unless convincing reasons to the contrary are adduced – as, of course, they sometimes can be when it comes to the introduction of a public good or the curbing of a public 'bad'. Although the operations of free markets and decentralised enterprise cannot of themselves prevent a gradual degradation of the quality of life or an erosion of moral values, they are surely more congenial to the exercise of effective economic and political freedom than is the concentration of economic power in the hands of giant corporations or, worse, in the hands of the state.

Nevertheless, in spite of the manifest resentment of ordinary citizens at the scale and frequency of government intervention, and in spite of the articulate apprehension of liberals everywhere, in spite even of the occasional resolutions of government spokesmen, the size of the public sector has continued to grow remorselessly in all Western countries since the turn of the century. As recently as the early 1930s, total US government expenditure (federal, state and local) barely amounted to 10 per cent of net national expenditure. By 1940 it had risen to 25 per cent; by 1950 to 29 per cent; and by 1970 to 42 per cent. Although it has not yet topped 50 per cent, the critical proportion beyond which, according to Hayek (1944), the government 'controls indirectly the whole economic life of the nation', and although it is still far from the 60 per cent share of the British government, it does seem to be moving in that direction.

Chapter 40

A Neglected Avenue of Inquiry

The question which, therefore, has to be faced is whether – in addition to the impetus provided by the enthusiasm of planners and technocrats, and by the empire-building propensities of bureaucrats – there is, in fact, a secular tendency for government to expand at the expense of the private sector – in particular, whether this tendency is itself a consequence of rising levels of affluence.

Here, then, is a rich vein of inquiry that has too long been neglected. Its terms of reference may be expressed as follows. Does the process of economic growth itself cause both a diminution in the private sector of the economy and a diminution of individual liberty? Two things may be noticed about the wording of the question.

The first is that an explanation in terms of economic growth does not preclude other, and possibly complementary, explanations. Among the more remarkable social phenomena of the postwar period is the emergence in the West of a shameless manifestation of gross appetite expressing itself in a veritable passion for equality, one that is marked by a growing impatience with privilege or authority whatever its source. The 'revolution of expectations' is transforming itself into what Daniel Bell (1975) calls the 'revolution of rising entitlements' – in effect, a revolution of mass sentiment expressing itself in the demand that the state provide and guarantee whatever discontented majorities or aggrieved minorities deem to be right and proper.

This phenomenon is not surprising. The extension of democracy along with the growth of affluence over the last 100 years has encouraged the spread of egalitarian opinion. Indeed, the demand for the universal extension of opportunity to compete for the economic prizes – popular among the Established Enlightenment before World War II – has been transformed today into a demand to share in whatever economic prizes are won; a demand that is being met, however, not so much through direct income transfers but rather through burgeoning public expenditures on health, education and welfare services generally.

Such an explanation of events – in terms, that is, of democratic and egalitarian forces – is not uncongenial to the liberal mind since it offers hope for the future. The good fight against persistent government encroachment could hardly be waged with conviction unless it were believed that this seeming trend could be checked, if not reversed; that is, unless it were believed that the factors making for more government are not decisive and need not, in the last resort, prevail against the express desires of that enlightened electorate which it is the task of the good liberal economist to bring into being.

From this liberal perspective, at any rate, the public sector in modern democracies grows in response to popular egalitarian demand. And this demand, as it happens, is linked to a strong preference for the government provision of specific services rather than for the straightforward money transfers that are favoured by liberal economists.

Complementary to this explanation in terms of egalitarian or populist sentiment is another: namely, that the growth of government expenditures is directly facilitated by the operation of existing progressive income-tax systems.

Although there is no necessary logical connection between economic growth and the growth of progressive tax systems, there is indeed an historical connection. In Western democracies, at least, economic growth over the last century has been accompanied by greater progression of nominal income-tax rates. This phenomenon is one that many economists regard as one of the direct causes of government expansion. For a progressive tax structure in a growing economy enables the government to collect over time an increasing *proportion* of the national product, especially – as we now know to our cost – in times of inflation. This is the result simply of moving income earners into higher tax brackets. From time to time, of course, nominal tax rates are lowered. But they are not lowered by enough to counteract the aforementioned trend – a fact that makes it easier for governments to expand their activities.

For this reason alone there is a strong case for proportional taxation, though one that will not be argued here,[1] the point of these remarks being only to acknowledge this characteristic property of the progressive tax structure in facilitating and encouraging government expansion.

The second thing to notice about the wording of our inquiry is the phrase 'a diminution of individual liberty'. There is an obvious sense in which, as Milton Friedman (1962) and others have argued, any extension of government activity at the expense of the private sector of the economy itself reduces both the variety of choices open to the citizen and the economic power at his disposal. But the implication of the phrase goes further than this. For, without any significant increase in the government sector of the economy, there can be substantial reductions in individual liberty arising directly out of repressive legislation. What is more, this untoward development may well be inescapable. It may be an unavoidable consequence of the very direction and pattern of economic growth.

The fact that this possibility has not occurred to the liberal economist must be attributed in some part to his ideological commitment to that material progress which he continues to regard, despite the accumulating evidence to the contrary, as a potent solvent of all social obstructions and personal frustrations. In some part also it is due to the economist's habit of thinking about economic growth in terms of a rise in the level, or flow, of an abstract 'real' income.

At best, economists have been satisfied to think about economic growth in terms of better consumer goods which, it is said 'expand the area of choice open to the individual'. Even those liberal economists who recognise the impact of economic growth on environmental amenity favour faster economic growth. To quote Samuel Brittan's remark in his *Capitalism and the Permissive Society* (1973): 'One very attractive way of taking out the fruits of faster economic growth would be to make the working environment itself less abrasive, even at the cost of some sacrifice in production.' As a result, economists have paid little attention to the particular kinds of technological innovation that, accompanying the process of economic expansion, have come to increase, directly and indirectly, the power and reach of the modern state.

The nature of the connection between economic growth and, more specifically, technological growth – the latter being the chief component and characteristic feature of modern economic growth – and the secular growth of government economic activity that will be illustrated in the following pages, may be mentioned here. The decline in personal freedom is not merely a corollary of this reduction in the private sector of the economy. More importantly, it takes the form of conscious surrenders of personal rights and freedoms, these being the unavoidable reactions of society to the consequences of particular kinds of technology. If the thesis is correct, it follows that the libertarian economist cannot consistently claim also to be a pro-growth economist.

Let us place this thesis in historical perspective, first by affirming that the slower the changes taking place within any civilised society, and the greater the degree of moral consensus within it, the smaller is the scope for legislation. *Per contra,* the more rapid the changes, and the less the moral consensus, the greater is the amount of legislation required. Moreover, in such conditions, the resulting legislation, passed in haste and based, as it will be, on compromise and expediency, is likely to please few and disgruntle many. The latter statements are clearly descriptive of the political situation prevalent in the Western democracies. And a moment's reflection about its causes takes us to the heart of the matter.

Rapid economic development over the last century has been responsible not only for an unprecedented expansion of populations the world over but also, and especially in the richer countries, for the growing mobility of their populations. Among the consequences have been a rapid increase in the size and crowdedness of urban areas, and a continuing change in their composition. Moreover, the concomitant innovations in industrial processes and products that (measured by conventional indices) have multiplied 'real' incomes in the West, have been productive also of powerful side effects which, for our purpose, can be divided into two overlapping categories: those which expose humanity to hitherto-unknown dangers, and those adverse spillovers which, in modern nation states, are continually translated into overt conflicts of interest. Both the dangers and the conflicts are, at best, contained by legislation, but generally at the expense of individual choice and, therefore, at the expense of individual freedom.

Chapter 41

New Sources of Mutual Annoyance

Let us turn first to those innovations both of consumer goods and of industrial processes that have incidental but direct and substantial effects on the wellbeing of others – effects which are known, in the economist's slang, as 'spillovers'. This analysis by economists turns on the concept of a divergence between social and market valuations and on methods for reducing this divergence.[2] In the light of our thesis, however, we must now take note of the propensity of these spillovers to augment the power of the state.

Grouping transport innovations, we can begin with the private automobile which, apart from severely restricting the freedom of the would-be pedestrian, happens also to be a lethal weapon. Through its intensive use, Americans continue to kill off their countrymen at the rate of about 50,000 a year, in motor accidents alone, and to maim for life more than twice that number. Apart from that its manifold nuisance value defies calculation. Society's half-hearted attempts to protect itself from the excesses of its beloved monster have already issued in a number of minor infringements of personal freedom. As automobiles continue to get in each other's way, they are subjected to closer regulation: to speed limits, parking prohibitions, one-way streets, no-entry precincts, and so on. Stricter controls on exhaust emissions and engine noise are on the way and, to enforce them, a variety of electronic devices and a growing army of traffic police.

The expansion of air traffic, both commercial and private, has also brought with it detailed regulatory legislation that can only grow over the future. The popularity of air travel, however, has other consequences. The promotion of mass tourism has already run into the incipient resentment of populations in the host countries, or of host regions within a country. Pressures on legislatures, both local and national, to limit the freedom of people to travel where and when they wish, are becoming increasingly effective. Certainly within the richer and more populated countries, motorised travel to national parks, wilderness areas and lake districts will soon have to be rationed, either by price or by more direct means, if they are to be preserved from irrevocable spoilation. Traffic congestion is not, of course, the only issue. Owing to the so-called package revolution, legislation is being enforced in some countries, and is being contemplated in others, in the attempt to control the growing litter (much of it synthetic and non-degradable) on the streets, on the beaches, in parklands and in lakes and streams.

One might continue down the list of despoiling technology. For the postwar growth of other motorised pastimes, involving the use of such things as motorcycles, speedboats, snowmobiles and private planes, has started a reaction among the more amenity-conscious citizenry – frequently identified by pro-growth economists as élitist middle-class kill-joys; a reaction that is manifestly on the increase, and which is sure to result in further restrictions on freedoms hitherto enjoyed by the motorised multitude.

The mounting concern over the last decade with air, water and soil pollution arising from new industrial processes and their products – in particular with the fouling of the air in metropolitan regions, with the destruction of forests, wetlands and everglades, with the dumping of sewage in estuaries and of oil on the high seas, and with the wanton use of pesticides and chemical fertilisers – has led to an increase in controls in all countries, the import of which has not yet been fully appreciated. Certainly in Britain they have excited little attention. In the United States, in contrast, the environmental interest has been vociferous enough to precipitate a rash of restrictive legislation, both state and federal. In 1970, for instance, the powerful Environmental Protection Agency was added to the existing number of federal regulatory bodies. Today, American businessmen no longer have the freedom to choose their most profitable type and scale of industrial plant, or its most profitable location.

Again, in the attempt to escape the clamour and suffocation and crime of their vast urban agglomerations, millions of Americans each year seek the solace of the great outdoors – though not without all the appurtenances of creature comforts also. Alas, modern highways make it disastrously easy for the motorised traffic to pour into once-secluded areas. And with the resulting threat to the destruction of wildlife and the natural terrain, official attitudes have become increasingly restrictive.

For instance, according to recent reports of the Worldwatch Institute (1976):

'In the most popular U.S. national forests and parks, rangers have become more like policemen than nature guides, campgrounds are tent cities, and supermarkets sprout up in the woods.

'The "pleasure ground" envisioned by the founders of the National Park Service is sagging under the weight of more than 200 million visitors a year. Summer attendance in 1975 was up 14 per cent from the previous summer. Unique American treasures in 38 national parks are being eroded by the people-crush. Campgrounds are often filled by 10 a.m. and facilities are jammed.

'As campsites and cabins proliferate, more water treatment, sewage disposal, and garbage disposal facilities are needed, as well as more roads, more employees, and more policing. Campers and trailers clog the existing roads and, collected together in campsites they can make pineclad hills look more like aluminum shantytowns. Human traffic now endangers the plant and animal life that parks were designed to protect.

'With a record 240 million visits to national parks in 1975, the National Park Service was forced in various situations to require permits for backpacking, to ban the collection of firewood, to prohibit autos, and to discourage large groups like Boy Scout troops from camping together. Such pressures alter the way people can hike, camp, and sightsee, but increasing restrictions are essential if the natural conditions are to be maintained.'

In view of their excessive mobility and enterprise, it is not, of course, surprising that Americans are more conscious of these problems than other nationals. Some of them have also begun to perceive uneasily the shape of things to come. Thus, in the introduction to a report commissioned by Congress, economist Ronald Ridker wrote in 1972:

'Conservation of our water resources, preservation of wilderness areas, protection of animal life threatened by man, restrictions on pollutant emissions, and the limitations on fertilizer and pesticide-use, all require public regulation. Rules must be set and enforced, complaints heard and adjudicated. True enough, the more we can find means of relying on the price system, the easier will be the bureaucratic task. But even if effluent charges and user fees become universal, they would have to be set administratively, emissions and use metered, and fees collected. It appears inevitable that a larger proportion of our lives will be devoted to filling in forms, arguing with the computer or its representative, appealing decisions, waiting for our case to be handled, finding ways to evade or move ahead in the queue. In many small ways, everyday life will become more contrived.'

Chapter 42

The Great Pay Scramble

We turn our attention now to an area of current controversy among economic specialists: the genesis of the new inflation. Since my more leisurely reflections on this topic have already been published elsewhere[3] we restrict ourselves here to tracing a connection between the shape of economic growth and the associated change of institutions in the West, on the one hand, and, on the other, the scale and potential of pay claims that today appear to be making it all but impossible for governments not to intervene actively, and continually, in industrial disputes or not to impose price and/or wage controls.

First let us bring to mind those innovations in transport, communication and industrial plant that have increased the size and economic power of both corporations and labour unions, national and multinational. There are some economists who choose to believe that the American economy is no less competitive today than it was fifty years ago, and on some kinds of definition this can be held to be true. But despite the growth of wealth and population, there are certainly fewer industrial firms today and, what is more significant, the larger corporations are very much larger than those of fifty years ago, whether measured in terms of value added, of capital used or of number of employees. Their power to influence voters and governments to support policies favourable to the corporations' business – through the buying up of advertising space or time, through highly organised lobbies, and through scarcely concealed bribes to journalists, labour leaders and public office holders – is too well known to require documentation. Nor need one waste time instancing the methods used by aggressive labour unions to intimidate individual workers, and to bring pressure to bear on smaller labour unions that threaten their monopoly.

This growth of national monopolies on each side of industry

has strengthened the propensity of both capital and labour to conspire against the public by raising production costs. It is a propensity that has been aggravated in the last two or three years by an unprecedented clamour for more money by the working populations in all Western countries. Owing to improved statistical techniques and to the employment of high speed computers – owing also to the spread of news media and to the postwar surge of material expectations, itself inspired by the growth gospel and encouraged by government pronouncements – workers in all occupations have now become hypersensitive to movements in their real wages and to their position in the pay structure. The ordinary citizen having been fed on the pap of 'rising expectations' for almost a generation, no group today suffers an actual reduction in its real pay without a deep sense of grievance and, currently, without continuing action to recover and advance its real earnings – even when, for the economy as a whole, some (temporary) decline in real standards may be unavoidable. Although economists are fully aware of this *de facto* intransigence of the working population, and have to work it into their traditional fiscal and monetary theories, it is a phenomenon without historical parallel.

Unfortunately, at the very time that workers have become acutely conscious of movements in their real and relative earnings, they have also become aware of their collective power to inflict injury on their industry and, more important, to impose inconvenience or even hardship on local or national communities. Since developments in communication have been such that management, representing all the firms of 'the industry' in question, negotiates with labour leaders representing all workers in that industry, the most likely outcome is one that concedes the bulk of the wage claims even if this entails a rise in the price of the industry's outputs.

The likelihood of this sort of solution is strengthened in the conditions of near-full employment, and of upward wage and price drift, that have prevailed since World War II. For if, in any important economic activity, industrial conflict looks imminent (or if any existing dispute is beginning to drag on), democratic governments, with their eyes always on the next election, are tempted to intervene.

Industrial peace in such cases generally entails concessions to labour. Since wage settlements, in one economic sector after another over the last few years, have invariably been in excess of productivity increases, prices have continued to move up. What is more, the resulting inflation becomes self-generating in as much as each wage settlement triggers off the pay claims of others whose positions in the pay structure are thereby disturbed.

These developments culminated in rates of inflation that during the years 1972–5 caused alarm and despondency in Britain and other countries. (It is no use blaming the inflation on the steep rise in oil or food prices since 1973, as, in all countries, it preceded such price movements.) Through a combination of reduced employment and increased government controls, which varied from one country to another, the rates of inflation began to subside towards the end of 1975, though it would be rash to regard this as part of a trend back to price stability.

Nevertheless, the significance of recent developments is clear. Given the existence of the welfare state and the commitment of all political parties to the 'full employment' objective, it seems highly unlikely that monetary and fiscal policies alone will suffice, over the foreseeable future, to maintain price stability. As events are moving, such policies look to be made subordinate and ancillary to an extension of price and wage controls. Even if this interpretation is inadequate, the tacit conspiracy against the public interest by capital and labour in the chief industries – a conspiracy that is one of the institutional outcomes of economic growth – is sure to strengthen the role of the central government as broker, as mediator and, in the last resort, as the wielder of countervailing power. Certainly price stability, the democratic welfare state and free collective bargaining no longer appear to be mutually compatible.

Chapter 43

A Future World of Moral Anxiety

The direction of current research in modern medicine is such as to make doctors' decisions increasingly painful and difficult, especially in view of the trend towards the dissolution of traditional values. In consequence, governments will be called up to play a yet larger role in the social control of medicine. At least three trends are discernible which look as if they will culminate in increased government intervention.

(1) The growing dependence of the medical profession upon expensive machines for diagnosis and treatment.
(2) Continuing improvements in the techniques of organ transplants and in those for preserving people in a non-sentient state for indefinite periods.
(3) The progress being made by research in RNA and DNA – the acid substances that store and pass on as heredity the blueprint for production of proteins by the cell.

Concerning (1), it may be assumed that physicians will want to invest in the new machines, for they believe (rightly) that their competence will be judged by the impressiveness of the equipment on display in their offices or clinics. Once they are bought, however, doctors will be under strong financial temptation to make maximum use of them, and they will, moreover, become increasingly dependent on them over time. With this development, a system of private medicine is more likely over the near future to threaten the private citizen with inordinate medical expenses and, in consequence, to induce him to favour an extension of state medicine. Universal recourse to insurance schemes, even ideal ones, will not prevent this development since the premia will have to rise in proportion to the rise in medical expenses. State control of medicine, however, can take the profit out of using elaborate equipment, and can otherwise regulate its use.

Another implication of this same development is that something akin to moral decisions have now to be made by medical staffs in hospitals where, because of their exhorbitant price, there are not always enough lung or kidney machines available for all patients who may benefit from their use.

Trends (2) and (3) also entail moral decisions of this nature. The enthusiasm of some surgeons for organ transplant operations has, according to press reports, led to the premature removal of the vital organ. Recently, for example, the victim of a motor accident was discovered to be still alive during the removal operation. So long as 'fresh' corpses are required by emergency wards, permission has to be sought from the close relations of the accident victims. Since it is now obvious that the information they receive should not come from the medical men who are anxious to exercise their skill in transplant operations, procedural rules will have to be formulated and enforced. Again, since medical evidence of death can be associated with the cessation of heart, lung or brain activity, there must also be criteria for determining whether or not a person is 'really' dead; whether and for how long to keep alive a person in a dormant state of being (a 'human vegetable'); or whether, and for how long, to keep a person alive when there is little hope of releasing him from continuous suffering, or when there is practically no hope of his ever enjoying life again. Thus disturbing moral problems are raised by advances in modern medicine whose resolution, however, cannot be left to the discretion of the medical profession – least of all, at a time of eroding moral consensus.[4] In the last resort the rules will be shaped through the political process, and their application enforced through government agencies.

We can, finally, imagine the public consternation as scientists begin to uncover the secrets of the genetic code. Discoveries enabling them to breed clones[5] or, most potent still, to influence the genetic compositions of human offspring, or to control it in 'test-tube' babies – so that, among other posibilities, highly superior or inferior beings could be bred or, alternatively, animal or human beings that are 'freaks' in that they are highly specialised for particular purposes – may seem far away just now. But there can be no doubt that scientific research is moving in that direction. The moral problems to be faced would be painful, particularly, if it were also feared that some other government, or group of scientists or fanatics, were planning to use the findings of such research for sinister ends. In the circumstances, only the most far-reaching powers of investigation and control wielded by governments acting in concert would suffice to allay such fears.

A moment's reflection will confirm that these are not idle fantasies. The most sensible course of action for mankind, it might be agreed, would be to prohibit further research in this dangerous area. But in the world of today international approval and operation of such a ban would be difficult on both political and 'scientistic' grounds. The import of the latter term has reference to the ideological presumption in favour of untrammelled scientific discovery, strengthened at times by the unwarranted belief that scientific freedom and personal freedom are closely intertwined. These grounds are reinforced by broad humanitarian appeals whenever the public becomes uneasy about their possible social implications. As indicated earlier, the 'good' uses of the research in question are always stressed; the possibility of the relief of suffering is an argument that is never omitted. Thus it was in the recent decision of the British government to permit microbiologists and other scientists to continue their experiments in creating new mutations of bacteria – provided, of course, that 'proper safeguards' were observed. And so the research goes on until substances and instruments of fearsome potential come into being.

Chapter 44

A Secret File on Everybody

Let us now consider some instances of those innovations in which the element of increasing hazard is the more immediate factor in the reduction of individual liberty. We may begin, arbitrarily, with a glance first at those developments, based either on microfilm or on computer technology, which have vastly facilitated the storage, the processing and the retrieval of information. Such developments have provided corporations and governments with inviting opportunities for extending the range of inquiry about their employees, their customers or the public at large.

As Jacques Ellul observes in his *Technological Society* (1965), if a thing is technologically feasible, a use for it will sooner or later be discovered. 'Invention is the mother of necessity.' It is now becoming technically possible, and not too costly, for a government in an industrially advanced country to store information on the economic and political activities of all its citizens, and to exchange such information with other governments. We can, according to Ellul's generalisation, confidently anticipate the phenomenon.

Although any scheme specifically designed to extend the detail and coverage of information about the private lives of citizens would be viewed with alarm by the public, it would not be at all difficult to rationalise such a scheme in the name of Efficiency, and even in the name of Humanity; as, for example, enabling assistance to be forthcoming more expeditiously to any victim of accident or hardship, or as a powerful aid in the detection and combatting of crime and fraud. In view of the phenomenal growth in crime since World War II, and the increasing danger it poses for society – about which more anon – it is not likely that such measures will be successfully resisted.

Apart from their existing uses by the police and the military, and their prospective uses indicated above, the need for more comprehensive dossier systems will grow with the economy's increasing dependence on the complex machines used in the control of modern plants. Computers, for example, perform such vital functions today as guiding missiles and airliners, and controlling the operation of steel and chemical plants. Their employment also in the operation of telephone exchanges, or in the provision of other public utilities such as gas, water and electricity supply, is sure to grow over the future. Since, in the interests of economy, a single plant can be made to serve a vast metropolitan area, a breakdown (or even a serious error in the operation) of such machines is exceedingly costly and could be disastrous. The same might be said of much simpler devices. Just imagine the consequences of a failure of the fail-safe device controlling the colours of the traffic lights of a large city!

Recognition of these new hazards must, of necessity, produce a system of closer checks and tighter controls on the personnel employed in the day-to-day management, maintenance and repair of such machines; a system which, for its effective enforcement, will come to depend, among other things, on the family histories and detailed psychological knowledge of the personnel in question. The intimate knowledge required to implement these necessary precautions will increasingly be provided by specialised agencies, public or private, having highly developed methods of prying into the private lives of ordinary citizens. The extreme distaste with which, today, such developments are regarded by liberals, cannot, however, prevent their continued growth. Indeed, the compilation of such personal histories will be facilitated by the co-operation of those citizens whose employment opportunities come to depend upon the availability of such records.

Chapter 45

High Consequence Risks

In this category appear those risks falling on the public that arise from the day-to-day applications of science to industry. Economic 'progress' in chemicals and synthetics, and in the food and drug industry, is being made in a state of virtual ignorance.

Apprehension is not confined to the general public. Modern medicine advances with extraordinary rapidity as a result of a variety of non-medical specialists, trained in chemistry, biology, mathematics, physics, engineering, biochemistry and so on, all working on one or other narrow aspect of the subject, making their tentative findings available to the medical profession. But such is the profusion of new discoveries that the physician, especially if he is a general practitioner, has neither the time nor the training to form an independent judgment with respect to the new drug, new method of treatment or new medical equipment in question. As is well known, many just read the leaflets sent to them by the drug companies and prescribe the drugs to their patients.

The sort of consequences that can arise in those circumstances can be illustrated by an event which occurred about the turn of the century. German scientists, working in the Bayer Company, succeeded in synthesising a crystallised compound from morphine which was marketed under the trade name of Heroin. It was regarded as non-addictive and was recommended in medical journals as a means of treating morphine addiction. Ten years had to pass before Heroin was recognised by the medical profession as highly addictive and dangerous.

Since the 1960s, Methadone, a synthetic drug developed in World War II – also, incidentally, by German scientists – has been used as a substitute drug in the treatment of heroin addicts. After encouraging reports of success for many years, investigations undertaken by the US Drug Enforcement Administration revealed in 1974 that deaths from illicit Methadone surpassed those from heroin, and that Methadone constituted a substantial share of the illegal traffic in drugs.[6]

Not only have we practically no knowledge of the probability of any particular risk's occurring, but also, for the most part, we know nothing either of the nature or the extent of the damage that could be associated with the production of the synthetic in question. The world simply has had no previous experience of it, and the experiments, if any, to which it has been subjected are perforce limited. Thus, although it is conceivable (though hardly likely) that the full range of adverse consequences, and the probability distribution of each of them, will come to light in the course of time for each new substance and each *combination* of substances, the social problem is that of creating or adapting institutions to cope with the dangers to which people are being currently exposed.

Consider, for instance, the problems of a government department in determining the risks of food additives. Among the reasons given for the difficulties encountered by the US Food and Drug Administration (FDA) are:

(1) The often inadequate scientific data-base (rapidly advancing scientific technology soon makes obsolete last year's level of detection of harmful substances).
(2) The lack of agreement by scientists on the significance of the safety data available.
(3) The fact that there is 'no public or scientific consensus today on the risk or uncertainty acceptable to justify the marketing of any substance as a food or drug'.

Admitting that subjective judgment necessarily plays a large role in safety decisions, the FDA has sought divergent viewpoints to help reach a consensus on particular issues.[7] In order to meet these problems, which can only grow with time, the FDA has to expand its personnel, extend the scale of its operations, and intervene more actively in the private sector of the economy.

Slowly and haltingly, we are beginning to realise the dangers that abound. Every so often – and sometimes, as in the Thalidomide case, more by luck than by systematic investigation – some new synthetic, drug or food additive comes under official suspicion and, after some preliminary inquiry, it is withdrawn from the market.

It is far from improbable that there are a number of Thalidomide-type drugs widely in use having deleterious genetic effects that operate more slowly over time, making them difficult to detect. Indeed, a recent issue of the *Sunday Times* (25 May 1975) carried an article reporting that about 100,000 women each year in Britain had been taking pregnancy tests with drugs that are currently suspected of giving rise to the birth of deformed children.

Sometimes the damage already wrought is irrevocable; sometimes not. What is certain, however, is that thousands of new drugs and synthetics come on to the market each year – a vague, persistent and growing threat to our health and survival. The risk of some genetic or ecological catastrophe carried by any single new chemical, used alone or in combination with others, may be slight, but at their present rate of accumulation on the world market we should be moving, over the years, closer to the certainty of some such catastrophe – unless the state comes to exercise far greater powers over the activities of farmers, and over the food-processing and chemical industries. Whether or not such powers will suffice to ward off the dangers, they will surely be ceded. Nothing rouses the indignation of the consuming public so surely as a threat to its health. And the demand for firm government action, which entails expansion of existing government bureaucracies, will swamp any libertarian considerations.

Chapter 46

New Weapons for Old

Let us now turn to a more obvious source of danger: the upward trend in military expenditures the world over.

In 1913, US national defence expenditure was about 0·7 per cent of national expenditure. By 1940 it was 2 per cent. By 1950 it had grown to 7·5 per cent, and by 1970 it was over 10 per cent (or $84 billion, valued in 1974 dollars). This trend in defence expenditure is directly related to economic growth via the technical innovations that maintain its momentum. It is not, therefore, the result merely of military ambitions, of administrative laxity, or of financial opportunism and corruption in high places. The arms race between the powers, especially that between the 'superpowers', the US and the USSR, does not take the form of accumulations of military hardware or of expanding military personnel. It takes the form of massive investment in developing and producing more expensive and deadlier weapons. For every weapon of offensive capability there is soon designed a weapon of defensive capability, the response to which is yet a more destructive offensive weapon, and so on. In the words of Charles Schultze (1970), an American scholar in this field: 'continually advancing technology and the risk aversion of military planners, therefore, combine to produce ever more complex and expensive weapons systems and ever more contingencies to guard against'. Without technological progress, that is, these huge expenditures on research and development for the production of yet more complex and lethal weapons could not continue to spiral upwards.

The consequent rise in the level of general anxiety, though subversive of social welfare, may not seem directly relevant to our thesis. But this spiral of self-sustaining research inevitably produces scientific secrets and technical equipment of value to enemy agents. The resulting fears, real or imaginary, of ubiquitous enemy

intelligence will go far to sanction the use of special powers for counterespionage activities, including powers to investigate the private lives and political opinions not only of government employees but also of every resident in the country. There is precious little a government, even a liberal democratic government, cannot do today in the name of 'national defence' or 'military necessity'.

Two broad technological developments, in particular, should be noted, since they have served to increase the vulnerability of Western democracies. The first is our growing dependence over the last half-century on radio and television communication, not only for our understanding of our rapidly changing world, but also for receiving official information and advice. The second is the shift, over a century, from the diffusion of a nation's defence potential, conceived as depending, in the last resort, upon the leadership and the morale of patriotic men bearing small arms, to its concentration functionally into specialised task forces and, geographically, into key areas within which technical experts and complex computers control gigantic and elaborate weapons. Such developments offer temptations to an unscrupulous enemy, a fact of which we are becoming uncomfortably aware without, however, being altogether aware of its implications on our freedom. But, again, the belief (whether true or not) that there are large numbers of enemy agents operating within the country, ready at the word of command to participate in a surprise attack – to seize broadcasting stations and military installations and, perhaps, also electricity-generating stations and other public utilities – would be enough to confer on the police, or on a special corps of investigators, such powers of interrogation, surveillance and arrest as to amount virtually to a suspension of *habeas corpus.*

From external security, let us now turn to internal security, bearing in mind the alarming trend in crime statistics. Notwithstanding the cherished beliefs of liberals and humanists, the growth in the West of material abundance – accompanied as it has been by a vast extension of state welfare services, in particular by an extension of educational opportunities – has not, in the event, brought about the anticipated decline in criminal activity. Quite the contrary, crime has grown without interruption since the end of World War II.

We have suggested, earlier, that this unhappy trend itself may be attributed to modern economic growth, especially to such factors as the contemporary emphasis on material status and 'the good things of life', and on the concomitant neglect of traditional values and the decline of moral constraints[8] resulting from the diffusion of secular education, both formal and popular. We need not pursue

the matter here. It is enough to remark that the economic growth of the last two centuries has had the incidental effect also of expanding the opportunities and the facilities for a life of crime. The rapid enlargement of town and city in the nineteenth century can be traced back to the 'Agricultural Revolution' and the Enclosure Acts of the eighteenth century which broke up hundreds of small farm communities throughout the land. A succession of innovations, in communication, in transport, in sanitation and in the provision of public utilities, transformed the new industrial and commercial centres into huge urban agglomerations that sometimes ran to hundreds of square miles, the breeding grounds for hordes of petty criminals and thugs. These conurbations, as they are now called, are ideal also for the operation of large criminal organisations. Against the anonymity of the teeming multitudes and the endless swirl of motorised traffic, their movements are difficult to detect. After some daring robbery or brutal crime, which today nearly always depends upon the fast get-away car (one of the great modern innovations), the criminal can hide for weeks within the big city, moving at short notice from one area to another. Within the hour, he can be on a commercial airliner or private plane on his way to foreign parts.

However, what is more pertinent to our thesis is not the increase in the incidence of crime that has been facilitated by economic growth, but the increase in power conferred on organised crime by technological innovation. It is by now abundantly clear that continued scientific research not only produces more expensive and complex missile systems or deadlier rays, gases and bacteria. It also produces critical simplifications in the design of smaller thermonuclear or bacteriological bombs that place them not only within the capacity of the smaller and less politically stable nation-states, but also within the capacity of the modern multinational criminal organisation.

At a time when criminals and political fanatics – their effectiveness multiplied by swift travel, radio communication, 'bugging' and other devices – are becoming more active in intimidating the public by the kidnapping, and by the torture or murder, of hostages, the fear instilled in the ordinary citizen is made keener by his recognition also of the increased vulnerability of the large city or conurbation in which he dwells. For, as indicated earlier, in order to avail itself of the economies of large scale production, the population of a city or of a whole region has come to depend increasingly upon a single source for each of a number of vital services: for example, its water supply. And mere suspicion by the public that a few pounds of radioactive waste has been thrown into the city's water supply would be enough to cause consternation. Perhaps, the greatest vulnerability springs from the dependence of densely populated regions on a single source of electricity – this versatile form of power itself operating a host of subsidiary services critical to the functioning, indeed the survival, of the city or region.

Quite apart from the risk of a breakdown in one of these vital services, one has to reckon today with the growing likelihood of their sabotage or attempted sabotage by criminals or urban guerillas, or even by gangs of delinquents. The anxieties created by the apprehension of such hazards will issue inevitably in an extension of police powers. For the desire for security exceeds the desire for freedom; indeed, security is a precondition of freedom. Once the millions of people crowded into the cities begin to realise just how helpless and exposed they have become, there will be little resistance to telephone tapping by the police, to closer monitoring of international and perhaps internal travel also, to the surrender of more arbitrary powers of search and arrest, and, above all, to the pervasive surveillance and control that become more effective as scientific progress is made in chemical and other methods of identifying, tracing and incapacitating people.[9]

Chapter 47

The High Price of Nuclear Energy

The last item I shall touch on here, the peacetime use of atomic power, serves only to reinforce the foregoing conclusions.

The prospect of peacetime atomic power is usually discussed in the context of 'the nation's energy needs', where the figures for 'needs' are all too often no more than an extrapolation of the existing upward trend in energy consumption. Strictly speaking, there are no 'needs' in economics. There are only choices – individual or collective. And, clearly, collective choices made through the political process can alter the direction of any trend. A rise in electricity prices or petrol taxes, a ban on automobile advertising, plus the creation of an atmosphere in which (as in wartime Britain) manifest austerity is regarded as virtuous, could check and reverse the secular demand for energy. Such measures not only serve a policy of conservation but also, by reducing the current depletion rate of conventional energy supplies, improve our chances of developing the technology necessary to make solar energy available at low cost.

Ecologists, preservationists, and others concerned with environmental pollution obviously prefer this latter solution to the so-called energy problem. Businessmen and technocrats, on the other hand, impatient to restore and maintain the pace of economic growth, argue for a rapid expansion in the production of atomic energy through nuclear fission in the hope of making the economy independent of conventional energy sources within two or three decades. This latter course is, at the time of writing, much the more likely one. For although controversy has begun to spread as information leaks down to the more alert segment of the public, such is the momentum of technology, such is the fear of slipping behind in the 'industrial race', that only a miracle can prevent the expansion of the nuclear fission industry.

Two sorts of risks are prominent in the current debate. First, there are the possible failures of the emergency cooling system which functions to avert civilian disaster in the event of reactor accidents arising from loss of coolant. Second, and more important, there is the production of biological poisons, of two kinds (a) long-lived radioactive fission products and (b) the production of plutonium – one of the deadliest elements handled by man.

Concerning the first sort of risk, Walter Jordon (a pro-nuclear member of the old US Atomic Energy Commission)[10] has suggested that a 'tolerable level' of risk is something of the order of less than one chance in 10,000 of having a serious accident in a year. But he admits that we have as yet no idea of the probabilities, having accumulated so far only some 100 reactor years of accident-free operation of commercial nuclear electric stations in the United States – which is a long way from 10,000. The only way we shall know what the odds really are, he says, is by continuing to accumulate experience in operating reactors. He believes it is worth the risk.

In a comment on these views in 1972, John Gofman, Professor of Medical Physics at California University, has written:

'If we look forward to a future of 500 reactors in operation (even more are planned) and take Dr. Jordan's one in 10,000 "tolerable" risk, we calculate one major, serious accident per 20 years. Since a serious accident may mean losing a city like New York or Philadelphia, one might wonder about his criteria of "tolerable" risks. Of course, Dr. Jordan makes it very clear we are far from even knowing that the risk is as low as one in 1,000, let alone one in 10,000.'[11]

The second risk is connected (a) with the disposal of radioactive wastes (after their separation by a reprocessing plant). At present, and simply as an 'interim' measure, the fission products, which form a 'soup' of virulent radioactive acid that will be dangerous for hundreds of years, are stored in concrete-encased refrigerated stainless steel tanks. This soup also contains heavy elements, 'actinides', that will be dangerous for hundreds of thousands of years.

No less alarming is (b) the calculation that in a fully developed US nuclear economy some 200,000 pounds of plutonium will be generated annually. Bearing in mind that the half-life of plutonium is about 24,000 years; that a mere half-pound of it, dispersed into the atmosphere as fine insoluble particles would suffice to inflict every living mortal with lung cancer, the plutonium 'inventory' that accumulates over the years will constitute a carcinogenic hazard for 1,000 human generations. Clearly a containment level of 99·99 per cent would hardly be enough to avert disaster. Yet in as much as plutonium is a necessary material for the fabrication of nuclear weapons, and is expected to be a lucrative item of illicit traffic, such a containment level is likely to prove unfeasible.

With such facts in mind the recent statement by Dr Hannes Alfven, the Nobel Prize-winning physicist, looks conservative. Writing in the *Bulletin of Atomic Scientists* in May 1972, he said:

'Fission energy is safe only if a number of critical devices work as they should, if a number of people in key positions follow all their instructions, if there is no sabotage, no hi-jacking of the transports, if no reactor fuel processing plant or reprocessing plant or repository anywhere in the world is situated in a region of riots or guerilla activity, and no revolution or war – even a 'conventional' one – takes place in these regions. The enormous quantities of extremely dangerous material must not get into the hands of ignorant people or desperados. No Acts of God can be permitted.'

To be more explicit, the extent of the vigilance required by the planned expansion of the nuclear energy programme will entail an unprecedented extension of the internal and international security systems. Among other measures, this will involve armed protection of the transport network along which move containers of atomic materials, a vast increase in internal surveillance and, inevitably, the surrender to the police or, possibly, to specially trained forces, of extraordinary powers of entry, arrest, detention and interrogation, if – as they will claim – they are to move fast enough to prevent highly organised criminals, psychopaths and fanatics from capturing positions from which they can effectively blackmail a nation, or cause, inadvertently or deliberately, irreparable disaster.

Chapter 48

In Dismal Conclusion

In sum, then, the growing threat to liberty arising from adverse spillovers is the direct result of the direction being taken by scientific and technological innovation. Some innovations take the form of industrial processes that generate a variety of dangerous pollutants; others take the form of new products that confer on the user a direct power to cause harm or distress to others, especially in large urban areas where people are inevitably in each other's way; yet others will bestow on society such dreadful powers of control as to induce in it a state of continuing anxiety. The resulting demand for government regulation and control is reinforced by the spread of new hazards produced by the very pace of modern research and the haste to market its products.

Whether the hazards created by new weapons systems ought to be classified as 'spillovers' is a question of definition. What can hardly be doubted, however, is that sustained research into yet more effective weapons of offence and defence is itself an important example of the broad thesis that the advance of science, though it enhances man's power, also makes his world an increasingly dangerous place to live in. There is now so much more that can go wrong. And the consequences of some mishap or misdeed can be terrifying to contemplate.

True, there has been no attempt at comprehensiveness in this review of recent developments. But I do not think that the examples used to illustrate my thesis are altogether singular or unrepresentative. Obviously not all innovations create significant spillovers, and not all significant spillovers act to augment government powers and to reduce liberty. But many of those which are familiar to us, and many which are confidently expected to occur, do indeed appear to have these tendencies. And none I can think of has strong countervailing tendencies.

Indeed, the longer one reflects on the matter, the surer becomes the vision of the human race being borne along by an irresistible tide towards an ocean deep-mined with unknown perils. As the perils loom closer, and as men come to apprehend their increasing vulnerability, the instinctive desire for self-preservation – found in organised societies as well as in individuals – will prompt them to cede to governments far greater powers of surveillance, control and repression than are compatible with contemporary notions of personal liberty.

If there is to be any hope of circumventing or mitigating this ignominious fate, it can arise only from a growing public awareness of what is taking place.

NOTES FOR PART VI

Chapter 40

1 The case is cogently argued by Milton Friedman (1962, pp. 172–6).

Chapter 41

2 A popular account of the economist's approach to this phenomenon is given in my article, 'The spillover enemy' (1969).

Chapter 42

3 See my article, 'The new inflation' (1974); and an exchange of notes and letters on the subject in subsequent issues of the same journal.

Chapter 43

4 The moral dilemma of the physician at a time when traditional values are in dissarray is well described by Alasdair MacIntyre (1975).

5 The difficult moral and legal problems that would arise in the event of successful cloning techniques are discussed by Leon Kass (1972).

Chapter 45

6 A critical account of Methadone's history is given by E. J. Epstein (1974).

7 In this connection see Rita Campbell (1974, especially pp. 3–7).

Chapter 46

8 Some confirmation for this conjecture is provided in an article by Mark Abrams (1974) on recent social surveys in Britain.

9 Improved methods for identifying, tracing and incapacitating people is among the list of the 100 most likely innovations compiled by Herman Kahn and A. J. Wiener (1967).

Chapter 47

10 Since 1975 this federal organisation has been succeeded by the Energy Research and Development Administration (ERDA).

11 See John Gofman, in *The Case for a Nuclear Moratorium* (1972).

Doubts about reactor safety are to be found today in innumerable publications. The interested reader is advised, first, to consult an excellent and well-documented critique of the nuclear industry by physicist Amory Lovins, *Nuclear Power* (1974).

Part VII

Final Reflections

Chapter 49

Digest of Contents

We begin this volume by reviewing, in Part I, the sources of complacency in the conventional economic approach to the measurement of social welfare. In particular, the longer term changes in GNP are shown to be unreliable, indeed, misleading, indicators of a nation's overall economic efficiency over time, and to bear no clear relation to changes in its social welfare.

Mention is made in Part II of the increasing doubts in the minds of the thinking public with respect both to the physical possibility of continued economic growth and to its ultimate beneficence as a guiding norm of social policy. Such doubts have been precipitated or aggravated by a growing public awareness of a new gauntlet of hazards to the survival of our civilisation created by the discoveries of science and by the scale of their application.

Reasons are given for concluding that serious inquiry into the connection between continued economic growth and social well-being cannot be conducted by reference to economic criteria alone; nor by reference to thoughts on the subject by modern economists since the factors they consider seldom extend beyond 'technological externalities' and distributional issues. A far-ranging debate is called for in which scientific expertise of any kind has only a limited role to play. Yet in order to prevent diffuse argument, wayward contention and inconclusive controversies, it is necessary, first, to secure agreement on basic assumptions of fact concerning human nature and, second, in making welfare comparisons, to focus, in the main, on developments over the last few decades.

Having more closely specified the nature of the debate, there are expositional advantages in appraising the relevance and cogency of the arguments advanced in much of the recent pro-growth literature, prior to a more systematic consideration of the links between economic growth and social welfare. Thus Part III is confined to a critical examination of a selection of the more popular pro-growth allegations, with the aim of revealing their irrelevance to the debate as defined, while Part IV subjects the chief hopes reposed in further economic growth to sceptical examination.

The core of this volume, to which the matter in Parts I to IV is preparatory and supportive, are Parts V and VI on the constituents of the good life. Continual juxtaposition in these two Parts between, on the one hand, the attributes of a good or civilised life and, on the other, the existing and the emerging social consequences of economic growth, tends to an overwhelming impression: that continued economic growth in the West will remove us yet farther from the good life, indeed, from *any* good life.

Two tasks remain to be discharged in this final Part, each requiring a chapter for the purpose: the first is to make sure we have not overlooked some emergent factor, recognition of which should cause us to revise our conclusion. Is there not, as has been alleged by some writers – for example, Charles Reich in his *Greening of America* (1970) – some grains of hope to be gleaned from the new attitudes of the young today? The second is to appraise the eventual political feasibility of a change to a steady state economy, assuming that the incipient disillusion with economic growth today continues to spread.

Chapter 50

How Different are the Young Today?

Notwithstanding the growing incidence of crime and corruption in the wealthier countries since World War II, optimistic voices can be heard on both sides of the Atlantic. They talk of the new awakening among the young, especially among the middle class young in America, who have become increasingly cynical of the Protestant ethic of their fathers, and who largely reject their materialism and their striving for respectability and status. As the young themselves see it, they are breaking the fetters of traditional values and seeking a freedom from the pressures of society; a freedom to experiment in 'lifestyles', a freedom to 'do their own thing'. 'Hippy' colonies, less popular today than they were in 1970, account only for a small proportion of the growing army of seemingly easy-going footloose youngsters, ready to talk to anyone and to try anything. These latter characteristics of the young, taken alone, are, incidentally, far from novel in the United States. But whatever their causes, and whatever the advantages claimed for them, they also reflect an indiscriminate affability which has no affinity with, and indeed is antithetical to, the cultivation of those enduring friendships that grow only with time and care and sacrifice.

If any reader is pinning his hopes for a brighter future on this development, let me urge him to think again. For if the colour of the garment that the young choose to wear differs from that of their parents, the shape is much the same. This becomes clearer, once it is understood that the motto I once associated with the spirit of economic growth, 'enough does not suffice', has relevance not only to the acquisition of material goods, but also to any object or objective that compels the attention of the citizens of the new affluence, old or young. For the essence of the growth ethos is not materialism; it is insatiability. Although there has been a perceptible shift of emphasis from absorption in material accumulation to absorption in 'lifestyles', there has been no diminution of appetite. The young may preen themselves on being in a different league to their fathers, playing for different prizes. But whatever the prizes, the more of them the better. From head to foot, from crown to toe, they are maximisers.

Their apparently unlimited tolerance is chiefly a product of the moral vacuum in which they are reared; in the main, it reflects their growing insensibility and promiscuity. Their inordinate fondness for 'mixing' with the world takes them by land, sea and air, in every kind of vehicle and in every kind of company, to every city and resort over the globe – there, like disoriented termite colonies, to swarm into parks and squares, to pour through castles, palaces and galleries, and to squat and sprawl, smoke and munch, over the once-hallowed steps of spired cathedrals. Travelling in groups, large or small, they extend their experience from the best hotels to the worst, seeking consciously to be equally at home everywhere; to 'slum' with the rich and 'slum' with the poor; to ape the clothes both of other countries and of other periods of history; to eat the food, borrow the accents, play the instruments and adopt the customs of other cultures; to enter the tabernacles and revel in the rituals, alike of primitive tribes and of ancient civilisations; in short, to be excluded from nothing that might pass for experience, bright or dull, good or evil, sublime or seamy.

Thus the young of the affluent countries are today among the most ruthless and persistent plunderers of the earth's vanishing variety. Their unchecked gluttony, intensified by commercial interests, is today one of the most active forces at work combining to produce an admass civilisation and to promote a cultural entropy; one that is in the process of dissolving all hierarchies, flattening all barriers, blurring all distinctions, erasing the mosaic pattern of centuries, transforming the once-rich diversity of our universe into an inextricably blended monotony.

The effect on the character of the young may seem to be of less consequence, but it is no less pernicious. For this craving for endless experimentation, for savouring new 'lifestyles', for tasting new experiences, is of the nature of a compulsion among them; a determination to wriggle like mad in every newly detected current of experience in the avid pursuit of hedonic satiation – a determination perhaps partially hindered by the few years of cramming necessary to acquire a university degree, but later diluted only by economic constraint. It is an attitude that, incidentally, generates its own brand of envy; envy of the faster-living, faster-spending groups, who have come into possession of private yachts, 'planes, and other pleasure-seeking facilities.

On reflection, I find these new postures, and the attitude that informs them, both less promising and less laudable than the stodgy 'bourgeois' values which are, allegedly, being rejected. Not only do they entail activities that are, conservatively speaking, no less profligate of natural resources, but, in addition, they are a good deal further out on the scale of human folly. For the fashion among these more emancipated spirits is, in effect (after sitting through a number of sandwich courses on 'personality development', 'assertive-training', 'cognitive-amplification', 'trust-building', 'stereotype avoidance', 'creative-relationship formation' and other bits of psychological bubble gum currently littering the extra-curricular departments of American campuses), to select their maxims and arrange their thoughts and feelings so as, above all, to be able to 'travel light', unhampered by affective ties. The goal of maximising pleasurable experiences requires that the risks of sorrow or pain, which arise from emotional commitment, be shunned simply by shunning emotional commitment. Indeed, as observed by H. Hendin (1975), all too many of the young at American colleges are unabashedly resolved to avoid falling in love and, generally, to resist surrender to feelings of love and trust, since these feelings are perceived to retard pace and 'turnover', so encumbering the search for pleasure. Yet no psychological sophistication is needed to see that the repression produced by such contrived behaviour can only arrest emotional development and lead eventually to loneliness and despair.

The genesis of this trend among the young, however, has many connections with technological growth, of which some of the more obvious can be mentioned. First, there is the waning influence of religion and moral restraint in a predominantly science-based civilisation and, as a corollary perhaps (especially in the open and commercial societies of the West), the rising influence of the erotic and the pornographic in modern literature and entertainment. The net effect has been a dissipation of the theme of romantic love in our age, and a greater preoccupation with the immediacies of carnal experience. There are also specific innovations, transport and recreational, without which the footloose style of life among the young would be impossible, to say nothing of the spread of the affluence necessary to support it. The transport revolution, along with other technological developments, has had the additional effect of battering all sense of community out of our towns and cities which, since the War, have been transformed into concrete and gas-filled conurbations hoarse with the echo of motorised traffic. A number of traumatic responses can be associated with this resulting urban environment, not the least understandable being a desire to escape, to take off, to get away – at least, to keep moving.

Chapter 51

The Political Feasibility of Moving from the Growth Path

If the reader accepts my interpretation of recent developments (though not perhaps without some reservations of his own), and concurs in the broad conclusion that nothing very promising can be detected along the horizon towards which we are moving, he will surely be wondering whether the radical changes required to move us from the growth path are, in fact, politically feasible. Assuming, always, that popular opinion becomes increasingly sceptical of the ultimate beneficence of economic growth, will Western civilisation, which has for centuries been guided by the idea of progress – expressed in material plenty, in the advance of knowledge, and in free institutions – be able to wrest itself gradually from the responses ingrained in its way of life? Will it be able to place science and technology under permanent constraint, and otherwise reshape its institutions in order to realise a saner and more viable economic system?

Attention to three features of the modern world tempt me to doubt it: the conventional rationalisation, entrenched interests and international distrust. We take them up in that order.

CONVENTIONAL RATIONALISM

Conventional rationalism can be described as the dogged persistence in the belief that, irrespective of the past record of science and technology, it is to science and technology we must continue to turn for salvation. Certainly, if the application of some new technology results in distress or disaster, the remedy is always to be sought in more technology, never in less. This uncompromising spirit is epitomised in a sentence of Sir Peter Medawar's address to the British Association in 1969: 'The deterioration of the environment produced by technology is a technological problem for which technology has found, is finding, and will continue to find solutions.' While admitting the difficulties which technology would have to overcome, Sir Peter ended, inevitably perhaps, with an affirmation of faith in Science. He scornfully dismissed the faint-hearted with the words: 'To deride the hope of progress is the ultimate fatuity, the last word in poverty of spirit and meanness of mind.'

I should have thought that the charge of 'the ultimate fatuity' ought, instead, to be reserved for that hubris which blinds a scientist to the enormity of the risks to which his continued research is subjecting the human race. Nonetheless, the fact is that many thoughtful people today would echo his sentiments. For to many scientists, the risks being incurred do not suggest the existence of limits to empirical research beyond which we trespass at our peril, but rather suggest the existence of unsuspected mines strewn along a zone through which we must pick our way carefully before entering the promised land. As for members of the larger public in the affluent society, many of them are still high with hopes that, sooner or later, science will unearth some breath-taking discovery – some new pill or potion that prolongs youth, maintains sexual potency, or makes us gurgle with happy sensations. Perhaps it will effect some genetic breakthrough which will enable us all to have brilliant children. Perhaps it will learn to decode signals received by radiotelescopes telling of a superior form of life on some not-too-distant planet, which form of life, we naturally hope, will be benignly disposed to us.

The newspapers, of course, keep these hopes simmering by occasional headlines announcing some miraculous scientific achievement or other. And although our apprehensions also are aroused by popular reports of things to come, there are so many of us today who suffer from a sense of vacuity, an absence of purpose in life (for which 'motivation' is no substitute), that we cannot but hope that the future will have something to offer us. In fact, much of the popular support of science can be attributed to the discontents and ambitions that are both the product and the precondition of sustained economic growth. Indeed, every form of personal hardship or frustration has come to be regarded by large numbers of people as intolerable; as evidence of an urgent need for state provision and for the enactment of new rights.

But with a growing awareness that institutional changes alone may not suffice, and that much of the inequality among people is basic and seemingly ineradicable, hopes turn towards a Science for which, it is claimed, nothing is impossible. From today's massive research, it is believed, ways and means will eventually be discovered for removing all the pain and frustration from people's lives, and for making them whole and beautiful again. There is, then, rationalism enough in this discontented world of ours for public support of scientific and technological research.

Such rationalisations offer more solace than do the portentous conclusions being drawn by some of the antigrowth opposition; in particular, the conclusion that further economic growth in already-prosperous countries is likely, on balance, to be inimical to society's welfare irrespective of any 'new direction' we might reasonably hope to impart to it. General acknowledgment of the real possibility of such an outcome is not easy to establish in spite of its increasing articulation. For what an almighty crash there would be if ever we dared, officially so to say, to topple the awesome Growth God, so long enshrined in our temples of worship! And when the dust cleared, the void left could be so immense as to paralyse us. Thus we stay our hand for fear to suffer, once more, the pangs of anguish and slow desolution that must follow the crumbling of an ecumenical faith that for so long has infused the spirit of Western man, and tinged his endeavours with hope and purpose.

This understandable resistance to abandoning the growth myth is, in fact, augmented by apprehensions of the enormous psychological difficulties involved in any attempt to adjust ourselves to the economic and social requirements of a no-growth society, apprehensions that weaken our resolve to face up to, and come to terms with, the cruel realities.

How, in fact, we are likely to respond if and when 'the awful truth' dawns upon us, even though we might well understand what we ought to be doing, is a matter of rueful conjecture. For our economic institutions are all polarised along the growth axis; they all pull in the growth direction. Our vast educational establishments, from infant schools to postgraduate research departments, have acquired an orientation which produces the research mentality. The spirit of innovation, in matters great and small, pervades our society. Habitually, unthinkingly almost, we seek more efficient ways of doing things. To use the current slang, we are 'hooked on' efficiency. We are corrupted by an unquestioned imperative to work 'improvements' into everything; into every article, every substance, every material, every machine, every process, every idea. Indeed, what keeps our civilisation going are successive 'shots' of innovation. Nothing compels our attention so much as the oft-claimed 'scientific breakthrough'.

Two centuries of unprecedented technical development have, it seems, left an indelible impress on the mind of modern man. Compared with pre-industrial man, the transformation wrought on his way of looking at the world is such as might be attributed to some powerful drug, one for which he has now a strong addiction. It is natural enough that the victim should extol the virtues of the drug which sustains him whenever he fears it may be withdrawn. And so, today, there is this new-found ardour in praise of the 'efficiency ethic'; in praise of that compulsive search for novelty and innovation that produces lives as filled with motivation as they are void of meaning. In sum, the pain of disengaging our mind and character from ingrained attitudes and values arising from two centuries of material progress is so great, and the effort so exhausting, that the temptation to rationalise the existing ethos and culture is overwhelming.

We conclude, then, that careful deliberation about the range and magnitude of the more untoward consequences of economic growth, although it can be counted upon to induce serious misgivings about the wisdom of persisting along the growth path, may not, after all, serve the purpose. The tide of disenchantment has indeed begun to flow, but it may not flow deep enough, or carry the force necessary, to dislodge entrenched institutions, or to wear away habitual attitudes ingrained in the fibre of our being. The forces of economic and technological growth may not then be stilled, debate them as we may. And those of us who have given the matter careful thought may have to resign ourselves to the prospect of a future we should prefer to avoid. For the sort of life that is emerging as a byproduct of the irrepressible processes of innovation looks to be far less congenial for ordinary mortals than it is at present and than it was in the more recent past.

If nothing more than this sad resignation is likely to result from our inquiries, we might feel some diffidence about pressing them. To a convinced determinist, to a man who believes that men have no power to alter the broad course of events, there would, indeed, be a case for desisting. If the worst is sure to come, foreknowledge of it can only blight the present. If, on the other hand, one believes that, in the last resort, man can influence the shape of the future, and that, no matter how powerful are the forces they have unleashed, they might yet contrive to bring them under control, such inquiries are worth pursuing. For there is then a chance – although in the circumstances depicted above, a very slender chance – that some of the worst developments can be avoided and, more hopefully, that as a result of prolonged reflection and social experiment, institutions can be brought into being which are more compatible with men's basic wants and aspirations.

ENTRENCHED INTERESTS

'Entrenched interests' is a term that brings to mind the organised power of wealthy stockholders, business magnates, landlords, bankers, industrial executives and state bureaucrats – supporters of the 'Establishment' all, and fearless growthmen at that. Their vocational purpose, as they see it, is to foster the growth of something; whether private profit, or sales, or revenues, or exports, or numbers of employees, branches or customers. This great exhilarating numbers game absorbs them thoroughly, from day to day and from year to year, the social life they lead being ancillary and subservient to the game; indeed, that social life is an extension of it through which connections are made and maintained, and power is exercised and exhibited. The very spirit of the individual caught up in this game becomes expansionist, thrusting, restless, rejoicing in the rise of the relevant indices and impatient of 'setbacks'. He may pay lip service at public meetings and conferences to emerging social ideals, but the full implications of the economics of the steady state are anathema to him.

In sum, the seemingly most powerful economic group in the modern nation state is unwaveringly committed to continued economic growth. It may be 'purified' growth, 'humanised' growth, 'harmonious' growth or any other variety; it may be given a new title, a new set of credentials and 'a new direction'. But growth it has to be.

Although their day-to-day occupation is not so charged with expansionist impulse as their executives, the bulk of the working class – using the term to cover both blue and white collar workers, skilled and unskilled – have as yet hardly begun to question the growth gospel. What is more, with price and wage indices sprouting from every research centre, the members of every paygroup have come to take the liveliest interest in their material prospects from one week to another. After three decades of engorging themselves from a burgeoning cornucopia of 'the good things of life' (enabling them incidentally to wreak havoc upon the environment in which they are immersed), and of quaffing periodically at the fount of unlimited expectations, workers in the affluent West are all but convinced that they are entitled by natural law, if not by common law, to a yearly rise in their real pay. Indeed, however difficult the economic circumstances, an interruption of this customary postwar process, even for a year or so, is apparently not to be brooked without every manifestation of impatience and displeasure. Some of the more thoughtful workers may have begun to appreciate the possibility of an eventual change to the economics of a steady state. But the Western world will have to suffer some pretty terrifying experiences before the unions will be ready to give their official blessing to the idea of a steady state economy.

Strong though these economic interests are, however, they are not the most powerful. They would not, I think, prevail against sustained resistance by today's 'Third Estate': the scientific community in the West, whose influence in society is undoubtedly on the ascendant. Despite the emergence of dissident voices over the last ten years, it is within the scientific establishment that the support for economic growth is most deeply entrenched. Not directly, of course; not as a crude support for faster rates of GNP. But more fundamentally, as a demand for 'freedom of inquiry' – which can be translated today into a demand for continued support and expansion of the immense facilities needed for research and development (R & D), facilities which are provided currently by industry, by governments and by the universities. Add to the sacred principle of 'freedom of inquiry' the spur of 'social need', the problems galore which, in many instances, arise from the applications of science itself, and the case for sustaining the expansion of R & D – which, of course, supports the scientific community and provides its members with social privilege and influence – becomes irresistible.

But, of course, one of our conclusions is that the continued expansion of research and innovation is ultimately incompatible with the good life. I would not go so far as to argue that only if *all* scientific and technological progress were to be halted could there be any hope of creating a good life. To do so would be to claim both too little and too much: too little, because there are already in existence enough of the products of technology as to make the good life impossible; too much, because one cannot exclude the possibility of stumbling upon innovations that are wholly beneficial on any reasonable criterion, even though we cannot foresee them. What, instead, I would argue, on the basis of the observations and reflections in this volume, is that the sum of enduring happiness cannot be much augmented by further scientific discoveries even under the most favourable circumstances.

If this much is conceded, an essential part of a social policy for the good life would be the enforcement of a general ban on all scientific research, on all new technology and on all new products – exception being made, on appeal, only for research closely directed towards discoveries serving clear humanitarian purposes. If, for example, there were the strongest grounds for believing that specific kinds of research would eventually discover remedies for a particular malignant affliction, permission to undertake or continue it might be granted provided, always, that safeguards against possible accidents and side effects were regarded as paramount considerations.

The implied controls on scientific freedom of such a policy would, however, be so drastic as to amount to a virtual ban on empirical research and technological innovation. For all practical purposes, economic growth would come to an end.

But imagine the plight of scientists in a steady state economy. Scores of thousands of them would have to move from their prestigious niches in industry, or in the university, to far humbler tasks. Hundreds of thousands of academics would have to abandon their hopes of status and recognition. The ambitions of an army of technocrats would be permanently thwarted. Design departments in every industry, in every country, would close down. Research laboratories of every size and description would go to rust. Complex and ponderous computers would cease to hum. Stackfuls of learned journals would no longer appear. It would seem to many as if the vital core of society's machinery were being dismantled, and that collapse must surely follow. One has but to contemplate the prospect, and the consternation it would produce, to dismiss it almost out of hand; to conclude, then, that scientific research and its translation into technological progress will, indeed, continue to impel us forward into the future of increasing hazard and anxiety that we have already described.

INTERNATIONAL DISTRUST

Finally, even if wisdom were somehow to prevail – as a providential result, we could suppose, of a succession of well-publicised near-catastrophes arising from new synthetics or technologies, none of which, mercifully, was fatal to mankind – a policy evolved to establish a steady state economy would run into another formidable obstacle: the universal apprehension that any steady state control of technology would cause the country adopting it to slip behind in 'the arms race'.

I, myself, doubt whether these apprehensions are warranted. Technological innovation is no longer what it was in earlier times: namely, a product of the spread of enterprise and the growth of markets. Today, it is increasingly the outcome of highly organised R & D, controlled and directed towards specific objectives. Western governments, disposing annually of scores of billions of dollars on military defence, could in principle, maintain an up-to-date war technology in virtual independence of the rest of the economy. They could organise research on any required scale, and build large scale plants for all specific weapons.

Whether this view of the matter is substantially true or not, we shall probably never find out. For the experiment is not likely to be undertaken. The notion of 'spin-off' – the notion that innovations in one branch of industry become an important source of progress in others – is a very persistent one. And, in the last resort, so long as the defences of the West are the primary considerations, the military can convincingly argue that serious attempts to swerve from traditional pro-growth policies cannot but introduce some element of risk.

It is not possible, then, to end on a note of even qualified optimism. Nor would it be responsible of me to contrive to do so. But if the outlook is grim indeed, it does not follow that we should feel depressed and impotent. The growth in our understanding of what has happened, and what is happening, to our civilisation does of itself afford some satisfaction. At least, we are not as sheep lost in the wilderness. Each of us can cling to his individual sanity even amid the collective insanity.

What is more, our forebodings need not encourage an attitude of quietism. And although one possible reaction would be to 'eat, drink and be merry' for tomorrow comes the holocaust, it is not a reaction that I should expect. For one cannot bring oneself entirely to rule out hope – if only because human beings are incurably obstinate, and because they still believe in miracles. Although slender in all conscience, what filament of hope there is depends upon the creation of a growing public awareness of the forces at work in society; awareness of the traditional rationalisations of science and technology, and awareness, too, of the entrenched material and intellectual interests which support them. Without that growing public awareness, without a growing disbelief in the prevailing attitude that, by and large, all is well – or, with some modest adjustments, could be made well – the little hope that there is would dwindle to nothing.

Postscript

Our journey ends here. Although I have purposed to broach all the chief issues that are pertinent to the economic growth debate, it is not impossible that I have omitted some important factors or misrepresented their import. But unless my interpretation of recent developments is seriously misleading, it is not possible to avoid the conclusion that something quite fundamental has begun to go wrong with Western civilisation. Thus, from a close consideration of the likelier social consequences of continued economic growth, and from their comparison with the characteristics of the good life, a sombre picture has emerged. Its broad outlines are as follows:

Modern economic growth, and the norms and attitudes it establishes, have produced a highly complex industrial and urban organisation, albeit one that is increasingly vulnerable largely because the spread of affluence, the diffusion of the products and processes of technology, and the sheer rapidity of change, have combined, unavoidably, to undermine the influence of the complex of institutions and myths that invested all pre-industrial civilisations with stability and cohesion. The existing libertarian order in the West is no longer rooted in a consensus that draws its inspiration ultimately from a common set of unquestioned beliefs. The legitimacy of all its institutions are perpetually under assault. Social order is visibly disintegrating.

In the circumstances, only an extension of state power and a diminution of personal freedoms will prevent a disintegration into social chaos. And this process, also, is under way. The growing fears today of violence, terrorism and urban disruption, the public's apprehension of the grave threats posed by the new technology, and the intensification of group conflicts within our 'pluralistic' societies – all of these untoward features, traceable (as indicated in the text) to the technological revolution of the past century, have weakened popular resistance to the assumption of wider powers of control by modern governments. An instinct for survival is impelling the Western democracies along the road to the totalitarian state.

There is, of course, a terrible pathos about what is happening that I have failed to capture in the text. I could, perhaps, come closer to describing it if I were permitted to take a leap in imagination for which I need not answer.

In his search for mastery over nature, and addressing his intelligence to specific and immediate ends, man has been all-too-successful. And his appetite has fed on his success. Today there are no bounds to his ambition and no limits to his rapacity. They have begun to wreck the social order as surely as they have begun to wreck the ecological order.

Since the beginning of the nineteenth century, and far more rapidly since World War II, industrial societies, in order to surge ahead economically, have thoughtlessly disencumbered themselves of myths and institutions that have grown over centuries and millennia. The great belief systems, the idea of a divine lawgiver, the sanctity of the family, the rich tapestry of custom and propriety, the ceremonies and festivals, the rituals and benedictions – all that, despite hardship and occasional disaster, gave purpose, pageantry and ultimate dignity to the communities of earlier ages, today lie in ruins and rubble. In our haste to throw off the burden of this heritage so as to give free rein to appetite, we failed to recognise its providential rationale: the provision of an intricate arterial system along which the irrepressible currents of human love – filial love, romantic love, the love of man for man and of woman for woman, the love that comes of respect and reverence, and the love that comes of sadness and remembrance – can flow easily along appointed channels, fitting to the custom and occasion.

In consequence of the technological eruption in the West there are today almost no institutions embedded in tradition through which love and respect can easily and regularly be given vent. While revelling in sexual permissiveness, we are inhibited in the expression of love for our fellows. Surely there was never a time in history when, between men, it was more awkward to express, and more difficult to experience, an unalloyed affection. From the pangs of such frustrations man's lust for power currently distils its frenzy, and sparks his hopes with technological fantasies that can only remove him further from fulfilment. The resulting despair begets a craving to pierce more wantonly the seemingly repressive integument of the social order, a craving expressed in the fevered search for novelty and excitement which is fostered and met by commercial interests. One result of these combustible forces is the popularisation of sexual display and abandon and, inevitably, also a growth in the taste for sadistic violence and obscenity.

To punish mortals the gods grant their wishes. But whether seen as nemesis or not, the vision evoked by this interpretation of events is a frightening one: that of Western civilisation, the civilisation of the Enlightenment, the civilisation of Science, a civilisation born of high hopes and auspicious heralding, today frothing with power and glee – and being piped gaily to the brink of the abyss. And all that yet might stay the fatal plunge lying in the mud, discarded and in decay.

References

Abrams, Mark, 'Changing values', *Encounter* (October 1974).

Arts Council of Great Britain, *The Obscenity Laws,* report of the Working Party (London, Andre Deutsch, 1969).

Banfield, Edward C., *The Unheavenly City* (Boston, Little, Brown & Co., 1968).

Bannock, Graham, *How to Survive the Slump* (London, Penguin, 1975).

Barnett, Harold J. and Morse, Charles, *Scarcity and Growth* (Baltimore, Johns Hopkins Press, 1963).

Bauer, Peter, 'The myth of foreign aid', *Encounter* (April 1974).

Becker, Gary, 'A theory of the allocation of time', *The Economic Journal* (1965).

Beckerman, Wilfred, 'The need for economic growth', *Lloyds Bank Review* (November 1971).

Beckerman, Wilfred, 'Economic growth and welfare', *Minerva* (October 1973).

Beckerman, Wilfred, *In Defense of Economic Growth* (London, Jonathan Cape, 1974); reviewed by E. J. Mishan in *Journal of Political Economy* (November 1975), pp. 873–8.

Bell, Daniel, *The Culture Contradiction of Capitalism* (New York, Basic Books, 1975).

Brittan, Samuel, *Capitalism and the Permissive Society* (London, Macmillan, 1973).

Bruce-Briggs, A., 'Against the neo-Malthusians', *Commentary* (July 1974).

Campbell, Rita, *Food Safety Regulations* (Washington DC, 1974).

Cline, Victor B. (ed.), *Where Do You Draw the Line?: An exploration into media violence, pornography, and censorship* (Provo, Utah, Brigham Young Press, 1974); reviewed by E. J. Mishan in *New Universities Quarterly* (April 1976).

Commoner, Barry, *The Closing Circle* (New York, Knopf, 1971).

de Grazia, Sebastian, *The Political Community: A study of anomie* (Chicago, University of Chicago Press, 1948).

de Madariaga, Salvador, *Democracy versus Liberty* (London, Pall Mall Press, 1958).

Easterlin, Richard, 'Does money buy happiness?', *The Public Interest* (Winter 1973).

Ehrlich, Paul R. and Arne, H. *et. al., Human Ecology* (San Francisco, Freeman & Co., 1973).

Elkins, Stanley M., *Slavery,* 2nd edn (University of Chicago Press, 1968).

Ellul, Jacques, *The Technological Society* (New York, Knopf, 1964).

Epstein, E. J., 'Methadone: The forlorn hope', *The Public Interest* (Summer 1974).

Freeman, Albert M. and Haveman, Robert J., 'Clean rhetoric, dirty water', *The Public Interest* (Summer 1972).

Freud, Sigmund, *Civilisation and its Discontents* (London, Hogarth Press, 1930).

Friedman, Milton, *Capitalism and Freedom* (Chicago, University of Chicago Press, 1962).

Fogel, Robert W. and Engerman, Stanley L., *Time on the Cross: The economics of American negro slavery,* 2 vols (Boston, Mass., Little Brown, 1974).

Forrester, Jay, *World Dynamics* (Cambridge, Mass., Wright Allen, 1971).

Fuller, John G., *We Nearly Lost Detroit* (New York, Readers Digest Press, 1975).

Galbraith, John Kenneth, *The Affluent Society,* 2nd edn (London, Hamilton, 1969).

Galbraith, John Kenneth, *The New Industrial State*, 2nd edn (Boston, Mass., Hamilton, 1971).

Goodman, Edward, *A Study of Liberty and Revolution* (London, Duckworth & Co., 1975).

Hardin, Garrett, *Exploring New Ethics for Survival* (New York, Viking Press, 1972).

Hardin, Garrett, 'The fateful quandary of genetic research', *Prism* (March 1975).

Harrod, Roy F., 'The possibility of economic satiety – use of economic growth for improving the quality of education and leisure', in *Problems of United States Economic Development* (New York, Committee for Economic Development, 1958), I, pp. 207–13.

Hayek, Frederick A., *The Road to Serfdom* (London, Routledge & Sons, 1944).

Heilbroner, Robert, *An Inquiry into the Human Prospect* (New York, Norton & Co., 1974).

Hendin, H., *The Age of Sensation* (New York, Norton, 1975).

Hirsch, Fred, *Social Limits to Growth* (Cambridge, Mass., Harvard University Press, 1976).

Holbrook, David, *Sex and Dehumanization* (London, Pitman, 1972).

Kahn, Herman and Wiener, A. J., *The Year 2000: A framework for speculation on the next thirty-three years* (New York, Macmillan, 1967).

Kapp, K. W., *The Social Costs of Business Enterprise,* 2nd edn (London, Asia Publishing House, 1963).

Kass, Leon, 'Making babies', *The Public Interest* (Winter 1972).

Keynes, John Maynard, *Essays in Persuasion* (New York, Norton, 1963).

Klein, Rudolph, 'Growth and its enemies', *Commentary* (June 1972).

Klein, Rudolph, 'The trouble with zero economic growth', *New York Book Review* (April 1974).

Klein, Rudolph, 'Trouble with a zero-growth world', *New York Times Magazine* (2 June 1974), pp. 14–15 ff.

Kneese, Allen and Schultze, Charles L., *Pollution, Prices, and Public Policy* (Washington DC, Brookings Institution, 1975).

Lave, Lester and Seskin, Eugene, 'Acute relationships among daily mortality, air pollution and climate', in Edwin Mills (ed.), *Economic Analysis of Environmental Problems* (1975).

Lovins, Amory, *Nuclear Power* (London, Friends of the Earth, 1974).

Linder, Staffan, *The Harried Leisure Class* (New York, Columbia University Press, 1970).

MacIntyre, Alasdair, 'How virtues become vices', *Encounter* (July, 1975).

Maddox, John, *The Doomsday Syndrome* (London, Macmillan, 1972).

Marris, Robin (ed.), *The Corporate Society* (London, Macmillan, 1974).

Meade, James E., *Efficiency, Equity and the Ownership of Property* (London, Allen & Unwin, 1964).

Meadows, Dennis and Donella, *et al.*, *The Limits to Growth* (New York, Universe Books, 1972).

Mills, Edwin S. (ed.), *Economic Analysis of Environmental Problems* (New York, NBER, 1975).

Mishan, E. J., *The Costs of Economic Growth* (London, Staples Press, 1967).

Mishan, E. J., *Twenty-one Popular Economic Fallacies* (London, Penguin, 1969).

Mishan, E. J., 'Heretical thoughts on university reform', *Encounter* (March 1969).

Mishan, E. J., 'The spillover economy', *Encounter* (December 1969).

Mishan, E. J., 'The postwar literature on externalities: An interpretive essay', *Journal of Economic Literature* (1971).

Mishan, E. J., *Making the World Safe for Pornography: And other intellectual fashions* (London, Alcove Press, 1973).

Nordhaus, W. and Tobin, J., 'Is economic growth obsolete?' in Milton Moss (ed.), *The Measurement of Economic and Social Performance* (New York, NBER, 1972).

Okun, Arthur M., *Equality and Efficiency: The big trade-off* (Washington DC, 1975).

Olson, Mancur, *The Logic of Collective Action: Public goods and the theory of groups,* Harvard Economic Studies vol. 124 (Cambridge, Mass., Harvard University Press, 1965).

Olson, Mancur (ed.), *Toward a Social Report* (Washington DC, US Department of Health, Education and Welfare, 1969).

Olson, Mancur, and Landsberg, H. (eds), *The No-growth Society* (New York, Norton & Co., 1973).

Packard, Vance, *A Nation of Strangers* (New York, David McKay Co., 1972).

Page, Talbot, *The Economics of a Throwaway Society* (Washington DC, Resources for the Future, 1976).

Popper, Karl, *The Open Society and its Enemies*, 1st edn (London, Routledge, 1945).

Reich, Charles A., *The Greening of America* (New York, Random House, 1970).

Ridker, Ronald G. (ed.), *Commission on Population Growth and the American Future,* Vol. III (Washington DC, 1972).

Schultze, Charles, 'Re-examining the military budget', *The Public Interest* (Winter 1970).

Schumacher, E. F., *Small is Beautiful: A study of economics as if people mattered* (London, Blond & Briggs, 1973).

Scitovsky, Tibor, *Papers on Welfare and Growth* (London, George Allen & Unwin, 1964).

Scitovsky, Tibor, *The Joyless Economy* (Oxford, OUP, 1976).

Scitovsky, Anne and Tibor, 'What price economic growth', in Tibor Scitovsky, *Papers on Welfare and Growth* (1964).

Slater, Philip E., *The Pursuit of Loneliness: American culture at the breaking point* (Boston, Beacon Press, 1970).

Taylor, Gordon Rattray, *Rethink: A paraprimitive solution* (London, Secker & Warburg, 1972).

Taylor, Gordon Rattray, *How to Avoid the Future* (London, Secker & Warburg, 1975).

The Public Interest (Winter 1971).

Thurow, Lester, 'Education and economic opportunity', *The Public Interest* (Summer 1972).

Tullock, Gordon, 'Does punishment deter crime?', *The Public Interest* (Summer 1974).

Vacca, Roberto, *The Coming Dark Age* (New York, 1972).

Veblen, Thorstein, *Theory of the Leisure Classes* (New York, Vanguard Press, 1928).

Ward, Barbara and Dubor, Rene, *Only One Earth: The care and maintenance of a planet* (New York, Norton & Co., 1972).

Weisskopf, Walter, *Alienation and Economics* (New York, Dutton, 1971).

Wick, Warner, 'Sour apples from the Tree of Knowledge', *The University of Chicago Magazine* (Spring 1976).

Wilkinson, Richard G., *Poverty and Progress* (London, Methuen, 1973).

Zeckhauser, Richard, 'The risks of growth', in Mancur Olson and H. Landsberg (eds), *The No-growth Society* (1973).

INDEX